The New Social Entrepreneurship

This book is dedicated to Alessia and Francesca

Ad rivum eundem lupus et agnus venerant
Siti compulsi: superior stabat lupus
Longeque inferior agnus. Tunc fauce improba
Latro incitatus iurgi causam intulit.
«Cur» — inquit — «turbulentam fecisti mihi
Aquam bibenti?». Laniger contra timens:
«Qui possum, quaeso, facere, quod quereris, lupe?
A te decurrit ad meos haustus liquor».
Repulsus ille veritatis viribus:
«Ante hos sex menses male, ait, dixisti mihi».
Respondit agnus: «Equidem natus non eram».
«Pater hercle tuus, ille inquit, male dixit mihi».
Atque ita correptum lacerat iniusta nece.
Haec propter illos scripta est homines fabula,
Qui fictis causis innocentes opprimunt.

Phaedrus (20 B.C. – A.D. 50)
I Lupus et Agnus,
Phaedri Augusti liberti fabulae Aesopiae, Liber Primus.

The New Social Entrepreneurship:

What Awaits Social Entrepreneurial Ventures?

Edited by

Francesco Perrini

Bocconi University, Milan, Italy

Edward Elgar

Cheltenham, UK • Northampton, MA, USA

Published by
Edward Elgar Publishing Limited
Glensanda House
Montpellier Parade
Cheltenham
Glos GL50 1UA
UK

Edward Elgar Publishing, Inc.
136 West Street
Suite 202
Northampton
Massachusetts 01060
USA

A catalogue record for this book
is available from the British Library

Library of Congress Cataloguing in Publication Data

The new social entrepreneurship : what awaits social entrepreneurship
ventures? / Francesco Perrini, [editor].
    p. cm.
    Includes bibliographical references and index.
1. Social entrepreneurship. 2. Social Change. I. Perrini, Francesco.
HD60.N46 2006
361.7'65–dc22

               2006002694

ISBN-13: 978 1 84542 781 8
ISBN-10: 1 84542 781 5

Printed and bound in Great Britain by MPG Books Ltd, Bodmin, Cornwall

Contents

Figures

Tables

Boxes

Contributors

Geoffrey Desa

Doctoral Student, Technology Entrepreneurship, Department of Management and Organization, University of Washington Business School, Seattle. Email: gdesa@washington.edu

Sandro Fazzolari

PhD from the University of Minnesota. Professor of Executive Training ESL Courses in Milan, Italy at leading industrial companies, investment banks, services, legal and consulting firms. Consults with the editorial staff at Bocconi University and Confindustria (Italy's industrial lobby group). Email: fazzolari@tin.it

Kai Hockerts

Kai Hockerts, Associate Professor, Centre for Corporate Values and Responsibility (CVR), Department of Intercultural Management and Communication, Copenhagen Business School (CBS), Denmark. Email: kho.ikl@cbs.dk

Joan Hoffman

Associate Professor of Economics and Co-ordinator Economics Division John Jay College of Criminal Justice, City University of New York (CUNY), New York City. Email: xhoffman@bestweb.net

Barbara Imperatori

PhD in Business Administration and Management at Bocconi University. Professor of Human Resource Management, SDA

Bocconi School of Management. Research fellow, Institution of Organisaztion and Information, Bocconi University. Email: barbara.imperatori@unibocconi.it

Beth Jenkins

Senior Consultant at Booz Allen Hamilton. Researcher for the Corporate Social Responsibility Initiative of the Kennedy School of Government. Founded the Corporate Responsibility Council. She has worked on the development of 'bottom of the pyramid' business models with the World Resources Institute and Ashoka. Email: jenkins_elizabeth@bah.com

Ferit Karakaya

Tourism Policy consultant at the World Wildlife Fund (WWF) Mediterranean Programme Office and has been instrumental in incorporating 'Conflict Resolution' to produce the declaration of 'Sustainable Tourism Development in Turkey' with the cooperation of UNDP. Email: ferit1@gmail.com

Suresh Kotha

Professor of Management & Organization, Douglas E. Olesen/Battelle Excellence Chair in Entrepreneurship, Technology Entrepreneurship, Department of Management and Organization, University of Washington Business School, Seattle. Email: skotha@u.washington.edu

Ian C. MacMillan

The Dhirubhai Ambani Professor of Innovation and Entrepreneurship; Professor of Management, Director, Sol C. Snider Entrepreneurial Research Center, Director Wharton Entrepreneurial Programs (WEP), The Wharton School, University of Pennsylvania, Philadelphia. Email: macmilli@wharton.upenn.edu

Johanna Mair

PhD Insead. Assistant Professor of General Management at IESE Business School, University of Navarra, Barcelona, Spain. She teaches strategy and social entrepreneurship in the MBA program, executive programs and the PhD program. Email: JMair@iese.edu

Alessandro Marino

Researcher of Management at the 'Findustria Center', Department of Management (IEGI), Bocconi University. Professor of Innovation Financing and Management, Bocconi University and University of Milan. Email: alessandro.marino@unibocconi.it

Jane Nelson

Senior Fellow and Director of the Corporate Social Responsibility Initiative at the Kennedy School of Government, Harvard University, and Director, Business Leadership and Strategy at the Prince of Wales International Business Leaders Forum. Email: jane_nelson@harvard.edu

Ulku Oktem

Adjunct Professor at the Operations and Information Management Department and a Senior Research Fellow at Risk Management and Decision Process Center. She teaches 'Environmental Sustainability and Value Creation' at the MBA program, Wharton School, University of Pennsylvania. Email: oktem@wharton.upenn.edu

Francesco Perrini (Editor)

Associate Professor of Management and CSR, 'G. Pivato' Department of Management (IEGI) and Senior Professor of Corporate Finance and Real Estate Department, SDA Bocconi School of Management, Bocconi University, Milan, Italy. Email: francesco.perrini@unibocconi.it

Dino Ruta

PhD in Management, Assistant Professor, Institute of Organization and Information Systems, Bocconi University. Professor of Organization Design, SDA Bocconi School of Management. Email: dino.ruta@unibocconi.it

Christian Seelos

Senior Researcher and Lecturer at IESE Business School, University of Navarra, and other European schools in Business Strategy and Social Entrepreneurship. Ph.D. University of Vienna and MBA University of Chicago, GSB. Email: cseelos@sscg.org

James D. Thompson

Lecturer and Associate Director, Wharton Entrepreneurial Programs. Director, Societal Wealth Program, The Wharton School, University of Pennsylvania. Email: jamestho@wharton.upenn.edu

Clodia Vurro

PhD student of Business Administration and Management at Bocconi University. Research Assistant at SPACE Bocconi, Research Center on 'Security and Protection Against Crime and Emergencies', Department of Management (IEGI). Email: clodia.vurro@unibocconi.it

Preface *by Ian C. MacMillan*

Last year, I launched a class on 'Entrepreneurship and Societal Wealth Generation' at the University of Pennsylvania's Wharton School. In preparing the class syllabus, a group of students and I reviewed other such courses and at the end of our review came to the conclusion that there was just not enough reach for our ambitions. The feeling was: 'All this is great stuff but where is the real impact? How are we going to cover the real issues in wealth generating entrepreneurship – enterprises that will help thousands, and enhance societal wealth?'

Corporate social responsibility, corporate citizenship, and corporate philanthropy are concepts that have been a topic of study for years. But now scholars and professionals in the USA, like their international colleagues, are approaching agreement on the principle that entrepreneurship can apply to the public sector, among nonprofit initiatives, or even to philanthropy.

As we say in Chapter 8 of the book below, governments and philanthropists in the rich nations spend billions of dollars each year supporting causes pertinent to the manifold social problems of the world. Some of their efforts, with cumulative donations in the hundreds of millions of dollars each year, support start-up firms and small entrepreneurial businesses, and are motivated by the belief that the creation and growth of new enterprises fuels the growth of the economy, particularly through increased employment. To date, however, few people have considered the role that entrepreneurial activity can play beyond employment creation, like attacking issues of health, nutrition and education. We contend that this expanded focus of entrepreneurial effort can directly address manifold social problems and create new societal wealth.

We now have delineated a facet of entrepreneurship that acts as a market-based catalyst to profitably confront social problems as societal entrepreneurship and propose this phenomenon as a distinct and critically important alternative to public-sector initiatives. As we argue later in the book, our basic thesis is that many social problems can be addressed with entrepreneurial solutions, for instance, the creation of opportunities for underprivileged members of society to launch ventures that generate profits and thereby alleviate some societal problems. Among the 'champions' of societal entrepreneurship are, for example, LocalFeed in Southern Africa or Teleserenità in Italy, young start-ups that measure their success in terms of social indicators in addition to traditional economic indicators.

In essence, this represents a shift in much activity attending to societal problems from the public domain; that is, governments and nongovernmental organizations, to the private domain, in other words businesses and private individuals. If the entrepreneurial effort succeeds, a virtuous cycle results, motivating the entrepreneur to generate more profits and the more profits made, the more society benefits.

This concept, because it is relatively new, calls for some fundamental research and perhaps some very creative approaches. The fact is that societal enterprising is going to be difficult. In fact, a cynic might argue that if there were an obvious entrepreneurial solution, some entrepreneur would already have found it!

Our position is that we may be able to mobilize the talents of universities and business to undertake a new mode of research via 'exploratory enterprising'– to use the technologies and talents resident in great universities to conceive of, design, and plan societal wealth enterprises, to seek out philanthropists to help seed these enterprises, and then recruit local entrepreneurs to launch and manage them. The profits they can make, though small by the standards of developed economies, will be adequate for local economic circumstances.

This experiment in exploratory entrepreneurial philanthropy is already being undertaken by the Snider Entrepreneurial Research Center (SERC) at the University of Pennsylvania's Wharton School. Some pilot businesses have been developed, and redirected as necessary as part of the experimental learning process. Like all entrepreneurial efforts, success is not guaranteed. We nonetheless will persevere, because the prize is great – if successful these exploratory enterprises will reduce problems of nutrition, health and education for thousands of unfortunate people.

We have arrived at the following objectives for this book:

- to offer an interesting and thoughtful analysis of the societal entrepreneurship;
- to examine current understanding of societal entrepreneurship and locate this within the extant body of research dealing with the relationship between the profitable maximization of business and that of social welfare;
- to propose an effective review of the academic debate;
- to develop a descriptive conceptual framework for new societal enterprises.

We hope this book will provide a rich and helpful perspective on this deeply important topic.

Ian C. MacMillan
Philadelphia

Acknowledgments

No project can be accomplished without the active support of a wide variety of people. Their insights, suggestions, experiences, and critiques have shaped my thinking and provided me with inspiration for this book. Though too numerous to mention, you have made this a stimulating and entertaining journey.

I would like to acknowledge first of all the authors, for their extraordinary support and contribution to the realization of this book, and for their collaborative spirit that has been decisive in creating a fruitful exchange of ideas.

Thanks to the colleagues of Bocconi University of the 'Giorgio Pivato' Institute of Corporate Economics and Management (IEGI), the Centre for Research on Security and Protection against Crime and Emergencies and Sustainability (SPACE), the Centre for Finance and Industry Studies (Findustria), the Centre on Entrepreneurship and Entrepreneurs Research (EntER), the Italian research Centre for Social Responsibility (ICSR), and the Corporate Finance and Real Estate Department of the SDA Bocconi School of Management.

I wish to thank my colleagues at the Business Ethics and Legal Studies Department, the Management Department, the Exploratory Entrepreneurial Philanthropy Program, the Wharton Entrepreneurial Programs, the Wharton Global Family Alliance, and the Sol C. Snider Entrepreneurial Research Center at the Wharton School of the University of Pennsylvania; the Haas School of Business and School of Information Management and System at University of California, Berkeley; and the Corporate Social Responsibility Initiative (CSRI) at the Kennedy School of Government of Harvard University.

I would also like to thank participants in seminars at the Legal Studies and Business Ethics Department Faculty Research Program Seminar Series, the Wharton Social Impact Management (SIM) Initiative, the International Social Entrepreneurship Research Conference (ISERC), the Academy of Management

Annual Conference, the Strategic Management Society Annual Conference, European Academy of Business in Society (EABiS) Conferences; the students of the Wharton MBA class on 'Entrepreneurship and Societal Wealth Generation', 'International Business Ethics', and 'Corporate Responsibility and Ethics', the PhD class on 'Entrepreneurial Finance'; and all colleagues at the international research group in which I am involved at INSEAD, Copenhagen Business School, HEC Genève e L. K. Academy Warsaw, ESADE Business School, Norwegian School of Management, Cranfield Business School, Vlerick Leuven Gent Management School, IESE Business School, Darden School of Business at the University of Virginia, and Michigan Ross School of Business at the University of Michigan.

All of them have supported me directly in my work on this book, and indirectly over the years that I have known and worked with them.

I am also grateful to all those who have responded most kindly and patiently to my pressing requests for help: many thanks to all the collaborators at Edward Elgar Publishing Ltd, and to the English editor for their continuous support throughout the editing process.

I would like to thank the 'Claudio Demattè' Research Division of SDA Bocconi School of Management and the Research Committee of Bocconi University for their financial support of part of this project.

Finally a special mention has to be made to the Internet, e-mail, the low cost of voip, and the time zones, which have supported my shuttling between Italy and the US, often translating delays into opportunities. Without them this project would not have been feasible.

May this book inspire at least one new social entrepreneurial idea.

Francesco Perrini
Philadelphia, 11 November 2005

Introduction

A new wave of entrepreneurial ferment is taking hold around the globe. Social entrepreneurship (SE) is riding the crest, supported by the long debate on the role and responsibilities of business in society that has been taking place for at least fifty years. The scale and scope of concrete experiences in the field of 'innovation in service of social change' make this moment in time rich in learning. The daunting challenge of this book is to capture and share at least some of those insights, starting from a clear, sharp, and focused vision of SE: it entails innovations designed to explicitly improve societal well-being, housed within entrepreneurial organizations, which initiate change in society.

This book is not about any one of the many exciting new initiatives being launched under the 'social entrepreneurship' rubric. Rather it is about the sea change they represent, the promise they hold, and the hurdles that must be overcome if their performance is to match that promise. Aside from the widespread affirmation of concepts such as Corporate Social Responsibility (CSR), Corporate Citizenship (CC), Corporate Philanthropy (CP), and so on, all claiming a proactive and dynamic corporate attitude towards society, its needs, and its expectations, little attention has been devoted to those organizations existing expressly to face social demand in an entrepreneurial way. In other words, the broad coverage of issues concerning business in society has on the one hand raised awareness of SE and created excitement about its potential, but on the other hand has also blurred the general understanding of what SE is and what it hopes to achieve.

However, although SE is a new field of inquiry and most of the extant literature focuses on a preliminary 'definer level', in the last ten years literature on social issues in management, entrepreneurship, and strategic management have devoted increasing attention to SE. Even the Academy of Management has recently introduced an SE area within both the Entrepreneurship Division and the Social Issues in Management Division, corroborating the relevance of the subject and the presence of a cross-border interest in the development of the field. Moreover the number of MBA programs and research centers devoted to the topic is mushrooming globally, and a well-defined supportive environment is now evolving out of the incubation phase into mature and increasingly accepted practices. In this context Venture Philanthropy (VP) represents the last frontier behind the emergence and proliferation of innovative social entrepreneurial ventures (SEVs), fostering the shift from the traditional nonprofit model of tackling social problems to an entrepreneurial orientation that sees valuable opportunities where others see black holes.

If we accept the deep change in what business looks like, this does not correspond to a comparable change in the way the main characters are set up and classified. The traditional criteria based on organizations' legal status remain, distinguishing simply among nonprofits, for-profits and public actors. SE is neither a matter of organizational form, nor one of legal status. Entrepreneurship, innovation, venturing, and social purpose represent, in our view, the basic ingredients of the SE 'formula' and the main focus of this work.

In the chaos that characterizes the literature on business and society, it is possible to find interesting clues that link SE to the larger, acknowledged theoretical debates on the validation of a social role for corporate actors. These are unavoidable hints in the process of defining the domain of the SE field. By now, however, SE, as an unusual 'contact point' among entrepreneurship, innovation, and social change, has attained a wider and more enthusiastic acceptance in corporate thinking and practice than in the literature.

This double line of reasoning, partly theoretical and partly practitioner-based, drives the bottom line of the book. In the first part we look for a consistent answer to a muddle of still-unresolved questions: How can SE be defined? How can SEVs be identified? What are the main dimensions along which organizations vary and what factors lead to success? What does success mean? Does the way in which an SEV is designed matter? Does it make sense to talk about a social business plan? Is an SEV aligned with traditional sources of financing? And so on. In the second part of the book, we change perspective, examining several practical examples of how perspectives on SE are translated into concrete phenomena.

The premises above are the pillars of a multi-year research project, from which this book emerged. Bocconi University, Bocconi School of Management (SDA Bocconi), but above all the Wharton School, University of Pennsylvania, and the MacMillan class on 'Entrepreneurship and Societal Wealth Generation' represent the sources from which we developed the ideas in this book. Our work anticipates the road ahead, and further research initiatives are expected in order to expand our knowledge on SE.

INTENDED AUDIENCE

The New Social Entrepreneurship is intended for both academics and professionals. In fact the first part of the book is grounded on academic sources and aims at clearly defining boundaries and intersections of SE research. In so doing, it provides a map, a critical and comprehensive framework, and aims at stimulating current and future debate on the role and main features of SE research. The second part of the book is case-based and provides insightful examples, at the practical level, of how SE works. In this sense the book is intended for those who want to enlarge their knowledge of start-ups in the field of SE, on the dimensions that can affect success regardless of the field SEVs insist on. In other words *The New Social Entrepreneurship* has a didactic aim, as a student handbook for those who are in the final years of a course in Business Administration and Management, at a master's degree level as well as in MBA classes. The book is also useful for those who are interested in applying SE philosophy or adhere to a new form of financing to support SEVs.

AN OVERVIEW OF THE BOOK

The New Social Entreprenuership is divided into two main sections.

The first six chapters focus on the theoretical issues surrounding SE.

Chapter 1 critically examines contemporary understandings of SE and locates them within the extant body of research dealing with the role and responsibilities of business in society. The main purpose is to formulate a definition of SE that is descriptively robust and conceptually distinct from existing concepts in the literature. In so doing, the chapter aims at developing a descriptive conceptual framework for research on SE, articulating the elements of social innovation and conceptualizing SE as entailing innovation designed to explicitly improve societal well-being, housed within entrepreneurial organizations that initiate this level of change in society.

Delving more into particulars, chapter 2 describes the links between the identification of social gaps, the exploitation of entrepreneurial opportunities, and social innovation through the process of organizational launching. The focus is on those dimensions along which SEVs vary. In particular at the organizational level, the role of visioning, the orientation towards scalability, and economic robustness are considered as the main factors affecting the way SEVs pursue social change. The relationship between organizational dimensions and outcomes is then moderated by three environmental factors: the extent to which economic environment is developed, the composition of the competitive environment in which SEVs operate, and the presence of supportive actors in the field.

Chapter 3 argues that the process of creating new social enterprises is not unlike the process of launching an enterprise in other fields. We begin by describing a hypothetical entrepreneurial 'path', within which we discuss some of the critical issues typically encountered when a social venture is undertaken. We then examine business planning and the key parallels between social and more traditional ventures.

Chapter 4 addresses the issue of finding financing for social start-ups. In particular it describes the emerging actors that could support SEVs through their participation as partners in business initiatives. Innovative financial instruments are then analyzed based on a re-reading of the traditional venture capital process from the point of view of SE.

The analysis of the new supportive actors in financing social entrepreneurial venture start-ups continues in chapter 5. Here different models of VP in practice are compared and contrasted, in order to highlight similarities in the way investment funds approach SEVs. Rather than considering foundations' investments in social enterprises simply as 'one-shot charitable giving', VP models are based on different phases, starting with the selection of a pilot portfolio and ending with a suitable exit strategy. The chapter focuses on investors' perspectives and analyzes four main areas: the choice of portfolio and the selection criteria; the relationship with the funded SEVs in terms of skills and resources transfer (capacity building); the criticalities in measuring performance and the different levels measurement refers to; and the path ahead in fostering VP practices.

The last of the theory-based chapters looks at the SE from an organizational perspective. The aim of chapter 6 is to point out peculiarities and organizational challenges that characterize the implementation and development of SE. Our main purpose is to provide indications for the organizational design, but we also underline the cognitive effectiveness – from an heuristic point of view – of the emerging new organizational configuration.

While from a theoretical point of view a homogeneous framework of complementary studies on SE can be created, the same level of consistency is not to be expected when SE is implemented in specific contexts of place and time. SE can emerge in several areas and therefore we include a set of heterogeneous studies representing some of the most debated practitioners' perspectives.

In particular we first present a set of papers concerning some private industries in different countries: LocalFeed (chapter 7) is a Southern African producer and distributor of animal feeds, founded in late 2000. Specifically the company produces high-quality feed mixes for poultry, cattle, and pigs in a region populated predominantly by small-scale and subsistence producers. The basic thesis of the chapter is that many social problems, if looked at through an entrepreneurial lens, create the opportunity for someone to launch a business that generates profits by alleviating that social problem.

The following contribution (chapter 8) is related to the tourism industry which, as stated in the United Nations Commission on Sustainable Development (UN-CSD) decision, is now one of the world's largest industries and one of its fastest-growing economic sectors. However, tourism is undoubtedly inseparable from the natural environment and has varying degrees of both negative and positive effects on the economic, social, and environmental aspects and wealth of a region. The mandate on Sustainable Development clearly encompasses tourism development as a whole and not in the form of trendy 'alternative tourism' schemes. The chapter is dedicated to a 'Sustainable Tourism Project' to demonstrate accomplishments one can expect as well as the challenges one must consider when undertaking such projects. The Çıralı project, conducted by WWF Turkey and the European Union Life Programme and covering the period between 1997 and 2000, was awarded the UN Habitat Dubai International Award for Best Practices in Improving the Living Environment in 2000 (Dubai Award List 2002). The main objective of the project was 'to promote environmentally and socially sound development through integrated planning, traditional and alternative economic activities and biodiversity conservation'.

In chapter 9 we describe the San Patrignano experience. The authors show how an entrepreneurial approach was adopted to realize one of the most successful communities for recuperating drug addicts and social outcasts in the world. After some 40,000 people have passed through the community and with an astonishing 70% recovery/societal reinsertion rate validating its effectiveness, studies both in Italy and abroad have attempted to figure out what makes San Patrignano different from other communities; if there is indeed a model that can be transferred to spread this success story where it is needed most. This case study considers three relevant factors that make San Patrignano consistent with the paradigm of successful SEVs and SE: geography, work skills, and restoring the individual's right to choose.

The next contribution, chapter 10, is an in-depth case study of Cafédirect Ltd. (London, UK). It briefly describes the state of fair-trade literature. So far the focus of academic interest has been on the actual developmental impact of fair trade, and the customer-acceptance perspective. The chapter goes on with a historical account of the development of fair trade in the UK over the past three decades, culminating in the description of Cafédirect's progress over the past ten years. Cafédirect is then discussed from three angles: its sustainability impacts, its entrepreneurial contribution, and its core competencies.

Then we shift perspective towards two private-institutional cross experiences. First Sekem's experience (chapter 11) shows how an entrepreneurial, step-by-step approach was adopted to realize a complex vision of holistic social, economic, and cultural development in Egypt. Sekem's founder, Ibrahim Abouleish, was the first entrepreneur to receive the Right Livelihood Award in 2003. After living, studying, and working in Austria for 21 years, he returned to Egypt and started from nothing – a piece of desert land north of Cairo. Abouleish showed tremendous resourcefulness, creativity, and perseverance. Today Sekem consists of a business conglomerate, medical center, schools, and an academy, and has set new standards and even changed laws.

We next include a contribution (chapter 12) on SE in Italy concerning the innovation in home assistance services for non-autonomous elderly people. According to projections by the Ministry of Labor and Social Policies, Italy is second only to Japan in the international ranking of countries that in the next 50 years will be most affected by population aging. The contributor examines how innovative operational models can be used to deliver health care services, whether by the public or by the private sector. Focusing then on the private sector, the author looks in detail at the experience of the social enterprise Teleserenità®.

Chapter 13 asks a key question: How does one manage technologies for social innovation in a resource-limited environment? Research in SE, with antecedents from nonprofit management and more recently from entrepreneurship and strategic management, is ideally positioned to identify the particular characteristics of technology management within a social venture. The authors study the evolution of seven projects within Benetech, an entrepreneurial incubator in Silicon Valley that designs technologies for under-served markets in the fields of disability access, human rights, literacy, and education. They then propose that as a social venture in technology evolves, sources of opportunity shift from founder resource endowments towards an interaction with the socio-political dynamic – the activist, philanthropic, and volunteer environments and the necessity of developing long-term relationships with stakeholders.

The following two chapters focus on the potential of collaborative SE practices. Sustainable development in general and watershed collaborations in particular are natural milieus for SE because the lack of correspondence between environmental flows and government boundaries requires new social arrangements to achieve both environmental protection and economic activity compatible with that need. Watershed collaborations, which are increasingly common in the US due to problems with non-point pollution, necessarily involve networks. The general properties of networks provide tools for understanding the interaction between SE and collaborations. In this case study (chapter 14) of the watershed collaboration between New York City and the Catskill/Delaware Watershed providing 90 percent of its water, the role of social entrepreneurs and networks is examined with regard to the shaping and implementation of the collaboration. Social entrepreneurs play a role in effecting dynamic change in the structure of networks involved in the shaping of the collaboration. How network properties both support and impede the achievement of SE goals for the collaboration is discussed. For instance the role of social entrepreneurs on the borders of the inner cluster of the collaboration network is seen to usefully extend the effective network and contribute to achieving collaboration goals. On the other hand, a characteristic of networks called Nadel's paradox, in which the local expectations for network nodes is viewed as conflicting with the general nature of networks, provides insights into inner tensions that undermine some of the goals of SE for this collaboration.

The second discussion of collaborative practices, chapter 15, starts by arguing that with a few notable exceptions, surprisingly little analysis has been done on the linkages between the corporate leaders and social entrepreneurs that drive them. This is especially the case in developing countries where there are both enormous development needs and great opportunities for increasing engagement between corporations and social entrepreneurs. This chapter looks at some of the innovative alliances that already exist in both developed and developing countries. It suggests a conceptual framework for thinking about the different ways in which companies can invest in SE, focusing on core business operations in the workplace, marketplace, and along the value chain; its activities relevant to social investment and strategic philanthropy; and its engagement in public policy dialogue, advocacy, and institution building. The chapter outlines the business case for how such investments can help companies meet their business goals and support their corporate values. And it offers a set of recommendations for business leaders, social entrepreneurs, foundations, and governments on how they can all work together to increase the scale and effectiveness of such alliances for their common good.

1. Social entrepreneurship domain: setting boundaries

Francesco Perrini

1.1 INTRODUCTION

Since Bowen (1953) wrote his seminal book *Social Responsibilities of the Businessman*, claiming that the obligations of the businessman are 'to pursue those policies, to make those decisions, or to follow those lines of action which are desirable in terms of the objectives and values of our society' (1953, p.16), the field concerning the role and responsibilities of business in society has grown significantly. Society and business, corporate social responsibility, social issues in management, corporate citizenship, and stakeholder approach are just some of the terms used to describe the relationship between business and society.

Despite this growth, little attention has been devoted to those organizations existing expressly to respond to social demand in an entrepreneurial way. Although progress toward defining the domain of the field is still slow, social entrepreneurship (SE), as an unusual 'contact point' among entrepreneurship, innovation, and social change, has attained wider and more enthusiastic acceptance in corporate thinking and practice than in the scholarly literature.

SE has in fact been introduced into the discourse on business's contribution to the improvement of societal well-being in the last few years, mainly at the instigation of corporate actors who began to associate themselves with SE. Others supportive in this process include academic research centers exclusively devoted to SE, foundations, specialized consulting groups, social venture capitalists, philanthropists, and others.

SE represents a totally new approach toward business and society relations. Organizations oriented toward the SE construct focus on social problems and initiate social change. Their specific concerns are still not considered in the academic research on socially responsible business management.

In this context, therefore, we must start by setting robust boundaries that are of necessity distinct from existing concepts in the literature. This is the first step in the process of legitimizing a new field in that it distinguishes between social entrepreneurial activities in different settings (mainly between SE and business entrepreneurship), and it represents the basis for comparisons within the parameters.

For example, an increasing number of companies are assigning more and more resources to philanthropy and social giving,[1] and some are even running these activities in a way that is close to entrepreneurial, but it is certainly not entrepreneurial per se. Similarly, when nonprofits adopt managerial techniques in order to become more businesslike, they are not categorized as social entrepreneurial actors. To put it another way, is SE just a variant of entrepreneurship or just the realization of corporate social responsibility (CSR)? How does SE differ from other business, government, or not-for-profit entities that deal with social problems? Finally, if SE is really different, then why are current theories of entrepreneurship, organization, and social responsibility inadequate to study and understand these 'new' organizations?

This chapter addresses these questions. To clearly define the field and the current dispute over SE, the chapter starts with these issues. The first debate concerns entrepreneurship itself. However much they may share with business entrepreneurship theories the 'entrepreneurial soul', new SE players differentiate themselves in terms of their ultimate goal – the enhancement of social welfare and social conditions, in terms of inclusion and cohesion, wide access to knowledge and information, community development, and so on. The second debate, closer to SE itself, concerns the crucial issue of SE's contributions to CSR and, in general, to the business and society literature.

The rest of the chapter falls into two main sections. In the first one the principal actors coaxing the progress and proliferation of SE are identified. The goal of this section is to clarify the specific mechanisms pertinent to the emergence of SE and the larger debates these refer to. The second section provides a definition of SE in an attempt to reframe the current literature on SE such as it is, while also referring to the classical theories of business entrepreneurship.

1.2 CONTEXT OF REFERENCE AND DRIVERS OF CHANGE

Most of the existing academic contributors recognize two decisive macro-dynamics in SE's emergence: the crisis of the traditional welfare state and the increased competition within the nonprofit sector.

The crisis of the traditional welfare state (Borzaga and Defourny, 2004; Matten and Crane, 2005; Matten, Crane and Chapple, 2003), characterized by a general slowdown in national economic growth rates and high unemployment, has been accompanied by a deep reconsideration of the social strategies employed by governments. This sparked, for example, the trend of privatization and decentralization that was so common in public policy during the 1980s. But the 'global shift away from a social welfare state approach to development and towards a neoliberal approach with an emphasis on market forces as primary mechanisms for the distribution (and redistribution) of resources' (Johnson, 2000: 2) has left unfulfilled an increasing number of social needs. As a result, we now see a growing demand for private providers who can match socially relevant goals with efficient and effective management practices.

In addition, cuts in public grants have compounded the problem, causing an unprecedented rivalry among nonprofit organizations, which, at the same time, are facing a greater demand for their services. Nonprofits have thus been compelled to reinvent themselves and their traditional *modus vivendi*. As a consequence of rising costs, more competition for fewer donations and grants, and increased rivalry from for-profit companies entering the social sector, not-for-profit organizations have been enlarging their 'range of activities', experimenting with cautious management practices, using tools found in the for-profit sector (that is, business planning or tools for evaluating economic performance), as well as new funding strategies. In other words, nonprofits are now shifting from a traditional philanthropic dependency toward more rigorous financial accountability, including identifying all potential commercial sources of revenue (Newman and Wallender, 1978).

In the above setting, the demand for SE clearly emerges as a direct consequence of a set of disequilibria: the slowdown in public supply of social products and services, increased competitive pressure in the nonprofit sector and, more generally, a concern for the seemingly unsustainable disequilibrium in the distribution of wealth and wellbeing across the planet (Prahalad, 2004; Bornstein, 2004).

With specific reference to Europe, an empirical research work (Borzaga and Defourny, 2004) promoted by EMES – European Network Research – and aimed at analyzing the current state of the art in the third sector, has demonstrated the existence of a proportional relationship between national economic and social development and the emergence of SE. In fact, in those countries characterized by a relatively low development level, the perceived need for social services is modest and the fulfillment of social needs is generally 'delegated' to the informal, family-based system. In these cases social entrepreneurship is mainly confined to the realm of work-integration.

In the meantime, competing in the same action field with public sector and traditional not-for-profit organizations, but as a latecomer, SE strength will be strictly related to the strength of the other competitors. For example, in North European countries that are characterized by a well-developed welfare state mainly oriented toward the minimization of the population's social risks, SE is confined to new market niches that benefit largely from public subsidies. But in those countries with a well-developed welfare state but without the direct provision of public services (Germany and Belgium, for example), SE will compete vigorously with traditional nonprofits and will succeed at the reciprocal development level.

More specifically, however, the breakdown of the traditional welfare state and the changes within the nonprofit sector are catalysts of the SE phenomenon. But neither accounts for the main theoretical debate concerning SE or why corporate actors are the proper societal group to tackle social issues.

Undoubtedly entrepreneurs are vital to the life of society. Whether they grew out of a business opportunity or a social need, as they fulfill their economic tasks, entrepreneurial organizations increase employment, stimulate innovation progress, and enhance material well-being. At the same time, given the importance of their economic function in terms of its impact on societal development, do entrepreneurs and entrepreneurial organizations have moral obligations to or responsibility within society?

This question represents the starting point of all studies on the relationship between business and society. As explained above, to date many aspects of the corporate-community relationship (Altman, 1998) have been studied, shifting from an initial, vague awareness of the relationship between companies and their social relevance to the identification of more defined taxonomies and identifiable streams of research. Although there is a variety of approaches, SE relates more closely to the theories of corporate citizenship (Altman and Vidaver-Cohen, 2000; Andriof and McIntosh, 2001; Matten and Crane, 2005).

The link between the crisis of the welfare state, the globalization phenomenon, and the deregulation process on the one hand, and the increasing economic and social power of some large multinational companies on the other, has convinced business and academics that corporate actors undoubtedly belong to a community and need to take its needs into account. In this context theories of and approaches to corporate citizenship focus on rights, responsibilities, and the possible partnership between business and society (Matten, Crane and Chapple, 2003; Wood and Logsdon, 2002). These are the specific ways of formalizing willingness to improve the local community. SE represents a further development of corporate citizenship in that it arises directly from the needs of society (that is, social problems) and aims specifically to enhance societal well-being by initiating social change.

Although the emergence of SE can be more directly linked to the debate concerning the role of corporations within society as a natural consequence of their increasing power over societal development patterns, arguments for the necessity of SE organizations can also be found in business entrepreneurship theory, and in particular in those studies focused on the link between entrepreneurship and economic advancement in developing regions (Baumol, 1986; El-Namaki, 1988; Harper, 1991). The bottom line is the opportunity to channel the development potential within entrepreneurship into the service of the urgent need for development in many regions of the world.

1.2.1 The Extant Debate on Social Entrepreneurship

The above discussion concerning the drivers of the SE phenomenon and the main streams of research it can be referred to, also explains the origin of the two different schools of thought that have been developing regarding the SE definition and boundaries. The first one – which I call the limited view of SE – considers SE as belonging to theories pertinent to nonprofits; the second one – which I call the extended view of SE – considers SE as a totally new, intersectoral field of study.

The authors claiming a limited view of SE (Boschee, 1998; Boschee and McClurg, 2003; Cannon, 2000; Dart, 2004; Dees and Elias, 1998; McLeod, 1997) delegate it to the category of nonprofit research, corroborating the belief that SE can be explained as a sort of 'recent innovation' in the field of social enterprise (Dart, 2004). This categorization is supported by the shift of managerial competencies and market-based attitudes to the not-for-profit actors in order to improve their operational efficiency and effectiveness.

In this sense, social enterprises and SE are viewed as a kind of 'encompassing set of strategic responses to many of the varieties of environmental turbulence and situational challenges that nonprofit organizations face today' (Dart, 2004: 413). This end of the spectrum emphasizes entrepreneurship as a way to make nonprofits more market-driven, client-driven, and self-sufficient – in other words, as commercialized nonprofits.

In other words, SE emerges as a third sector's (that is, not-for-profit sector) rational and strategically better response to a changed and challenged macro-situation resulting from a perceived breakdown of the welfare system (Cook et al., 2001), increased financial pressure on social-purpose organizations, increased costs in many areas of social sectors, and decreased public and private grants and donations (Boschee and McClurg, 2003; Dees and Elias, 1998). In this sense, the expectation that nonprofits will provide services and achieve social change on a large scale, while also diversifying funding resources, is motivating social entrepreneurs to invent hybrid nonprofit and for-profit organizations. In this context, the innovation, as it intrinsically relates to entrepreneurship (Bruyat and Julien, 2000), is seen as the ability of nonprofit actors to reinvent themselves within the nonprofit system.

At the opposite extreme – the extended view of SE – are a group of authors who espouse a broader view of SE theory. These authors (Grenier, 2002; Henton et al., 1997; Hockerts, 2004; Johnson 2000; Mair and Marti, 2004; Thompson, Alvy and Lees, 2000; Perrini and Vurro, 2005; 2006) believe that the phenomenon can be considered as opening up a new and independent (Dorado and Haettich, 2004), extremely intersectorial (Johnson, 2000; Mair and Marti, 2004) field of study; they additionally stress the entrepreneurial content of entrepreneurial initiatives. In this sense, only those innovators who are able to actively contribute to social change with creativity and innovation, typical of the classical entrepreneurial process, can be called social entrepreneurs, regardless of their specific organizational form (for-profit or nonprofit).

This extended perspective seems to apply to SE better than others because of the possibility both to give autonomy to the overall discipline and to explain those initiatives not usually ascribed to the not-for-profit sector, even when they have a prominent social mission and social purpose – for example, those activities that target the 'bottom of the pyramid' and aim at converting poverty into an entrepreneurial and profitable opportunity. Even if most of the companies are categorized as traditional and for-profit, their contribution to the enhancement of impoverished communities' social, cultural, and economic conditions has been proved to be relevant to SE (Prahalad and Hart, 1999; Prahalad and Hammond, 2002; Prahalad, 2004).

Overall, the literature pertaining to the more limited perspective on SE does not prove the necessity of a new classification. If SE was considered a mere innovation within the nonprofit sector, its innovativeness in dealing with complex social problems would not be considered (Johnson, 2000; Grenier, 2002), and it would qualify simply as a process used by nonprofits to become more businesslike. In other words, there tends to be little reflection on the notion of entrepreneurship and the potential for new meanings to surface. On the other hand, while the authors arguing for the extended view of SE appear to understand the entrepreneurial nature of SE and its strong links to opportunity exploitation, self-sufficiency, and innovation, we believe this literature has not gone far enough in clarifying a clear, direct, and unambiguous definition of SE. Table 1.1 sets out just a few of the many definitions of SE. It is evident, however, that despite the addition of the concept of

SE to the debate surrounding the entrepreneurial role of social business, its usage has not been consistent.

To date, the heterogeneity of these contributions presents SE as a multi-faceted, multi-perspectival phenomenon. This is consistent with the interpretative key of business entrepreneurship: diversity and the entrepreneur's ability to break up deterministic frameworks and predictable paths (Bruyat and Julien, 2000). Although we believe that the diversity of social entrepreneurial phenomena should be taken into account in modeling SE, we argue that conceptualization is more than necessary in this phase of boundary setting.

From this perspective, we next turn to differentiating among constructs and answering these questions: What is SE, in addition to the definitions and refinements outlined above? How can organizations consistent with the SE concept be labeled and recognized? Who is, in this field, the social entrepreneur and how is s/he different from her/his business counterpart?

Despite the lack of common reference points and a shared reading grid through which to distinguish among the conglomeration of corporate actors devoted to addressing social problems in an entrepreneurial way, there is an obvious and growing interest in the phenomenon. SE is therefore a topic worthy of discussion and heightened understanding. The following section elaborates on the importance of further study of SE.

1.2.2 The Need for Studying Social Entrepreneurship

The basic question concerning a new phenomenon undoubtedly aims, at least in part, at a general understanding of the relevance of the phenomenon per se. Our focus, SE, can be studied from both a practical and above all from an academic perspective

To address the basic question: while the world cries out for repair, for filling the gap between the business and social-welfare issues of society (Margolis and Walsh, 2003; Drayton, 2000), the business sector is more and more responding to these requests, seeking solutions in several different settings. As mentioned above, the process of reconciliation between business and society is taking different forms.

On the one hand, firms are increasingly shifting from a shareholder-centered view of business and profit maximization to a stakeholder-management approach (Carroll, 1989; McWilliams and Siegel, 2001) centered on maximizing the overall cooperation between the entire system of requests and needs, and the objectives of the firm (Donaldson and Preston, 1995; Freeman, 1984; Mitchell, Agle and Wood, 1997). In other words, starting from the acknowledgment that they are open-dynamic organisms that continually interact with a wider system (McGuire, 1963; Vogel, 1986; 2005), firms engage in socially responsible behavior linking their day-by-day operations to a process of social responsiveness, goaded by public pressure and societal expectations (Sethi, 1975; Wood, 1991).

Table 1.1 Social entrepreneurship: some definitions

Limited View of SE

The rules of the game for nonprofits have changed dramatically during the past 20 years [...] Smart nonprofit managers and Board members realize they must increasingly depend on themselves to insure their survival...and that has led them naturally to the world of entrepreneurship. [...] A social entrepreneur is any person, in any sector, who uses earned income strategies to pursue a social objective.
Boschee & McClurg, 2003

Social entrepreneurs are nonprofit executives who pay increasing attention to market forces without losing sight of their underlying mission, somehow balancing moral imperatives and the profit motives – and that balancing act is the heart and soul of the movement.
Boschee, 1998

The changes and transformations from conventionally understood nonprofit to social enterprise are stark: from distinct nonprofit to hybridized nonprofit-for-profit; from a prosocial mission bottom line to a double bottom line of mission and money; from conventionally understood nonprofit services to the use of entrepreneurial and corporate planning and business design and concepts; and from a dependence on top-line donations, member fees, and government revenue to a frequently increased focus on bottom-line earned revenue and return on investment.
Dart, 2004

Table 1.1 Continued

Extended View of SE

It's a process whereby the creation of new business enterprise leads to social wealth enhancement so that both society and the entrepreneur benefit. These benefits include the creation of jobs, increased productivity, and enhanced national competitiveness and better quality of life.

MacMillan, 2003

We define SE as the innovative use of resources to explore and exploit opportunities that meet a social need in a sustainable manner.

Mair & Marti, 2004

Social entrepreneurship is emerging as an innovative approach for dealing with complex social needs. With its emphasis on problem-solving and social innovation, socially entrepreneurial activities blur the traditional boundaries between the public, private and non-profit sector, and emphasize hybrid models of for-profit and non-profit activities.

Johnson, 2000

Social entrepreneurs play the role of change agents in the social sector, by: (a) Adopting a mission to create and sustain social value (not just private value), (b) Recognizing and relentlessly pursuing new opportunities to serve that mission, (c) Engaging in a process of continuous innovation, adaptation, and learning, (d) Acting boldly without being limited by resources currently in hand, and (e) Exhibiting a heightened sense of accountability to the constituencies served and for the outcomes created.

Dees, 1998

As well as business entrepreneurs, we need social entrepreneurs, people who realize where there is an opportunity to satisfy some unmet need that the welfare system will not or cannot meet, and who gather together the necessary resources (generally people, often volunteers, money and premises) and use these to "make differences".

Thompson et al., 2000

Corporate social responsibility (CSR) represents a strategy of dealing with the context and its constituencies (Vogel, 2005), initiating a process of reciprocal interactions in which social responsibility – defined as 'increased engagement and transparency about what the company stands for, how it creates long-term value for its shareholders, clients, and employees, and how it contributes to society' – translates into trustworthiness and, as a direct result, the ability to deliver profitable growth (Ackerman, 1975; Post, Preston and Sauter-Sachs, 2002; Preston and Post, 1975).

Despite this growing academic interest in exploiting the 'social side of business', theoretical and empirical attention to private organizations specifically conceived to deal with social dilemmas and promote social change is to date extremely scarce. But the number of actors interested in the practical exploitation of SE is growing rapidly. Moreover, several different emerging actors now compose an out-and-out 'SE sector.'

Table 1.2 exemplifies some of the actors currently using SE. It tries to cover the different viewpoints on the SE phenomenon and to provide an overview of the new categories of actors in the SE field. The list of examples provided is not, of course, exhaustive; rather, it aims to illustrate the diversity and scope of interests and perspectives related to SE. What emerges is a changing context, with several significant subjects insisting on it. Therefore, the absence of SE from our collective theories of firms and organizations makes our understanding of the business landscape incomplete.

1.3 DEFINING THE DOMAIN OF SOCIAL ENTREPRENEURSHIP RESEARCH

If we deduce that SE today is much more than a mere extension of the nonprofit sector, we can elaborate on the concept by creating distinctions. First, it is important to understand what the expression 'social entrepreneurship' implies, its roots, and how it differs from business entrepreneurship.

SE shares its business counterpart's strong drive toward innovation and change (Dorado and Heattich, 2004: 6) and the ability to discover unmet needs and entrepreneurial opportunities (Casson 1982; Leadbeater, 1997; Shane, 2000). On the other hand,

SE has its own distinguishing characteristics, one of which is different long-term objectives: the enhancement of global or local social conditions starting from a perceived social gap. At this point, one could argue that every private company, in particular the expressly socially responsible ones, has a social mission. This is certainly true, but SE goes farther, maintaining that those organizations consistent with the SE domain create economic value, but do so explicitly to 'stay in business' and continue their clear-cut social mission.

Table 1.2 Social entrepreneurship: new supportive actors

Academic Research Centers
Social Enterprise Initiative Harvard Business School http://www.hbs.edu/socialenterprise
Center for Advancement of Social Entrepreneurship Fuqua School of Business, Duke University http://www.fuqua.duke.edu/centers/case/
Center for Social Innovation Graduate School of Business, Stanford University http://www.gsb.stanford.edu/csi/
Skoll Centre for Social Entrepreneurship Said Business School, Oxford University http://www.sbs.ox.ac.uk/html/faculty_skoll_main.asp
Center for Business in Society IESE Business School, University of Navarra http://www.iese.edu/en/RCC/CBS/Home/CBSHome.asp
Canadian Centre for Social Entrepreneurship University of Alberta http://www.bus.ualberta.ca/ccse/
Exploratory Entrepreneurial Philanthropy Snider Entrepreneurial Research Center, Wharton School

Table 1.2 Continued

Supportive Actors	Mission
The Schwab Foundation for Social Entrepreneurship	The Schwab Foundation provides a global platform to promote social entrepreneurship as a key element to advance societies and address social problems in an innovative and effective manner. http://www.schwabfound.org/index.htm
The Institute for Social Entrepreneurs	The ISE is a for-profit consulting company that provides education, training and consulting services for social entrepreneurs in the United States and abroad. http://www.socialent.org/index.htm
The Robert Enterprise Development Fund	Using a venture capital approach to philanthropy, REDF applies techniques designed to create value in the for profit sector to its work with its nonprofit-run enterprises. REDF helps the twenty businesses within our portfolio grow toward sustainability in order to provide employment opportunities for over 600 homeless and very low-income individuals each year. http://www.redf.org/index.htm
New Economics Foundation	NEF is an independent think-and-do tank that inspires and demonstrates real economic well-being. We aim to improve quality of life by promoting innovative solutions that challenge mainstream thinking on economic, environment and social issues. We work in partnership and put people and the planet first. http://www.neweconomics.org/gen/
Venture Philanthropy Partners (VPP)	Venture Philanthropy Partners (VPP), a philanthropic investment organization, is working to improve the lives of children from low-income communities by pursuing two interrelated goals. First, we help strengthen nonprofit organizations, offering not just major

Table 1.2 Continued

Supportive Actors	Mission
	funding but also significant management expertise and other non-financial resources that are too rarely available to nonprofits. Second, we are joining with others in our field to inspire philanthropists, corporate and nonprofit leaders, and public policymakers to help increase the effectiveness and the flow of capital, talent, and other resources to nonprofit organizations meeting the core needs of children. http://venturephilanthropypartners.org/index.html
Community Wealth Ventures	Community Wealth Ventures is a social enterprise consulting firm that: Helps nonprofit organizations become more self-sustaining by generating revenue through business ventures and corporate partnerships. Helps corporations improve their bottom line through the design and implementation of community investment strategies. Through its consulting and research, CWV influences both nonprofits and corporations to think differently about market-based approaches to their social sector activity. http://www.communitywealth.org/index.htm

In order to mediate these aspects, we propose the following definition:

SE entails innovations designed to explicitly improve societal well-being, housed within entrepreneurial organization that initiate, guide or contribute to change in society.

Entrepreneurship, innovation, and social change represent the ingredients of the SE formula. The remainder of the chapter aims to better explain each of these and how they are linked to each other.

1.3.1 Social and Business Entrepreneurship

The concept of SE stands close to the field of entrepreneurship. The basic thesis is that many social problems, if viewed through an entrepreneurial lens, create the opportunity to launch a venture that generates profits by alleviating a specific social problem. This sets in motion a virtuous cycle – the entrepreneur is propelled to generate more profits and in so doing, the more profits made, the more the problem is alleviated (MacMillan and McGrath, 2000; Prahalad, 2004; Prahalad and Hammond, 2002). As such, the concept of SE remains strictly associated with and reciprocally determined by innovation, in that entrepreneurially driven innovations represent the crucial engine for propelling and stimulating change processes (Shane and Venkataraman, 2000). SE is the integration of entrepreneurial and innovative perspectives in developing and taking actions designed to create social wealth. In other words, even if we agree that entrepreneurship and innovation cannot be considered synonymous, SE is first and foremost concerned with a process of change and with the creation of new value.

At a more detailed level, it is widely accepted that entrepreneurship requires the presence of opportunities as well as enterprising individuals who wish to take advantage of them (Eckhardt and Shane, 2003; Gartner, 1985; Venkataraman, 1997). The entrepreneurial economy consists of a limited number of individuals and firms able to pursue entrepreneurial opportunity. Entrepreneurial opportunities always exist, regardless of the ability of individuals to recognize and exploit them. But what is an entrepreneurial opportunity and how can social and entrepreneurial opportunities be distinguished one from the other?

To date, scholars have identified social entrepreneurial opportunity as the major commonality between business and social entrepreneurialism. Yet SE stands out for focusing attention on a different set of possibilities: innovative ways to create or sustain social change, bringing two different cultures – business and nonprofit – together into one innovative and hybrid organization.

Mair and Marti consider entrepreneurial opportunities as 'opportunities to bring into existence new goods, services, raw materials, and organizing methods that allow outputs to be sold at more than their cost of production' (2004: 3) and affirm that a central way to differentiate between traditional business entrepreneurship and social entrepreneurship is by looking at their identification of opportunities. In this sense, even if social opportunities arise from unsatisfied needs (apart from their being social or not), in the SE process the interest is centered on the possibility to 'meet a social need in a sustainable manner, and thus to (partially) alleviate social problems' (ibid.). These social needs are not limited to a particular category (for example, poverty alleviation), but to the possibility to enhance social conditions and promote extensive social change.

With regard to SE opportunities, Hockerts goes farther, affirming how the exploitation of opportunities is based on the possibility of generating 'simultaneously economical rents and social benefits' (2005: 11). He considers the discovery process as the sole opportunity for SE ventures (SEVs) to survive 'in the limbo between social welfare and profit maximization motive' (2005: 11). Starting from these premises, Hockerts identifies three main sources of social entrepreneurial opportunities: activism, self-help, and philanthropy.

Instead of focusing only on external drivers, Guclu et al. see opportunity exploitation as the combination of internal and external factors. In particular, entrepreneurs' previous personal experience combines with social needs – 'gaps between socially desirable conditions and the existing reality' (2002: 3), social assets, and change to stimulate entrepreneurial ideas or innovations for social impact (Alvord et al., 2002).

There are two vision-oriented considerations. The first is personal experience. Transformative events (Barendsen and Gardner, 2004) both at the individual level (for example, living abroad and gaining perspective, directly experiencing a social breakdown, or dealing with a social issue) and at the organizational level help make organizations aware of the possibility to contribute to changing an existing social problem.

The second consideration refers to previous experience: past experience, at the organizational level that make organizations aware of the possibility of applying an acquired knowledge base to something different and socially significant (Dees et al., 2001).

Crisis-oriented factors also play a role. They include external, explicit, and implicit 'requests for help' or changes in the previous situation (changes in legal/normative situations, technological progress, market niches left uncovered, unmet social needs, new sources of monetary and non-monetary resources, the possibility of establishing partnerships with unexpected actors, etc.).

According to entrepreneurship and SE scholars (Kirzner, 1979; Casson, 1982; Mair and Marti, 2004; Hockerts, 2004), to be called entrepreneurial, an activity must entail a discovery of new means-ends relationships that generate a different image of the future. As business entrepreneurial opportunities, social ones represent the possibility to bring into existence new goods, services, raw materials, and organizing methods that allow outputs to be sold at more than their cost of production. Improvements in the efficiency of existing goods and services do not constitute true entrepreneurial opportunity. This is why we consider as incomplete that stream of research in extant SE literature that relates SE to the nonprofit management theories (Boschee and McClurg, 2003; Dees and Elias, 1998; Dees, Emerson and Economy, 2001; 2002; McLeod, 1996). The expectations for nonprofits to provide services and achieve social change on a larger scale, while also diversifying funding resources, arc motivating social entrepreneurs to invent organizations that combine nonprofit and for-profit structures. According to this view, there still tends to be little reflection on the notion of entrepreneurship and the potential for new meanings to surface.

Diverging from this stream of research, we affirm that only the introduction of new goods, services, raw materials, and organizing modes that allow output to enhance social well-being earn the term entrepreneurship. Because the entrepreneurial activity drives social change with new products, technologies, markets, processes, and organizational forms, it represents a significantly different activity from that of the traditional sector.

It is from this perspective that the innovation process represents the essence of SE. Schumpeter saw the entrepreneurial innovative force in the economy as a constant challenge to the status quo, and separated the entrepreneurial process from business management represented by traditional and routine managerial activities (Baumol, 1990; Eckhardt and Shane, 2003; Kirzner, 1997). According to the above definition of SE, innovation is concerned with the social realm in that it deals with developing, applying, or introducing new ideas, behaviors, products, and processes, and contributes to a reduction of social burdens, or in general to specified social targets.

While the previous discussion of entrepreneurial opportunities associates SE with entrepreneurship research, the different nature of social entrepreneurial opportunities distinguishes SE from business entrepreneurship. In other words, social opportunities arise from unsatisfied social needs that SE entails in order to alleviate social problems (MacMillan and McGrath, 2000). These social needs are not limited to a particular category (that is, alleviation of poverty), but depend on the possibility of enhancing social conditions and initiating social change. In business entrepreneurship, the exploitation of entrepreneurial opportunity is tied mainly to the expected value of the entrepreneurial profit. In other words, the decision to exploit and the choice of exploitation mode are linked to a sense of exclusivity and self-protection: the possibility to maintain the first-mover advantage as long as possible in order to preserve profit. As a result, the duration of the advantage must be increased by reducing the ability of others to 'imitate, substitute, trade for or acquire the rare resources required to drive down the surplus' (Shane and Venkataraman, 2000: 223).

In contrast with business entrepreneurship, SE overturns this mechanism, as well as the concept of expected value. We propose social expected value as the contribution of SE to the enhancement of social condition in the form of, for example, improvement of working conditions, access to technological progress, integration and participation within the community, and so on. If so, the interest in SE opportunities lies not only in achieving a competitive economic advantage, but above all in spreading the social innovation as widely as possible in order to maximize social change and the improvement of social conditions (Drayton, 2002). In other words, since SE focuses entrepreneurial skills on solving social problems, envisaging systematic change in all of society, it is necessarily distinguished by that set of opportunities that will allow it to turn all of society onto the new path.

1.3.2 Innovation in Social Entrepreneurship

The decision to exploit SE opportunities represents the first step for organizations in innovating within the social sectors. As a general consideration, innovation tends to occur in different fields. They range from microcredit services (that is, Real Microcredito, Brazil; CrediAmigo, Brazil; and Grameen Bank, Bangladesh) and community venture capital (Aavishkaar, Singapore), to new patterns in employment education (Artists for Humanity, Boston, Massachusetts; Global Education Partnership, Washington, DC; and Golden Gate Community, San Francisco, California) and the delivery of goods and services to the poorest populations (Casas Bahia, Brazil).

Often innovation is not related to products and services per se, but to market relations or new methods of organization and production. A clear example of this process is Aravind Eye-Care Hospitals. This organization was established as a more efficient way to bring eye care to the poorest people in rural and urban India (Prahalad, 2004) by reorganizing the workflow with a view toward cost-cutting and process efficiency. Today the organization has grown, with camps for those with visual problems, community-based rehabilitation projects, eye screening of school children, and other innovative services joining the initial winning innovation.

Jumpstart, an organization devoted to addressing the social, economic, and educational problems of school readiness, is another example. It began with a service innovation: delivering individualized tutoring to preschoolers in order to develop the literacy and social skills needed to succeed in school. From this initial innovation came an innovative business model made up of innovative production factors: a balanced combination of children (the 'clients'), their families (in order to support them during the learning process), and college students (the workforce) as tutors.

All this makes it difficult to find commonalities at a glance. I propose a definition of innovation as multidimensional, something pursued simultaneously or progressively on four different fronts: products and services or new qualities of products and services, methods of organization and/or production, production features, and market relations. SE can originate with a single innovation and progressively embrace other fields. Multidimensionality and the temporal dimension of innovation are crucial in the SE process.

1.3.3 Social Change

As stated before, the enhancement of global or local social conditions starting from a perceived social gap represents the main goal of organizations that conform to the SE model. In other words, SE gives back to the community and environment of reference in terms of specific social outcomes and long-term social change. At a glance, areas in which SE pursues change are diverse. Some of the fields in which social transformation is expected include arts, culture, and humanities; children and youth; community and economic development; disaster relief; education and research; employment training; environment and sustainable development; health enhancement; homelessness; hunger and poverty relief; and rehabilitative services.

Because these fields of action are so vast, it is helpful to group them in broad subcategories.[2] A first area of contribution is employment creation: *Juma Ventures* (San Francisco, California), *Pioneer Human Services* (Seattle, Washington), and *Rubicon Programs Inc.* (Richmond, California) exemplify how to create direct employment for at-risk people, otherwise excluded from the access to the marketplace. But SEVs contribution in this sense is not limited to the employment training field. They may 'help in developing both demand and supply, as well as in reconfiguring public expenditure composition' (Borzaga and Defourny, 2004: 359). The fact that SE often employs low-income or at-risk workers does not imply quality reduction. On the contrary, this is a major strength of the SE approach: to adapt traditional business practices to unexpected resources that are not necessarily low growth but simply need to be stimulated and balanced in accordance with innovative approaches. In more general terms, we could consider this area of social change as a way of building local capacity, thus enhancing local conditions by giving power to the underused local capacities.

Second, SE also focuses on information access and more in general on the reconfiguration of products, resources, and management practices into forms that fit better with specific local needs. All the activities at the bottom of the pyramid (BOP) market are rooted in this logic and in Prahalad's (2004) twelve principles of innovation for BOP markets (some examples include reinterpreting the relationship between price and performance; looking for hybrid solutions that can combine advanced technologies with existing infrastructure; developing solutions that can easily be translated into new markets, cultures, and countries (scalable solutions); focusing, from the beginning, on the environmental sustainability of the innovation; developing products starting from a deep understanding of functionality; focusing on both product and process innovation; and considering the existing resources and the overall country's skill level). Bay

Area Video Coalition (San Francisco, California) and International Network of Street Papers (Glasgow, UK) are specific examples of how to stimulate an inclusive flow of information. Gaining access to information through technological progress, particularly for those at the bottom of the pyramid, is the main driver toward enhancing democracy and reducing asymmetry, at every level (Prahalad, 2004). Third, SE can actually contribute to change patterns of interaction in order to enhance social cohesion through personalization and participative approaches, giving voice to marginalized groups.

As Borzaga and Defourny (2004: 360) observed:

> By contributing to solving or to alleviating the problems of specific groups, and by favoring the integration of disadvantaged people into the labor market, with higher wages than those paid by sheltered employment workshops and sometimes for-profit companies, social enterprises also contribute to improving life conditions, the well-being of communities and the level of social integration.

Finally, as innovation, social change is much more than a one-dimensional construct, and results can be both planned and unplanned. For example, the Rubicon Program Inc. is essentially an employment agency. However, related outcomes for community development should not be underestimated.

Certainly SE success cannot be measured only in terms of social outcomes and performance. The second dimension along which successful organization can be recognized is an economic one. Even if it has not been considered specifically in the definition of the SE construct, the ability to pursue a self-sustaining flow of resources together with profitability cannot be overestimated as a measure of SE success. This fact is emphasized by an increasing diffusion of measuring instruments that mediate between social and economic performance, such as the balanced scorecard.

1.3.4 Social Entrepreneurial Ventures and Socially Innovative Entrepreneurs

Throughout this chapter, the expression *organization* has been used to label actors that conform to the SE paradigm. It is now time to specify these actors and distinguish between them.

In that the entrepreneurial venture is the focus of the field of entrepreneurship (Bruyat and Julien, 2000), the term SE gives way to *social entrepreneurial venture* (*SEV*) (Dorado and Haettich, 2004; Henton et al., 1997; Kanter, 1999). Different from the construct of corporate entrepreneurship, in which strategic renewal represents the main outcome of innovation exploited through venturing (Zahra, 1996), SEVs represent a new breed of entrepreneurship, blending and integrating prominent social intentions and objectives (that is, social change) with innovative and rigorous venture-development practices.

The expression SEV has been introduced in order to give equal weight to the different components of the SE construct (that is, entrepreneurship, innovation, and social issues), as well as to avoid confusion by using a term taken from the nonprofit tradition – namely, social enterprise. SEVs share with their nonprofit counterparts the ability to serve members – not workers or stakeholders – and the community in general, the participatory decisional process, and, above all, the importance of stakeholder satisfaction with investors and profit distribution (Laville and Nyssens, 2004). As nonprofits, SEVs are cause-driven (Thompson, 2002) and community-based, but they remain profitable businesses.

SEVs in fact lose that typical 'charity label,' focusing on the efficient and effective production of goods and services. Their processes differ from those of nonprofits in that theirs are not supported by public goods (non-excludable and non-rival in consumption) nor collective goods (excludable, but non-rival in consumption), but by an 'individual demand associated with a perceived social utility' (Borzaga and Solari, 2004: 334). In addition, while nonprofits are required to distribute profits, SEVs are free to distribute or retain profits according to which option best fits their social mission.

Since the beginning of entrepreneurship research, theories have moved toward a more person-centred perspective, explaining entrepreneurship as 'a function of the types of people engaged in entrepreneurial activity' (Eckhardt and Shane, 2003: 334). SE follows this trend by offering a clear, distinguishable portrait of innovative social entrepreneurs. They are mainly innovators and, like their business counterparts, agents of change and drivers of social and economic progress (Leadbeater, 1997; Dees, 1998a; Johnson, 2000; Thompson, 2002), with a strong analytical capacity and problem-solving orientation. To date, when describing this category of entrepreneurs, the literature has focused more on entrepreneurial aptitude than social orientation (Johnson, 2000). For example, social entrepreneurs are not limited by the initial lack or scarcity of resources (McLeod, 1997). They also present a certain risk-tolerance and a strong desire to control the surrounding environment (Prabhu, 1999). In the words of Jeff Skoll, founder of The Skoll Foundation for Social Entrepreneurship:

> Social entrepreneurs both see and act on what others miss, the opportunities to improve systems, to create solutions, to invent new approaches. Like business entrepreneurs these folks are also intensely focused, self-driven and very determined in pursuit of their vision. The biggest difference, though, is that whereas business entrepreneurs are going after a problem from a purely economic viewpoint, social entrepreneurs usually have a vision of something that they would like to solve in the social sector (Dearlove, 2004: 52).

Indeed, social entrepreneurs exhibit qualities and behavior we usually associate with the business entrepreneur, but they start the entrepreneurial process by explicitly embracing social causes and place themselves where social, civic, or community-based gaps exist. Their main source of motivation is the desire to change society and a discomfort with the status quo (Bornstein, 2004; Prabhu, 1999). This makes them more sensitive to entrepreneurial opportunities that deal with social problems and unsatisfied social needs (Mair and Noboa, 2003). As Moore wrote (2002):

> [...] they create value by building portfolios of resources to address unmet social needs. They seek and find innovative ways of tackling the gaps left by the markets and/or the welfare state and commit themselves to addressing intractable social problems.

Equally important is their aptitude towards networking and cooperation (Thompson, 2002). Because they operate in an intersectorial domain, social entrepreneurs need a strong ability to establish and manage multiple relationships.

The ability to build external relations is also critical to establishing legitimacy with different constituencies (Prabhu, 1999) and to enhancing visibility, since best practices still do not exist.

Table 1.3 Summary of key definitions

Social entrepreneurship
SE entails innovations designed to explicitly improve societal well-being, housed within entrepreneurial organizations, which initiate, guide or contribute to change in society.

Innovation in social entrepreneurship
Innovation is concerned with society, in that it deals with developing, applying, or introducing new ideas, behaviors, products, and processes and contributes to a reduction of social burdens, or in general to specified social targets.

Social entrepreneurial opportunity
Social entrepreneurial opportunities arise from unsatisfied social needs that SE embraces in order to alleviate social problems. These social needs are not limited to a particular category (e.g., poverty alleviation), but depend on the possibility of to enhancing social conditions and initiating social change. SE focuses on entrepreneurial opportunities that deal with solving social problems, envisaging systematic change in the whole society.

Social expected value
SE contributes to the enhancement of social conditions in the form of, for example, improvement of working conditions, access to technological progress, integration and participation within the community, and so on.

Social change
Social change corresponds to the enhancement of global or local social conditions starting from a perceived social gap.

Social entrepreneurial venture
An organization that blends and integrates prominent social intentions and objectives (i.e., social change) with innovative and rigorous venture development practices. SEVs are the organizations consistent with SE. As nonprofits, SEVs are cause-driven and community-based, still remaining profitable businesses, with a focus on the efficient and effective production of goods and services.

In conclusion, a strong bridging capacity has been linked to the success of SE initiatives (Alvord, Brown and Letts, 2002).

We have just discussed how SE differs from traditional business entrepreneurs. Now we look at how they differ from their counterparts in the nonprofit world.

As emphasized by McLeod (1997), social innovators show a firm focus on outcomes and a market-based aptitude, reversing the traditional nonprofit accountability flow from a reliance on funding from organizations to accountability towards the overall stakeholder base. Furthermore, social entrepreneurs tend to be less fearful of failure and often abandon cause-marketing tactics in favor of quality-oriented entrepreneurial processes.

To sum up, we recognize two major distinguishing characteristics of the social innovative entrepreneur. First is the explicit, cause-driven social mission, which guides the social entrepreneur towards innovative activities. Second is the field of action: social entrepreneurs insist on the social sector as change promoter in society, they pioneer innovation within the social sector through groundbreaking entrepreneurial ideas, they have the ability to build capacity, and they concretely demonstrate the quality of the idea and measure social impacts, all with well-defined growth objectives. Table 1.3 summarizes all of the concepts introduced in this chapter

NOTES

1. According to Giving USA, charitable giving by for-profit corporations has risen from an estimated $ 9.6 billion in 1999 to $ 12.19 billion in 2002 (Kotler and Lee, 2005).
2. The examples presented in this section have to be considered as representative of organizations that conform to the SE concept as defined in this chapter. For more information, visit the following web sites: Juma Ventures, www.juma venture.org; Pioneer Human Services, www.pioneer humanserv.com; Rubicon Programs, Inc., http://www.rubiconprograms.org; Bay Area Video Coalition, http://www.bavc.org/; International Network of Street Papers, http://www. street-papers.org/.

2. Leveraging social change through entrepreneurship

Francesco Perrini and Clodia Vurro

2.1 INTRODUCTION

The fact that we expect all organizations consistent with that 'social entrepreneurship (SE) way of life' to seek the same goals does not mean that we expect all of them to attain that goal in the same way, with identical design, structure, or behavior. It is essential that we find universals, but equally essential to find patterns in variation. In this sense, social entrepreneurial ventures (SEVs) exist in that space where the nonprofit sector, the for-profit sector, and the public sector overlap. Harnessed together, the qualities of each sector ought to put the previously unreachable within grasp: innovative, entrepreneurial organizations, which focus on social problems and initiate social change. By the way, not all innovative social entrepreneurs who embrace an innovation, with an entrepreneurial mindset and a strong need for achievement, do it in the same way.

To clarify those elements that determine the effectiveness of a SEV, in this chapter we analyze SE focusing on critical issues that a socially innovative entrepreneur faces in creating and sustaining organizations. In other words, entrepreneurial orientation, innovation, and social change represent the constitutive elements of SE, but they still do not adequately define this complex phenomenon. SE process emerges as the integration of entrepreneurial and innovative perspectives in developing and taking actions designed to create societal well-being. It is first and foremost concerned with a process of change and with the creation of new social value. But in what ways do SEVs differ from one another? And is it always possible for an established SEV to run well?

In answering these questions, we suggest that the basic ingredients across which SEVs vary in the way they pursue social change can be grouped into two main divisions. The first one, the organizational set, is composed of three dimensions: a cause-driven vision, a scalable innovation, and an economic robustness. The second set – the environmental set – concerns those features that affect a SEV's success but that are hardly controllable by organizations directly.

The remainder of the chapter is structured as follows. First a brief review of the main contributions of the literature on SE as a process of venture creation is presented. Then we explain each one of the variables mentioned above. The analysis includes examples of SE best practices.

2.2 THE SOCIAL ENTREPRENEURIAL PROCESS: AN OVERVIEW

The contributions that specifically explain how SEVs work and are managed are in scant supply. Because SE is a new field of inquiry, most of the current literature focuses at a preliminary 'definition level'.

In particular the most recent debate on SE (Guclu et al., 2002; Hockerts, 2004; Dorado and Heattich; 2004) considers the SE process as one that originates in the discovery of a social entrepreneurial opportunity. In other words, by adopting an opportunity-oriented mindset, SEVs transform a viable idea into a functional organization. But beyond this the current research is even scanter, overlapping with literature on nonprofit management and enterprise (see, for example, Letts et al., 1997; Brinckerhoff, 2000; Dees at al., 2001 and 2002; Paton, 2003). In what follows, we identify a list of preliminary features that extant debate recognizes as typical of the SE process:

- SEVs' production of goods and services is ongoing, with a decided orientation towards problem solving and emphasis on the ability to obtain measurable results in real terms;
- SEVs are characterized by a low level of dependence, and therefore a high level of autonomy: they can receive public grants but they are not managed directly or indirectly by public actors;

- in SEV management, power does not depend on capital share: there is scant motivation for individual profit maximization, and company rights are widened and shared by all stakeholders (Borzaga and Solari, 2004);
- SEV operations are based on a complex mix of monetary and non-monetary resources (that is, volunteers) and are oriented towards collaboration and participation (Grenier, 2002). In particular the more visible and potentially controversial the SE initiative, the more important external relations and partnerships become. Alvord et al. (2002) draw some conclusions on the relationship between kinds of innovation and typologies of external relations. For example, those SEVs involved in capacity building pay more attention to local communities and resource providers. Those whose focus is the dissemination of innovation are concerned with the role and importance of users/customers. And finally SEVs that prioritize movement building are principally centered on their relationship with members and allies;
- in all phases of the SE process, training and capacity building are crucial because of both the difficulty of duplicating skills and the consequent necessity to build an organizational environment in which competencies and skills can easily flow around (Johnson, 2000). In general, because of the newness of this field, conventions for building organizational capacity have not yet been established. Even where SE initiatives vary considerably, the larger the organization is, the more sophisticated its systems and arrangements are (Alvord et al., 2002). In any case, at the moment, it is not the organizational form that determines the character of the SE (Mair and Marti, 2004), but rather the relationship between entrepreneurial aptitude, innovation, and social change and its unexpected and unpredictable results.

Most of the characteristics listed above refer clearly to nonprofit based SE. Independence, training, and capacity building, along with the ongoing production of goods and services comprise strategies opposed to the more traditional scenario of resource scarcity, increasing competition, and a push for more market-based solutions.

But if we agree that SE today is much more than a mere extension of the nonprofit sector, it becomes essential to reinterpret how SEV leverages social change thorough entrepreneurship. We argue that, in working towards social innovation through an SEV, the vision of the SE process embraces both nonprofit and business culture. Toward this end, SEVs leverage transferable skills and best practices. In so doing, they strive toward an instructive and participatory organizational structure.

The remainder of this section focuses on those elements we consider critical in affecting outcomes across the whole SE process.

2.3 GETTING OFF THE GROUND: CRITICAL ISSUES AND MAIN CHALLENGES

The SE process starts with the recognition and assessment of a SE opportunity. The idea for a new business can emerge through a deliberate search or a chance encounter. There is almost always a triggering event that gives birth to a new organization. An opportunity for socially innovative entrepreneurs concerns new ways to enhance and sustain societal well-being, as well as to pursue social change. As explained in chapter 1, those factors that make socially innovative entrepreneurs aware of the existence of a social gap to transform into an entrepreneurial opportunity are strictly determined by personal and environmental agents. Transformative events and previous experience as well as external, explicit, and implicit requests for help, the state of the economy, and the availability of resources are all part and parcel of a SE opportunity.

The decision to exploit such an opportunity, the next step of the SE process, is based on a joint and balanced evaluation of related social and economic potential. In other words, since entrepreneurship always involves assembling a unique package of resources that are never completely controlled by the entrepreneur, it is essential that the decision to actually exploit the opportunity be based on an understanding of its potential in relation to the effort that will be required. Specifically, an opportunity should, in general, earn an adequate return to justify an entrepreneurial risk. Adequate, certainly a relative term, depends on the amount of capital invested, the time-frame required to earn the return, the risk assumed in the process, and the existing alternative uses of both capital and time. Since circumstances will change over time (that is, changing technology, community needs and customer preferences, personnel turnover, and availability of resources), a good opportunity is flexible, open to additional options in a variety of different ways. SE does not represent an exception, although the assessment model is much more specific to the purpose of SE (Dees, Emerson and Economy, 2001): the enhancement of societal well-being and the attainment of social change. In this sense a good SE opportunity is characterized by adequate social potential in terms of contribution to social change, given the required resources.

The opportunity to satisfy an unmet social need, then, translates into a concrete innovation, which can embrace one or more of the following four main fronts: products and services or new qualities of products and services; methods of organization and/or production; other production considerations; and market relations. Certainly the effectiveness of an innovation in terms of potential to change society is strictly linked to a fitting business model, which represents the 'output' of organizational launching and functioning.

The SEV's entrepreneurial model should be oriented toward well-defined, measurable social and economic outcomes and wide innovation dissemination, consistent with the definition of SE. Both lead to the enhancement of societal well-being within communities, in terms of direct and indirect employment creation, access to information and knowledge, social cohesion and inclusion, and community and economic development. Social change is what remains at the end of the process and what sets in motion that virtuous cycle according to which the more the profit, the more a problem is alleviated, freeing up resources for prospective fulfillment of other social gaps.

As for business entrepreneurship, we argue that SE does not require, but can include, the creation of a new organization. As Fowler (2000) observed, SE can occur in different ways: as an integrated SE, when conceived from the beginning as clearly oriented toward filling in a social gap; as reinterpreted SE, when nonprofits try to integrate an SE perspective by diversifying their activities; and as a complementary SE, when the promoter of an SE initiative is a traditional business organization that decides to reorient part of its processes toward the achievement of a social mission. Figure 2.1 summarizes the main steps of the SE process.

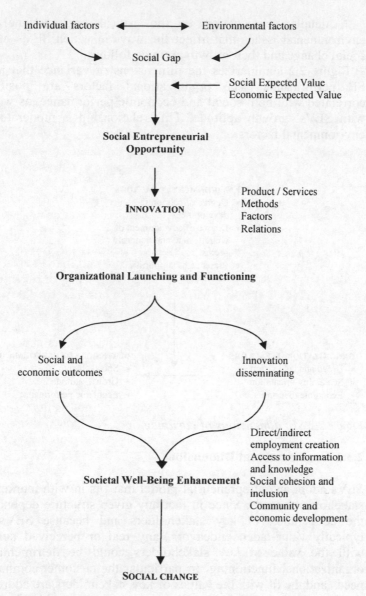

Figure 2.1 The SE process

A detailed explanation of the critical organizational and environmental issues that affect the ways in which SEVs pursue social change and their growth aptitude follows.

Figure 2.2 summarizes the dimensions of variance that affect SE performance. The organizational factors are positively correlated with both social and economic performance, as well as with SEVs' growth aptitude. This relationship is moderated by environmental factors.

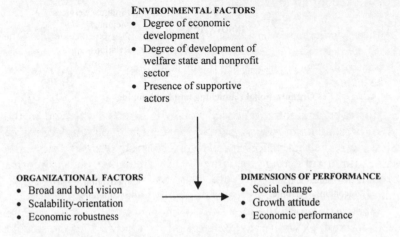

ENVIRONMENTAL FACTORS
• Degree of economic
  development
• Degree of development of
  welfare state and nonprofit
  sector
• Presence of supportive
  actors

ORGANIZATIONAL FACTORS
• Broad and bold vision
• Scalability-orientation
• Economic robustness

DIMENSIONS OF PERFORMANCE
• Social change
• Growth attitude
• Economic performance

Figure 2.2 SE: dimensions of variance

2.3.1 Organizational Dimensions

SEVs adopt an entrepreneurial model that fits in with market and stakeholders' needs. Since in fact any given structure depends on the cooperation of key stakeholders and because SEVs are typically value-laden endeavors, any real or perceived conflict with the value of key stakeholders could be detrimental to organizational functioning. In particular the customer/community needs and the fit with the values of key stakeholders are addressed through a set of organizational traits: (1) a broad and bold vision; (2) a scalability-orientation; (3) an economic robustness.

2.3.1.1 The role of vision in pursuing social change

Every change begins with a vision that sparks the decision to take action. A vision is the innovative social entrepreneur's prediction of a future state; it is seeing an opportunity where others see nothing, an opportunity to break established patterns and initiate social change. Inevitably the vision is strictly tied to the characteristics of the entrepreneur, and to his/her willingness to enact that image of the future, acquiring the necessary resources and harnessing the support of other key people (Thompson et al., 2000). According to Drayton (2002):

> There is no entrepreneur without a powerful, new, system change idea. The entrepreneur exists to make his or her vision society's new pattern. He or she is married to that vision, in sickness or in health, until it has swept the field (p. 123).

However, the entrepreneurial vision is directly reflected in the mission statement, which should be centered on the ability of SEVs to serve that vision in relatively concrete terms, while at the same time reflecting the three key elements that comprise organizations consistent with the SE construct: innovation, entrepreneurship, and motivation towards specific social change.

When navigating the web sites of pioneers of SE, the role of a well-defined, well-stated mission appears impressively straightforward. In other words, mission, vision statement, or company values are the most direct indicators of the organization's soul and belief. Describing the service area, service recipients, and the main outcomes the organization is expected to achieve, they signal that an organization has a new approach with which to tackle social problems and achieve social change.

At the same time, mission and value statements accomplish more than this. They help organizations to identify goals and expected returns from the beginning (Brinckerhoff, 2000). The mission represents the first step in the process of transforming entrepreneurial opportunities into concrete social outcomes and social change (Dees, Emerson and Economy, 2001; Dees, Battle Anderson and Wei-Skillern, 2004).

Finally, defining a mission forces organizations to identify service or product recipients. In other words, making explicit what SEV intends to achieve, guides them in overturning the

34 *The New Social Entrepreneurship*

accountability flow that typifies nonprofits. As McLeod (1997) argued:

> in traditional nonprofits, it was the funding organization that had to be satisfied first, then the executive director (usually the conduit to funding sources), then the employees and volunteers, and, only in the end, the people whose satisfaction was directly tied to the organization's mission in the first place (p. 4).

Contrary to this, SEVs start from their community of reference, and from the need and social gaps that are consistent with their community of reference.

Microcredit exemplifies what knowledge of the customer base means for SEVs and how a social gap can be turned into an innovative and effective vision of the future. Microcredit refers to all those programs that extend small loans to very poor people for self-employment projects that generate income, allowing them to care for themselves and their families. The key implication of microcredit is in name itself, 'micro', which alludes to the small size of the loans made, small size of savings made, the less frequent loans, shorter repayment periods and amounts, the micro/local level of activities, the community-based immediacy of microcredit, and so on.

Hence microcredit is not the solution to poverty, but rather an enabler and a menu of options that have to be put together based on local conditions and needs. Grameen Bank is a leading organization in the microcredit field. Its experience exemplifies the impact of a powerful idea. Box 2.1 provides a brief description of this successful SEV, which has translated SE into real terms and results.

BOX 2.1 The case of Grameen Bank

When Professor Muhammad Yunus founded Grameen Bank in 1983, he reinvented conventional banking model, removing the need for collateral or legally enforceable contracts, promoting credit as a fundamental human right, and making women and the poorest its first priority.

In contrast to most banks, which require endless paperwork, Grameen lent to people who were largely illiterate. And, rather than expecting people to come to it, it dispatched 'bicycle bankers' to rigorously select borrowers and their projects.The resulting banking system, mainly based on trust and accountability, relies on modest loans (microcredit), offered to to over 2.4 million mostly female borrowers in 42,000 Bangladeshi villages, with a loan repayment rate of over 98 percent. For these communities, microcredit represents a dose of hope and confidence, opportunities to respond to their circumstances with unique and relevant solutions, and typically, the difference between destitution and a productive life. Based on the premise that the poor have under-utilized skills, Grameen offers them microcredit for housing and income-generating, and self-employment-related activities, like small businesses in food production and animal husbandry. Community support networks are established to improve the success of these activities, and both obligatory and voluntary savings programs for borrowers accompany the award of loans.

Grameen also promotes community development by establishing groups and centers, and nurturing leadership through elections of group and centre leaders, and of board members when borrowers own institutions. In addition, it monitors children's education and encourages them to enroll, stay, and excel in school by offering scholarships and student loans for higher education. Grameen also runs other initiatives aimed at making information technology and energy accessible to rural areas through its Grameen Family of Organizations.

Since its establishment, Grameen has given loans of about US $3.75 billion through over 1000 bank branches. Impact studies by independent researchers credit Grameen with extricating about 5 percent of its borrowers out of poverty yearly, raising standards of nutrition, health, and housing, improving access to education, increasing the adoption of family planning practices, enhancing the status of women, and increasing participation in social and political activities.

Grameen, which is owned by its borrowers, is also a profit-making, financially self-reliant enterprise. Its success at employing microcredit as a sustainable developmental strategy and a viable business model that fulfils rather than subordinates the financial needs of the poor has spawned similar initiatives in nearly 100 countries.

As Yunus firmly believes,

Banks can and should lend to the disinherited of this Earth, not only out of altruism but out of self-interest. Treating the poor as outcasts is immoral and indefensible; but it is also financially stupid.

(Yunus, 1999; http://www.grameen-info.org)

2.3.1.2 Scalability orientation and the aptitude to grow

Growth aptitude in SE is mainly determined by the extent to which the innovation is scalable, in that scalability is one criterion for assessing the potential success of a socially oriented project. Scalability is relevant in this context because of the different nature of social entrepreneurial opportunity. Since its potential is evaluated in terms of expected social value (see Chapter 1), scalability is the criterion to keep in mind in the process of spreading social innovation as widely as possible and thus maximizing social change and the improvement of social conditions.

According to Dees et al. (2004), there are three main approaches to innovation scalability in the process of maximizing impact. The first one, dissemination, corresponds to spreading an innovation across new sites through a targeted new site-development plan. To put it another way, organizations help other communities to independently replicate an innovation, often limiting their involvement to providing information and technical assistance. This approach can be read as an attempt to maintain a constant level of customization in the pursuit of the social mission and avoid the proved ineffectiveness of standardized services to improve social conditions (Borzaga and Defourny, 2004).

The second approach, affiliation, corresponds to the creation of a more or less formal and identifiable network of organizations with the same purpose. Branching, the third way to spread the impact of an innovation, corresponds to the creation of local units coordinated by one large organization, the one that first introduces innovation for social change. These approaches can be viewed along a continuum, from a low to high degree of central coordination and required resources.

The specific scaling strategy has to be strictly determined by the organization's knowledge of its community of reference and by the specific characteristics of the innovation to be spread. But this is not enough. Dees et al. propose the five R's model in assessing different scaling approaches. This decision model is presented in Table 2.1. Notice that scalability necessarily implies the development of networking and partnership development strategies. The reasons can be diverse: from thorough shared facilities, services, or activities and the elimination of duplicative costs and excess capacity, to critical input combinations.

Table 2.1 The five R's

READINESS: Is the innovation ready to be spread?
RECEPTIVITY: Will the innovation be well received in target communities?
RESOURCES: What resources, financial or otherwise, are required to get the job done right?
RISK: What's the chance the innovation will be implemented incorrectly, or will fail to have impact?
RETURNS: What is the bottom line? Impact should not just be about serving more people – it should be about serving them well.

Source: Dees et al., 2004, p. 30

But partnership and networking can also increase the impact of the innovation through putting together complementary capabilities or, moreover, enlarging the market or client base. In addition new expertise and contractual power applied to funding the organization can also be acquired. According to Prabhu (1999, p. 143)

Networking with other organizations within their geographical operating area as well as with similar organizations operating elsewhere is crucial for social entrepreneurial leaders for receiving relevant information, mutual learning, getting appropriate personnel, and for joining together for common causes.

In more general terms, since SEVs are designed to leverage limited resources into major social change and since their action is

mostly catalytic rather than direct, extensive networks are crucial
to success (Waddock and Post, 1991). In other words, the complex
nature of social problems makes it necessary to involve a number
of different constituencies, each one with specific types of skills
and power to be used cooperatively. It is in this respect that SE
involves a strong propensity to forge partnerships and alliances
with nonprofit organizations, for-profit companies, and public
actors (Gartner, 1985; Katz and Gartner, 1988; Kodithuwakku and
Rosa, 2002; Waddock and Post, 1991).

Finally, building networks and partnership is critical for SEVs
to establish legitimacy with multiple constituencies.

In order to scale impact and foster partnerships and networking,
SEVs inevitably should base their operation on a participatory and
learning management philosophy. An additional reason for this
assumption regards the 'newness' of the SE phenomenon. The
scarcity of models and acknowledged best practices makes it
critical to build an organizational environment in which
competencies and skills can easily flow (Johnson, 2000). As such,
SEVs are characterized by an extremely adaptive culture.

This feature reminds us again of the newness of the SE domain
and the related necessity to achieve visibility, wide community
awareness, and eventually to gain new resources to replicate the
model (Thompson, 2002). Therefore we believe that the more
visible and potentially controversial the social entrepreneurial
initiative, the more important external relations and partnerships
become.

In conclusion we argue that, in operating social innovation
through a SEV, the SE process aims at creating an overall vision
that embraces both nonprofit and business culture in order to
maximize the impact of the innovation. Thus SEVs look for
synergy, leveraging transferable skills and best practices,
establishing their operations on a learning and participatory
organizational structure in order to succeed in achieving social
change.

Manchester Craftsmen's Guild (see Box 2.2) represents a prime
example of how a simple idea can be leveraged into a powerful
SEV, thorough scalability-orientation, diversification, and
networking aptitude.

BOX 2.2 Manchester Craftsmen's Guild case study

The Manchester Craftsmen's Guild began in 1968 as an after-school programme to redress the deteriorating socio-economic conditions of the predominantly African-American community of Manchester, Pittsburgh, by teaching pottery to at-risk urban youth. Wanting to re-create his own life-changing experience with pottery, and convinced that artistic endeavour inspires hope, fosters self-confidence, and saves lives, MCG founder Bill Strickland turned the basement of a donated Manchester row house into a classroom and a modest exhibition space for the youth he taught.

Today, the MCG is a 62 000-square-foot, multi-discipline arts education and performance centre built with money Strickland actively raised from foundations, corporations, and government sources, and offering music studios, a 350-seat concert hall, classrooms, and jazz performances. The Guild runs a host of innovative programmes in the facility and brings them through outreach efforts to Pittsburgh schools.

These programmes build on mentoring relationships with artists, educators, and counsellors, and employ disciplines such as music, photography, ceramic art, visual art, and drama to teach life skills and nurture creativity, self-awareness, intercultural understanding, and entrepreneurial potential. A typical lesson involves high school students constructing puppets to stage a fable they have watched and discussed as a play, or revisiting the Civil Rights movement to explore perspectives about major historical events and people through their own photography and writing.

The MCG also houses Strickland's other venture, the Bidwell Training Center Inc (BTC), a failing vocational school in a rundown Pittsburgh neighbourhood that Strickland took over. Through partnerships with corporations like chemical-pharmaceutical company Bayer and food industry giant Heinz, Bidwell has been transformed into a viable school, training displaced adults in high-skill fields including computer technology, horticulture, and pharmacy for meaningful job opportunities. Its culinary arts programme even operates a catering service and a 200-seat restaurant.

Together, the Guild and Bidwell reach about 400 underprivileged youth and nearly 500 adults yearly. And, about 80 percent of the high-risk high-school students who attend the MCG's after-school arts program have gone on to college, while 78 percent of the adults who graduate from this vocational programme find jobs.

The Guild's success can be attributed not only to Strickland's creativity and vision, but also to a sound business plan. In the early years, Strickland ran the MCG's after-school pottery programme on an annual budget of less than $50,000, relying on small grants and contributions by community leaders who had begun to support his work. Delivering results that built confidence in the Guild's organisational capability, and actively nurturing partnerships with business and community leaders, Strickland was able to diversify and multiply sources of capital, and dramatically expand the scope and reach of the Guild.

The MCG's innovative partnership with Bayer on the Bidwell project, for example, also resulted in a record label for the Guild's Jazz Performing Arts Program. Involving not only Bayer, which makes the plastic for the CDs, but also Sony Disc manufacturing, the label even boasts a Grammy Award, and has a deal with Starbucks Coffee to sell its CDs at their cafes worldwide.

In 2001, Strickland broke new ground again, unveiling plans to build a $4 million greenhouse and education centre near MCG. Sprung from his love of gardening, and realised through a partnership with California-based Zuma Canyon Orchids, and generous funding from the government, foundations, and corporations, the greenhouse grows hydroponic tomatoes and orchids to teach inner-city youth horticulture and prepare them for careers in this field. At the same time, it is a platform for an orchid growing wholesale business that Strickland hopes will generate more revenue to fund programmes at the Guild and Bidwell.

Keen to share his success with transforming social missions into sustainable profit-making enterprises, Strickland has also embarked on the Denali Initiative, a three-year fellowship programme funded by the Kaufmann

Foundation to teach non-profit leaders entrepreneurial and business skills.

Strickland's innovative model of community development through the arts, education, and enterprise now generates an annual turnover in excess of US$10 million.

http://www.manchesterguild.org/home/non.html

2.3.1.3 Pursuing social change through economic robustness

One of the most important ways in which the entrepreneur can create value is by doing more with less. This is even more relevant for the social sector, in which lack of resources is a founding attribute.

In this context, day-by-day operations should be sustained by an explicit, balanced understanding of cost minimization and efficiency, and overall maximization of quality.

The assessment of SEVs' efficiency and economic robustness goes hand in hand with the problem of measurability of results and balanced evaluation of social and economic outcomes. This issue is especially critical for social-purpose organizations in that they involve several different considerations that have to be taken into account. Values, for example, cannot be easily measured and often are tied to a long-term horizon. Significant diversity exists within each field of action and across different fields, in that each vision is highly community-based.

Since those considerations are case-specific, SEVs should share the ability to pursue a self-sustaining flow of resources together with profitability, as a measure of SE success.

A detailed analysis of the main measurement tools and success indicators is beyond the scope of this chapter. However, what we consider relevant in this phase is emphasizing the importance of adopting an efficiency-based entrepreneurial orientation starting from the very beginning. A self-sufficient and financially sound business strategy should inform the process of creating new ventures. One of the most interesting and well-known examples of an economically robust SE model is presented below. Aravind Eye Hospitals (Box 2.3) was established explicitly as a more efficient way to bring eye care to the poorest people in rural and urban India (Prahalad, 2004). Therefore the initial innovation regarded not service per se but organization of the workflow.

BOX 2.3 Aravind Eye Hospital case study

To combat one of the highest percentages of blindness in the world, and a lack of accessible, state-subsidised eye care, Dr G. Venkataswamy founded the Aravind Eye Hospital in Madurai, India, with just 11 beds in 1976. Today, as a network of hospitals providing over 190 000 surgeries and nearly 1.3 million outpatient services yearly, Aravind is – literally – a visible solution.

Aravind provides high-quality but affordable curative, preventive, and rehabilitative eye care, including cataract surgery to cure blindness. These services are provided through its hospitals, which have well-equipped specialty clinics with comprehensive support facilities, as well as through community outreach, which is integral to the organisation. Aravind partners local community leaders and service groups to organise screening eye camps, school eye-health programmes, village volunteer programmes, and campaigns to educate people about eye care. These initiatives provide different strategies for taking eye care service to the community's doorstep. This innovative system is delivered within a sustainable financial structure based on dramatic reductions in the cost structure that are passed on as savings to its consumers. Aravind's hospitals are served by their own manufacturing facility, Aurolab, which undertakes the research and development of manufacturing technologies to produce cheap pharmaceuticals, intraocular lenses (IOLs), and suture needles. Hospitals also put two or more patients in an operating room at the same time, and use bamboo rather than more expensive metal for its beds to cut costs. As a result, a cataract operation costs Aravind only about $10, compared to $1,650 in the United States.

Furthermore, only about a third of the patients who can afford it pay market prices to offset the cost of serving a third who pay about 65 percent of cost, and another third who pay nothing. This unique 'cross-funding' model, combined with low costs and effective management, have enabled Aravind's hospitals to enjoy a gross margin of 40 percent and become the most productive eye care organisation in the world, in terms of surgical volume and the number of the world, in terms of surgical volume and the number of patients treated. With less than 1 percent of the country's ophthalmic manpower, Aravind performs about 5 percent of all cataract surgeries in India. At the same time, its patients receive not only the gift of sight, but also opportunities to continue in the workforce, minimise lost wages, and increase economic productivity.

By providing high-quality eye care to the greatest number of people at the lowest possible cost, Aravind reaps long-term social and economic revenue for those it serves. At the same time, it challenges conventional business wisdom with proof that there is profitability in business opportunities involving the poor.

Dr V. has set its goals for Aravind: 'We want to be global. I think in these days of technological advancement, barriers of countries have been demolished. So I have set myself a target of eradicating needless blindness by 2010.'

http://www.aravind.org/

2.4 ENVIRONMENTAL DIMENSIONS

Even if socially innovative entrepreneurs have both the willingness and the abilities to enter the SE path, it is the environment in which they operate that will either kill or facilitate their development.

Three environmental factors influence the impact of SE dimensions on performance. The first one regards the extent to which the economic environment is developed. In this sense the level of economic development influences the demand for social services. Accordingly, in less developed countries, SE is more widespread and devoted to facing the main problems of these countries – for example the creation of jobs for those groups of people excluded from the labor market.

The second environmental factor that can affect the success of SE is the competitive environment within the organization, in terms of welfare state and nonprofit development. Although the type and quality of services they provide are innovative, organizations consistent with the SE construct operate in the same fields as do public authorities and other third-sector organizations, that is, nonprofits. Since SE organizations are the latecomers, it is quite obvious that their success depends on the strength of the other providers, on the resources and the characteristics of the welfare state, and on the state of development of the traditional third sectors.

The third element that has to be considered is the presence of a supportive environment. The main reference here is to the financial and consulting service sectors and their ability to provide adequate financial assets and technical assistance to SE organizations. In order to overcome the misalignment between the needs of social entrepreneurs on the one hand and the traditional financial sectors on the other, attention is extending to the role of social venture capital or venture philanthropy (VP) in supporting the diffusion of SE. Specifically VP has established itself since the nineties as an alternative form of charitable giving based on the application of venture capital principles to the first SE organizations (Porter and Kramer, 1999). It is the main result of this reinvesting process that drives current philanthropic practices. In other words, a private or alternatively a corporate foundation will want to develop a financing relationship with a social organization that has been able to distinguish itself for innovative spirit and high growth potential and impact in contributing to social change.

In this sense VP would seem to be an innovative expression of a classical financing relationship between foundations and nonprofits. In reality the premises change radically. In fact venture philanthropists no longer consider the theoretical social effectiveness of social projects but rather turn to a further, new dimension: the assessment of the concrete SE organization's ability to implement its social mission through an economically sustainable business model.

For too much time, the decision to assign financial resources to social programs has been based on a vague feasibility judgment rather than on the organization's actual ability to interact effectively with the environment of reference and achieve the mission.

Therefore social venture capital now represents philanthropic foundations' attempt at redemption, perfectly consistent with the definition of SE as a highly innovative entrepreneurial formula.

If we look for the main characteristic of VP, the first element that emerges is a permanent attention to SE capacity building, the development of organizational and managerial skills, from building a solid organizational infrastructure to hiring qualified personnel, and from the achievement of a clear definition of tasks to the development of a problem-solving orientation and a working business strategy. In addition VP is based on conceiving and implementing ad hoc measurement instruments to evaluate the degree of realization of economic and social objectives and the soundness of the firm's performance through specific indicators. Finally VP is characterized by a partnership approach to management and a collaborative approach toward its exit strategy, aimed at evaluating the ability of SE organizations to survive in the long term.

Financing therefore requires more than just giving money. As with start-ups, financing, mentoring, and incubation are critical to the success of SEVs. Engaged financing or VP-like models are necded.

3. The basis for launching a new social entrepreneurial venture

Francesco Perrini and Alessandro Marino

3.1 INTRODUCTION

Its hybrid, cross-industry nature and the lack of a consolidated reference framework that would make the meaning of social entrepreneurial venture (SEV) and its special features readily recognizable continue to hinder the development of social entrepreneurship.

Nonetheless, the process of creating new social enterprises is not unlike the process of launching an enterprise in other fields. In the section that follows, we begin by describing a hypothetical entrepreneurial 'path', within which we discuss some of the critical issues typically encountered when undertaking a social venture. We then examine business planning and the key parallels between social and more traditional ventures. The business plan is a fundamental entrepreneurial tool that neither traditional nor social enterprises can do without, particularly during start-up.

3.2 THE START-UP PHASE FOR A SOCIAL ENTERPRISE VENTURE

The creation of new enterprises is an essential part of overall economic growth, in that it stimulates innovation and development, creates new jobs and, in the case of SEVs, has a strong positive impact on the community. The actual start of operations is typically preceded by two macro-stages: the identification and assessment of the business opportunity; and business planning/development and acquiring the necessary resources. We now discuss the key elements of these preliminary phases, underscoring the special characteristics of 'social' start-ups.

3.2.1 Identify and Assess the Opportunity

In the earliest stages of the start-up process, the entrepreneur must determine whether a given business opportunity is sufficiently attractive. According to Drucker (1986), in order to be a truly innovative entrepreneur, one must be able to recognize certain signs that represent important, highly reliable indicators of changes that have already happened or that can be made to happen with little effort. In his view these include the unexpected; the incongruity between reality as it actually is and reality as it is assumed to be or as it 'ought to be'; innovation based on process needs; changes in the industry structure or market structure that catch everyone unawares; demographic changes; changes in perception, mood, and meaning; new knowledge, both scientific and non-scientific.

For social entrepreneurs in particular, the decision to take on a new venture can be based both on the identification of an economically attractive opportunity and on one's own system of values. In other words, social entrepreneurs are typically driven by the desire to make a contribution to society. However, they are aware that in order to do so it is necessary to come up with an organization which, unlike a more traditional enterprise, fully leverages the strong link that there must be between all potential stakeholders.

3.2.2 Defining the Business and Procuring Key Resources

Determining the feasibility of a business alone is not enough to start an enterprise, however. The entrepreneur must define a strategy that can effectively translate ideas into plans and activities. In other words, the initial development of the enterprise must be laid out and formalized in a business plan.

The plan therefore lays out the resources needed, for which certain key issues need to be resolved. The entrepreneur is at the center of a process aimed at defining a set of resources that are critical to the full exploitation of the opportunity. Usually, however, the entrepreneur does not control all of the necessary resources, so this gap must be bridged through important decisions regarding interaction with the outside world that will have a systemic impact on the internal organization of the enterprise. Such resources may include, for example, physical inputs, human resource inputs, technology inputs and social inputs (Brush et al., 2001). It is important to note, however, that financial resources are an essential, high-priority factor during start-up, primarily because of their natural fungibility. A lack of financial resources is often cited as the main cause of the failure of start-ups (Chandler and Hanks, 1998).

Defining the set of resources needed to start the enterprise is a complex process, given that it regards the entire scope of the venture. In fact, the entrepreneur develops a network of stakeholders that can quite easily turn hostile if they lose motivation owing to a lack of credible, rewarding development strategies. MacMillan (1983) underscores this aspect in speaking about entrepreneurial behavior that seeks to anticipate difficulties. The key to not delaying or actually impeding the initial entrepreneurial development is the ability of the entrepreneur to 'put together a keystone alliance with the key subset of stakeholders' and to anticipate any resistance by developing credible strategies.

This is of even greater importance for the social entrepreneur, who brings together a broader, more diverse community of stakeholders. This challenge can be overcome by placing a great emphasis on business planning. This process is a key factor in increasing the ability to communicate and dialogue with all of the interest groups associated with the enterprise. Before addressing this issue in detail, we take a moment to describe an entity external to the enterprise that can make a crucial contribution to the start-up phase: the business incubator. Business incubators can provide excellent support in procuring key resources. For SEVs, there are even 'social incubators' dedicated specifically to social ventures. This phenomenon is still in the very early stages of development, but is destined to stimulate a great deal of interest in the years to come.

3.2.3 Incubators as a Support Tool in Starting Traditional and Social Enterprises

As defined by Smilor (1987), a business incubator is an innovative means of supporting and accelerating the initial growth of an enterprise by providing services and leveraging skills, technologies, capital and know-how in order to implement viable entrepreneurial ideas. Therefore, an incubator is not a mere provider of services and infrastructures, but rather an organization that brings together support activities and resources from a network of individuals and organizations in order to assist new enterprises.

The literature classifies incubators in a number of ways. For example, Brooks (1986) and Allen and McCluskey (1990) define a continuum that links organization types and their objectives. They consider for-profit, non-profit and academic-related incubators, attributing to them the objectives of direct sale of services to incubator tenants, the creation of jobs and the commercialization of university research, respectively.

As such, business incubators nurture the initial development of the business idea – the key asset of the potential entrepreneur – with the ultimate goal of minimizing the risk of failure, which is very high at this stage of the process. The term 'incubator' itself evokes the idea of a sort of nursery in which newborns are nourished and developed.

An incubator typically works with the new venture for between 4 and 8 months. As a first step, the new product or service is created and supported through the initial stage of development. The company is then given help in the search for sources of financing, such venture capitalists, with whom the incubator normally has a well-established relationship. Sometimes, the incubator is a branch of a company or an investment fund, for whom it selects projects in which to invest. In this way, incubators serve to strengthen the new venture's bargaining power with investors.

Thus, incubators help provide numerous resources and services in a variety of business areas: space, technology, organizational consulting, market-entrance strategies, marketing and tax consulting. They are also involved in supervising the preparation of the business plan, forming the management team, and structuring financing. Their operations are based above all on the intellectual and technological resources of their managers, who typically have experience in the fields of business, finance and consulting. As noted, their contribution does not normally include financing the company, a task that is entrusted to more specialized entities, such as venture capitalists, that are nevertheless connected with the incubator's network. However, an incubator may sometimes provide a minimal level of financial resources needed in the pre-venture capital phase (that is, seed financing of the idea). Monetary payment is rarely requested for the assistance provided. Normally, they will ask for a stake in the new company. If the company succeeds, the incubator benefits from the significant capital gains that can be achieved by selling its holding.

Incubators that operate exclusively in the field of social entrepreneurship (SE) are known as 'social incubators' (SI), but, with the exception of their objectives, they do not differ from the more traditional model. In order to present certain special features, the following paragraph offers a description of the experience in Israel of the Joint Distribution Committee (JDC), a non-governmental organization in the social sector.

3.2.3.1 The Joint Distribution Committee's incubator for social entrepreneurship

The main reason for undertaking this initiative was the same as that encountered in other international contexts, that is, the existence of a gap in social support mechanisms: The social sector lacks the kind of institutionalized support mechanisms (such as venture capital funds, industrial parks, entrepreneurship incubators, entrepreneurship support centers) which are now common in the business sector for supporting and aiding entrepreneurs in every aspect of developing and implementing new ventures. It was therefore decided to create an incubator to establish a set of services and resources for the social entrepreneur. Generally speaking, this was not to be much different from the structures typical of the business sector, and its success was to be linked to its relative ability to improve service quality and efficiency and add value to the incubated initiatives.

As with many similar organizations, the initiative developed into a network with a number of strategic operational partnerships with government agencies, training organizations, companies and individuals in order to bring together services and resources that would be difficult to duplicate from scratch. The initiative got under way in 1997 without, however, the establishment of a separate legal entity.

The central decision-making role was played by a Steering Committee composed of members of the founding institutions. It had decision-making power over selecting initiatives and setting policy. Although not all applicant entrepreneurs were accepted in the program due to the nature of the initiative, they were provided preliminary assistance and basic consulting services.

The main service provided by the incubator was the creation of a network of partners and organizations that could be integrated into the development of the ideas presented. Entrepreneurs could, in various stages, contact and dialogue with the potential partners. In fact, the assisted entrepreneurs recognized the importance of the credibility provided by the program, which served to overcome the resistance of key institutions to establishing that initial contact with social entrepreneurs.

In that sense, the fundamental contribution of a social incubator is to accompany entrepreneurs towards adoption by interested partner organizations, as reiterated by the chairman of the initiative himself:

> The incubator needs to develop expertise in nurturing the initiatives that are not yet ready for adoption and to invest resources in them in order to bring them to the point where potential adopting institutions can decide whether they want to take them on.

Although this might appear to be a simple thing to execute, experience has shown how establishing actual, credible operational partnerships is a critical factor in the success of an incubator. In other words, the social value created by sustaining adopted enterprises must be widely recognized as a driver of interest and focus for the organizations that are a part of the network. A desire to participate in similar initiatives that is based solely on considerations of image or otherwise characterized by a lack of operational involvement makes the work of the social incubator inefficient and ineffective. Accordingly, social entrepreneurship has a special need to be promoted and supported by structures that operate from a robust, well-designed multi-stakeholder perspective. Table 3.1 offers a selection of projects that took part in the JDC initiative.

Table 3.1 Projects in the JDC Initiative

Idea	Entrepreneur	Treatment by Incubator
Using temporary foster families and community treatment teams as means of helping dysfunctional families rather than breaking them up.	Ph.D in Social Work who has developed the idea based on years of personal experience with the current system.	Accepted and adopted including funding, by one of the founding partners. The program is currently in its pilot stage.
Creating greenbouses and courses in gardening as a means of social rehabilitation among Bedouin resettled in towns in the Negev region.	Social worker and employee of the welfare department of the local council.	Accepted but no adopting institution found yet. Contacts made with Ministry of Interior, Jewish National Fund, National Social Security Institution.
Developing a multi-year traffic safety education program beginning in elementary school and utilizing simulated traffic parks.	Private contractor. Came up with idea after a member of his family was killed in a traffic accident.	Accepted in the Incubator but without a formal adopting institution. Attended roundtable and put in contact with officials from Ministry of Education and Ministry of Transportation.
Social supervision for private family daycare centers, training for family daycare, and consulting to consumers.	Two entrepreneurs. A social worker who formerly worked in the supervision of public family daycare. A psychologist.	Accepted in the Incubator. Given help in developing a business plan through collaboration with MBA students of entrepreneurship. Still looking for adopting institution or outside funding.

Table 3.1 Continued

Idea	Entrepreneur	Treatment by Incubator
Creating educational programs in non-violence and respectful communication.	Two retired educators and former officials in the Ministry of Education.	Application in process.
Developing telemarketing center in depressed communities in the geographic periphery as a way of combating unemployment.	Unemployed engineer who came up with the idea and began developing it on her own.	Accepted into the Incubator but the relationship was terminated by the entrepreneur due to disagreements over how the project should be advanced.
Program for pre-schoolers in sexual abuse.	Masters in eduction and experts in the field.	Accepted in the Incubator but rejecter the offer to be adopted by the Ministry of Education. No longer in the Incubator.
A ranch for therapy through horseback riding and contact with animals.	Undergraduate student.	Rejected by the Incubator after expert advised the Incubator that the idea already existed in other locations (i.e., not innovative)

3.3 SOCIAL ENTERPRISE PLAN: A STAKEHOLDER APPROACH TO UNDERSTANDING THE DIFFERENCE

The process of business planning and design plays a crucial role during the start-up phase. The reasons for this lie in the fact that it is during the start-up phase that the effects of planning begin to truly take shape. The impact of planning is reflected in operations much more quickly than in more mature companies. Furthermore, the set of objectives that normally guides a start-up is perceived by the entrepreneurs to be a direct and immediate result of their own action. This contributes to making the business planning process more effective and more motivating (Delmar and Shane, 2003). However, this affirmation has been countered by a number of studies that claim that business planning can be a distraction during the start-up phase: business planning is an obstacle to carrying out important activities that must be completed under considerable time pressure (Baron, 1998; Bhide, 2000; Carter et al., 1996).

Generally speaking, for companies that are already operational, business planning is an active process of uninterrupted definition of what an organization intends and is able to produce in the future and the expected outcomes (Mintzberg, 1994).

Other authors make no distinction as to the moment in the life of an enterprise in which a business plan should be adopted, considering it to be essential at all times. Hormozi et al. (2002) in particular see the business plan as a way of constructing an enterprise 'on paper'. They argue that this tool is essential if one hopes to achieve and surpass company goals and objectives in a consistent, organized manner.

The purpose of a business plan is twofold: internally, it is an entrepreneurial self-learning tool; externally, it represents the primary means of informing all stakeholders outside the company about its strategies, plans, and expected results (Marino, 2005). For the social enterprise venture, the basic concept remains unchanged. Its special characteristics are related to the different nature and configuration of the organization itself. In other words, the social purpose does not alter the underlying logic of the business plan. What changes are the relative weights used to aggregate and interpret the needs of the various stakeholders and, consequently, the relative emphasis placed on the various aspects of the plan.

The model presented below views the business plan as a mosaic of perspectives that the entrepreneur must paint in order to develop the system of relationships and to motivate the various interest groups towards the common goal of the enterprise. The stakeholder approach (Freeman, 1984) considers the active role in company management of all stakeholders, both within the organization and external to it. The business plan can be seen as an opportunity to represent the various stakeholders and their means of interaction. A typical business plan would be organized into the following areas:

- description of ownership, management and the workforce;
- description of customer relationships;
- description of relationships with competitors;
- description of relationships within other systems (suppliers, the community, the government, etc.);
- description of current and potential relationships with the external financial system.

In the remainder of this section, we discuss these aspects in more detail, pointing out the special issues that may arise when the activity outlined in the business plan refers to a social entrepreneurial venture.

3.3.1 Ownership, Management and Employees

The vast majority of the most authoritative literature on the subject (Sahlman, 1997) argues no other aspect of a start-up truly counts without the right entrepreneurial team. It is essential that the founders and management demonstrate that they have enough experience in the industry. In other words, it is traditionally considered very important for the entire business plan be built upon a foundation that is able to support it, that is, on internal skills that are able to implement the strategies: 'Bad management can make the best product a failure' (Elkins, 1996, pp. 60-61).

In a social enterprise, there is no difference in the emphasis that needs to be placed on the founders and management. Nonetheless, the description of the founders must emphasize the different attitude with regard to expected return in the form of profits: the social purpose is normally placed on the same level as the founders' profit expectations (Backman and Dees, 1994). This is not always the case, however, as there are certain borderline cases in which the entrepreneur demonstrates that there is no conflict between the two realms. This is a sensitive and often controversial issue, but one which must be explicit and not left to the guesswork of outsiders. The nature of the management of a social venture is also different from that of a more traditional enterprise. In many cases, managers are given less authority and responsibility over administration and strategies than in a traditional company. In fact, they tend to play more the role of stewards of the social mission, ensuring that the organization acts in the interests of all stakeholders in an efficient and appropriate manner (Backman and Dees, 1994). These aspects inevitably lead to a different way of configuring this area in the social enterprise plan without, however, changing its relative priority.

Separate mention must be made of the employees of the new company. In traditional business plans, non-managerial employees do not play a significant role. They are often cited as a key cost factor without particular emphasis on their characteristics or intrinsic needs. A possible reason for this lies in the fact that the needs related to the workforce of a start-up are not seen to be of immediate importance, but are put off until later stages of development. However, the rules change for social ventures, where employees become a more complex issue in the business plan. In particular, there is less of a direct association with cost, given that they are significantly motivated by non-economic objectives that are in line with those of the social enterprise (Backman and Dees, 1994). The boundary between founders, employees, and enterprise goals is fuzzier. Employees may not necessarily work on a volunteer basis, but they are an integral part of the social method that motivates all activities of the enterprise (Marino, 2005). Accordingly, one distinctive characteristic of a social enterprise is a more central, higher priority description of the workforce.

3.3.2 Customers and the Marketplace

The description of the current and potential market necessarily involves expressing the business idea in terms of new products or services. The challenges faced by entrepreneurs are many. They must determine whether the target 'market' is sufficiently large (either currently or in the future) and attractive. There must also be evidence that the customers' needs have been studied carefully and that the entire project has been designed on a credible scale. In other words, it is necessary to support plans with active market analysis at both the macro and micro levels. The positioning of the product or service in relation to the preferences of the target and the related pricing strategy must therefore be clear (Hormozi et al., 2002).

An effective social enterprise plan shifts the focus from a direct analysis of the customer's needs to the construction of knowledge based on the relationship. This makes it possible to define the manner in which the mission of the social enterprise can improve the lives of its intended beneficiaries (Dees et al., 2001). In fact, many potential 'customers' of a social enterprise have no idea what services might meet their needs. In other words, from the point of view of the start-up, the signals received from the market are typically faint and coded. Another distinctive characteristic of the definition of the product/market system is the different conception of the value offered to the customer. An SEV, in fact, has to create social value that 'more than offsets' the resources used to generate it. In other words, a social enterprise is required to 'co-finance' the transfer of value beyond the levels typical of traditional business models. Backman and Dees (1994) summarize the reasons behind this characteristic of the 'social method'. They notice that, in most cases, the targets are unable to pay for the product or service (the homeless, refugees, etc.) or unwilling to do so (for example alcoholics or drug addicts). The enterprise may also be unable to collect payment, or payment collection may be inappropriate (that is, in cases in which intangible 'public' goods are produced or when providing assistance to rape victims, respectively).

A concluding note regarding communication with customers should also be made. Many traditional communication channels may be largely ineffective. As we mentioned earlier, it is possible that the intended beneficiaries may not be able to recognize the link between the message and their own needs, rendering vain the communication efforts. Therefore, during the planning process, attention must be paid to defining credible strategies that create a direct bridge to the target audience. Primarily, however, one must ask the following question: what will prevent the intended recipients of my products or services from ignoring these solutions and continuing to do what they are currently doing? The answers are to be found in a serious, in-depth analysis of the social mission based on direct experience of the actual situation for which the enterprise intends to change the rules of the game.

3.3.3 The Competitive Framework and Other External Systems

For a traditional company, an analysis of the competitive environment is essential to building a credible business model. According to Porter (1983), the role of competitors is to be placed in direct relationship to the intensity of competition within the industry. This, in turn, depends on factors such as the degree of concentration of supply, product differentiation, the presence of barriers to entry and so on (for example, in highly concentrated industries, interaction with competitor stakeholders will be less intense, since only a few enterprises will control the lion's share of the market; or with highly standardized products, there will be a great deal of competition, since price will be the decisive factor in determining competitive advantage; and so on). Another of Porter's important contributions to the analysis of the competition is the recognition of 'latent' competitors that exert a potential competitive influence, that is, potential new entries and enterprises that produce substitute products or services. Since these parties are able to pose a threat to the enterprise, the key to success lies in its ability to set a price-quality ratio that can be adapted to the demands of the competitive landscape (Porter, 1983).

The business plan must specifically address these aspects with well-supported analysis based on observations of the environment in which the enterprise operates. The quality of this analysis has a direct impact on the ability to define the competitive strategy properly and, therefore, to identify the enterprise's competitive advantage (Lindsay and Rue, 1980). There is broad consensus in the literature that careful analysis of the external context is a crucial prerequisite to the maximization of business opportunities through planning (Mathews and Scott, 1995; Durate, 1993; Mintzberg, 1994; Temtime, 2003).

A social enterprise must be able to interact with competitors in a competitive manner: social impact cannot ignore economic efficiency in allocating resources and, therefore, confrontation with similar enterprises. This does not rule out the possibility of establishing forms of cooperation in order to set alliances or work on joint projects. Thus, an analysis of the competitive environment is an important element of preparing the business plan. It is also plausible that there will be less emphasis on this analysis than for traditional companies, and a greater focus on defining strategic and operational partnerships.

Perhaps the aspect that more distinguishes the business plan of a social enterprise is the emphasis placed on other categories of external stakeholders, such as government, the community, or society in general. Under the neo-classical and economic/industrial approach, attention should be focused entirely on the competitive landscape (Jones, 1980). However, leading scholars have argued that these categories of stakeholder are not different than any others, in that they are people or groups towards which the enterprise has a responsibility (Freeman, 1984; Alkhafaji, 1989). Although these positions represent the modern view of the enterprise as a socially responsible organization (Tencati, Perrini and Pogutz, 2004), traditional business plans typically leave little room for planning relations with these actors. The social enterprise venture, on the other hand, is naturally configured to work in the interests of all stakeholders, both internal and, above all, external. It is both plausible and desirable that a social enterprise plan should place a great deal of emphasis on these aspects, giving importance to the design of broad and high-quality relational systems. The quality of these aspects is a key success factor which has a direct impact on achieving the social purpose.

3.3.4 The Financial System and Measuring Performance: The Systems of the Social Enterprises

Relations with potential external investors can only take place after the entrepreneur provides a clear and exhaustive quantitative overview of the enterprise's expected performance. The section of the business plan set aside for this purpose typically includes the assumptions used to calculate financial requirements and the pro forma financial statements (balance sheet, income statement and cash flow statement). The four elements that determine financial needs during the start-up phase are:

- investments to develop the venture;
- structural investments to create production capacity;
- investment in working capital in order to support the start of business;
- additional investment to support subsequent development.

The sections related to financial analysis also provide the data for a quantitative analysis of whether and how the enterprise will be able to generate the returns required by outside investors. Consequently, an estimate of the risk implicit in the venture can be made. According to a study by MacMillan and Subba Narasimha (1987), the business plans that are less successful in obtaining outside investment are those that have a structural tendency to overestimate the performance of the enterprise itself. This tends to create the perception that the entrepreneur is unfamiliar with the actual business being proposed. As a result, it is a good idea to use many comparative indicators of similar industries or markets. The same authors underscore the fact that excessive attention to detail in the financial statements is not directly correlated with a high probability of obtaining financing. This is a key point: the business plan must be designed as a coherent whole, as this is the way it will be read.

Suppliers of financial resources are an important external stakeholder for the enterprise. This category of stakeholder comprises both those who provide debt financing and institutional investors in equity. These are very often the main audience of the business plan for the purposes of obtaining financing. Nonetheless, from the moment they decide to invest, they can no longer be considered as an external financial stakeholder, but rather as an actual 'partner' in the enterprise. Conversely, when a bank lends funds to an enterprise, it cannot be considered an internal stakeholder. Nonetheless, this does not make it any less important for the enterprise to manage relations with the bank as well as possible.

As noted earlier, it is crucial for enterprises (both traditional and social) to raise financial resources during the start-up phase. The methods for presenting the quantitative scope of the project are not different for SEVs than for traditional ventures. They are, however, supplemented with additional measurements aimed at communicating the size of the social impact that the enterprise hopes to generate as part of its mission. In fact, only providing financial data regarding traditional business turnover would be misleading in terms of the established objectives and their special, diverse nature. Many models for measuring social impact have been developed and tested, which can be used to pursue three secondary objectives. First, certain systems make it possible to monitor the social outcomes that are directly correlated with the correlated with the outputs of the business process. Management therefore implements methods for measuring active processes in order to obtain real-time indicators of their social impact. Another objective of measurement is to evaluate the differential impact generated by the very existence of the enterprise and, therefore, the results related to its operations. They can also be used to assign a monetary value to these results and to the social impact. For the first two objectives, measurement tools can include the balanced scorecard, the Acumen Scorecard, the social return assessment, and others. As mentioned previously, these tools focus on processes from a multi-dimensional point of view, which is therefore well suited to companies that are already operational and have established business processes. Limiting ourselves to the set of objectives underlying a new social enterprise, it would be fair to expect the use of measurement systems that give preference to the latter two objectives. In fact, because operations have yet to begin, it is more useful to emphasize the impact the enterprise may have in the future. The most widely used method is the forecast of social return on investment (SROI). This method is designed to integrate the typical calculation of return on investment with a monetary measurement of social savings and social expenses (Long et al., 2003). The first regard company benefits in terms of the creation of new jobs, social welfare programs, and so on. They can have a direct effect on income equilibrium through a more favorable fiscal position, for example. Social expenses, on the other hand, are those directly associated with the enterprise and its primary stakeholders. In any event, depending on the category in which the business falls, it will be necessary to develop a list of possible impact areas in terms of society or the environment. For example, this can include environmental issues (improving air, water, or soil quality; financial savings resulting from the elimination of the need for future environmental clean-up, etc.), health issues (improving health or the quality of life; increasing life expectancy by reducing illness, etc.), human capital or community development (reducing unemployment or increasing social justice, etc.), education, and so on. Adding such indicators enables us to calculate a new return on investment that may be either higher or lower than the more traditional number. At the same time, we may be able to measure the degree of achievement of the social purpose underlying the mission of the SEV. In a recent study, Lingane and Olsen (2004) propose a series of indicators based on an analysis of a number of business plans of social enterprises with regard to certain traps that entrepreneurs typically fall into when calculating SROI. In short, they have seen a tendency to include only the positive impacts and to ignore the negative. They also encountered the practice of attributing to one's own enterprise values related to the general impact of different enterprises, even if connected to the enterprise in question. Finally, conclusions regarding the relative value of SROI should take similar industries into account, and it is also a good idea to use sensitivity analysis to consider a variety of possible scenarios.

3.4 CONCLUSIONS

In the sections above, we described the typical start-up process and the main stages and challenges entrepreneurs encounter along the way. We then presented an overview of the special characteristics and distinctive aspects of the business plan of an SEV. The analysis began with an approach where the business plan is seen as a means of describing the policies through which the enterprise intends to pursue the interests of the various stakeholders. The result was a different ordering of priorities, with a redefined emphasis on the various sections of the document as compared with the business plans of traditional enterprises. This process takes place by adding new tools and new sets of analyses aimed at comprehensively supporting both the social and business purpose.

The following is a summary of the key points (see figure 3.1):

- ownership and management remain high priorities, but the role of the actors involved has changed. In particular, the workforce typically acquires greater visibility and importance. The business plan needs to recognize and present this new order;
- relationships with the market change. There is an emphasis on the critical nature of understanding the latent needs of the 'customer' and the manner in which they can be met. Considerable attention must be devoted to designing the business system. The concept of value also changes: it is necessary to demonstrate the ability to widen the difference between value created and value captured;

- relations with the competitors imply the introduction of new strategies and new players. The concept of relative value over competitors remains, but there is a greater emphasis on complementarity and partnership. In the social enterprise plan the system of external stakeholders, which is typically 'secondary' for traditional enterprises (the community, the environment, etc.), is given greater importance and a higher priority;
- the presentation of the quantitative dimension of company performance used to analyze the risk-return ratio for the purpose of interacting with potential stakeholders from the financial world is enhanced with new tools. In particular, in accordance with the intrinsically multi-dimensional nature of the social purpose, business performance is also measured in terms of the social impact the enterprise is able to generate.

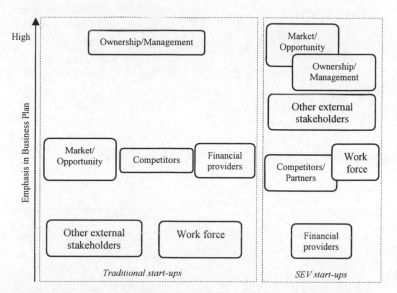

Figure 3.1 Differences in the areas addressed by the business plans of traditional and 'social' enterprises

Social innovation and the establishment of best practices require the ability of enlightened entrepreneurs to imagine the future and its implications with a high degree of accuracy. In this sense, the business plan can, and must, be a tool in both dialoguing with potential stakeholders and assessing the feasibility of the idea and the acceptability of the risk. Sahlman (1997) reminds us, 'One of the greatest myths about entrepreneurs is that they are risk seekers. All sane people want to avoid risk'. In an SEV, this concept not only remains a priority, but increases in importance given the number and diversity of the primary stakeholders equally involved in pursuing the social purpose of the enterprise.

4. The role of financing in ensuring growth

Alessandro Marino

4.1 INTRODUCTION: AN OVERVIEW OF SOURCES OF FINANCING FOR SOCIAL ENTREPRENEURS

Sourcing financing for start-ups is more complex than for existing businesses, since the lack of a track record makes it difficult to demonstrate their ability to be self-financing in the future. In general, entrepreneurs can turn to the following alternatives:

- subsidized financing, namely government incentives or grants aimed at supporting entrepreneurship and development. It is the least expensive form of financing and is best suited to enterprises in the start-up phase, in that they are unable to generate large cash flows;
- debt capital (bank borrowing or bond issues). This form of financing involves the assumption of a formal contractual commitment to reimburse the funds received, with the payment of interest on the outstanding principal;
- equity capital. This is a stable form of financing in that it is not encumbered by the obligation to repay the funds, with remuneration varying in relation to the profit distribution policies that management decides to adopt;
- intermediate forms (convertible bonds, mezzanine debt or participation loans). These forms of financing are especially appropriate for the development phase, thanks to their flexibility and the fact that they do not compromise the possibility of finding credit.

For the entrepreneur involved in launching a social enterprise, we need to offer a contingent framework of the main ways in which financial resources can be raised.

The vast majority of currently operational SEVs emerged in the third sector, relying on public subsidies in the start-up phase (Bank of England, 2003). Although such financing is generally inexpensive (or provided free as a grant), it has certain limits. Some comes with restrictions on its use or is granted for specific projects complementary to the enterprise's core business. The timing of disbursements may be misaligned with cash flows and funding needs. Finally, the bureaucratic nature of accessing public funds may require specific skills and considerable time.

The situation with debt capital is not any rosier. Banks are reluctant to lend to start-ups and usually require adequate collateral to secure the loan. The Bank of England study underscores the difficulties that banks encounter in assessing loan applications from SEVs. These are essentially linked to the specific features of the social entrepreneurship approach. More specifically:

- reputational risk: this is the risk that the potential failure of a social enterprise (which has a close relationship with its community) could be blamed on the excessively stringent terms imposed by banks;
- arrangement time: banks are usually reluctant to grant loans to social enterprises owing to the (real or perceived) slowness of the typical decision-making processes of a social enterprise. Processing times are lengthened by the participatory and collaborative nature of these enterprises and the need to combine financing in an especially complex range of funding sources;
- shortage of financial expertise: the lack of financial expertise that would help accelerate the bank's assessment process is perceived as a weak point of social enterprises.

This reluctance on the part of the traditional banking sector is, however, stimulating the emergence of specialized lenders. They focus their assessment of the risk profile of social enterprises on the joint examination of the social and economic components of the venture (the triple bottom line). Experimentation has also begun with innovative approaches to guarantees that exploit the economies of specialization and a thorough understanding of the sector to lower the initial assessment costs for each project.

The situation with equity capital is different. Of all the forms of financing that social entrepreneurial ventures use, recourse to equity capital is extremely limited at present. There would appear to be a clear divergence between the objectives of a social enterprise and the classic equity investor. This is primarily linked to the difficulty of determining the risk/return ratio with sufficient accuracy and to investors' uncertainty about exit strategies.

More specifically, the main problems that underlie the limited use of equity capital can be summarized as follows:

- the difficulty of establishing with any certainty the risk/return ratio of the investment owing to the divergence between the objectives of the social enterprise and the investor;[1]
- the possibility that the legal form of the social enterprise could restrict the use of equity as a form of financing;
- the complexity of exit strategies owing to the risk that maximizing the investor's capital gain could compromise the pursuit of the social objectives of the original social entrepreneur and control over the enterprise;
- the complexity of due diligence and assessing/monitoring the use of economic resources and time once the enterprise is under way.

Nevertheless, these limitations can be overcome by the emergence of specialized investors. Over the years both the composition of institutional investors in equity capital and investment strategies have evolved considerably.[2] This means that the logic underpinning the methods and processes of financial intermediaries (venture capitalists) does not need to be altered for investments in SEVs. However, it is necessary to involve appropriate institutional investors in subscribing investment funds (in this case, for example, foundations).

We propose a description of the emerging actors that could support SEVs through their participation as partners in business initiatives. As in other sectors, the drivers of success are the innovative content and robustness of the projects themselves. The following sections analyze innovative financial instruments based on a re-reading of the traditional venture capital process from the point of view of social entrepreneurship.

4.2 FROM THE VENTURE CAPITAL PROCESS TO THE SOCIAL ENTREPRENEURSHIP MODEL

As mentioned earlier, the most widely discussed innovations in financing social entrepreneurship are centered on specialized operators that take account of the dual profit and social objectives of SEVs. This form of investment has been dubbed 'patient capital' and includes all forms of financing to support the development of social enterprises' business capacity and sustainability. It represents a long-term investment that gives the recipient access to funds beyond the start-up phase (Bank of England, 2003). In line with the objective of social entrepreneurship, patient capital explicitly subordinates financial returns to the achievement of social output. Note that if this form of financing is provided in the form of equity investment, it typically involves limited ceding of control and no explicit exit strategy (Bank of England, 2003).

One form of patient capital is social venture capital or venture philanthropy, which in systemic and methodological terms does not differ substantially from the traditional venture capital process, although it has many special features.

The following sections present the traditional model of venture capital investment and a revised view of such investment in the light of the specific nature and contributions in the literature on social entrepreneurship (SE).

4.2.1 Equity Investment in Start-Ups

Private equity is risk capital provided to an enterprise by an external financial intermediary. The latter are usually specialized undertakings that also provide support to the entrepreneur in managing the enterprise. The term 'venture capital' is used when the financing is being supplied to recently-founded innovative firms with a view to fostering their development and expansion. These businesses may be at the start-up stage (start-up financing) or at the first stage of development (first-stage financing), but are normally not at any earlier stage (Marino, 2005; Perrini, 1998).

In general, venture capitalists take a minority stake in enterprises and provide their know-how in order to guide the development of the companies, allowing them to maximize their capital gains when they sell their holdings. The venture capitalist's investment is temporary, with a typical time horizon for disinvestment of 5 to 10 years.

The key characteristics of venture capitalists are:

- financing in the form of equity capital;
- investment in new small to medium-sized companies with high growth potential;
- the contribution of professional skills;
- a temporary time horizon for the investment.

The venture capital cycle or process (VCP) comprises all the actions undertaken by the actors involved, from the establishment of the venture capital fund (or the investment company) to its closure.[3]

We now describe the phases of the VCP, summarizing the key challenges that the involved actors face. Our attention will focus on investments in start-ups in order to link the framework to the context of SEs. The main actors in the process are (see figure 4.1):

- institutional investors (II);
- venture capitalists (VC);
- entrepreneurs (I);
- enablers (E).

The VCP begins with the managers of the investment company deciding to work together and develop a common investment strategy. This initial stage is followed by one in which the new management company contacts institutional investors in order to raise funds for investment in line with their proposed strategy. In the traditional model, institutional investors are represented by major banks, pension funds, investment funds, public investment companies and so on. After drawing up a contract governing relations between the investors and the VC acting as intermediary, the investors transfer an initial tranche of funds to the VC (first capital call).

The management company can then focus exclusively on finding target companies in which to invest. It is necessary to generate a flow of potentially attractive investment opportunities (deal flow management) and select those for investment (due diligence). Once all of the capital is invested, the VC manages and monitors the investees, seeking to leverage its experience in order to add value. This stage (managing) involves a principal (the VC) controlling the actions of the agent (the entrepreneur), imposing sanctions if the action of the entrepreneur diverges from its own interests (Perrini, 2000; Duffner, 2003). The key importance of the ability of the VC to improve the performance of the company and create value by offering management services is argued by a number of authors (Kanniainen and Keuschnigg, 2003). Some VCs manage their investments on a hands-off basis, limiting their involvement to financial support alone. By contrast, others take a more hands-on approach, following entrepreneurs in the development of their projects even after the initial injection of funds.

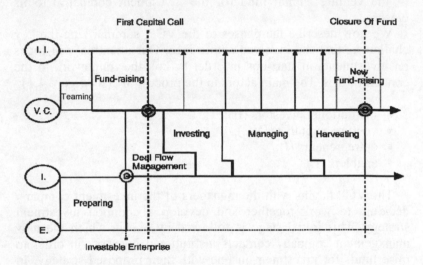

Figure 4.1 The venture capital process (Marino 2005)

During the managing stage, the VC also has to keep its institutional investors constantly informed, with regular reporting on developments. The most common forms of reporting are the consolidated income statement and balance sheet. However, it is also necessary to track other sources of information that can pick up changes in the competitive context. These reports might even be made on a weekly basis. VCs have developed customized models that go beyond the mere measurement of composite indicators (such as the internal rate of return) (Fenn et al., 1996).

Nevertheless, in practice the latter still serve a useful purpose as reference parameters.

At the end of the process, after a number of years, the VC reaches the stage where it gradually sells its investments or writes them off if they have failed to perform. The capital gains are distributed to the investors net of the VC's fees. Disinvestment can be carried out in a number of ways (Cumming and MacIntosh, 2000):

- an IPO (initial public offering), with the sale of the investment through a public offering on a regulated market;
- a trade sale, which involves a private sale of the investment to new industrial shareholders or through a merger with another company. This is also called a secondary sale or replacement capital when the buyer is a financial company;
- a secondary buy-out, where the investment is sold to the majority shareholders or to management, or the company acquires its own shares;
- a write-off: the investment is fully written down if it has lost its value.

If the fund is not wound up once the investment phase is completed (normally when the investments have been an overall success), the VC can start the process anew.

Examining the process from the point of view of the entrepreneur who wants to launch an innovative start-up, in most cases it is not possible to contact a VC at the idea generation stage. In order to attract the interest of VCs, entrepreneurs normally have to take a number of key preparatory steps to move from the embryo stage to start-up. This preparatory stage involves a range of new actors (we have called them enablers). This broad category (also known as venture-to-capital (V2C) practitioners) includes many of the actors already present in the informal equity capital market. They share a number of common features (Bygrave and Timmons, 1992; Seppae, 2000; Seppae and Rasila, 2001): they provide basic financing to the enterprises, supporting them in strategic decision-making and accessing additional resources. After an initial development stage, they also contact venture capitalists in order to present companies now ready for more substantial investment (Jungman and Seppae, 2004). The critical success factors regard their ability to develop their entrepreneurial projects effectively, lowering the risk threshold for subsequent investment by VCs. The category includes such players as business angels, accelerators, advisors, public-sector initiatives (both financing and the provision of services) and incubators (with the collaboration of universities).

4.3 VENTURE PHILANTHROPY AS THE BASIS OF A NEW SOCIAL ENTREPRENEURSHIP MODEL

Social venture capital or venture philanthropy first emerged in the 1990s as an alternative form of charitable giving. In many respects it resembles traditional venture capital but the beneficiaries are social enterprises. We examine this form of investment using the same approach taken in the previous section, pointing out differences, similarities and possible areas for future development. The new interpretation can be characterized as a social entrepreneurship model.

Generally speaking, under the venture philanthropy model, a private or corporate foundation[4] – the venture philanthropists – decides to develop a long-term relationship with a social organization that stands out for its innovative spirit and high potential social impact. This conception is a recent development. In the past, traditional donations by a foundation to a social organization did not involve the formulation of an exit strategy, restricting the relationship to fund-raising, deal flow management and investing. The transition from philanthropy to venture philanthropy has prompted a far-reaching reshaping of the logic underlying investment decisions and the phases of the investment process, absorbing the perspective underpinning the traditional venture capital model, including its cyclical and dynamic nature. As with the model presented earlier, the main practitioners can be grouped as follows:

- institutional investors, which provide funding to the foundation on the basis of shared objectives and a common social sensibility;
- venture capitalists: the venture philanthropists (VPs), that is, the private or corporate foundation explicitly formed as an 'investment company' to take a stake in the equity capital of a social enterprise. Alternatively, they may be a traditional

foundation that decides to change its investment rules for social entrepreneurship;

- entrepreneurs: social entrepreneurs with a strong orientation towards social innovation and a managerial approach to problem-solving;
- enablers: intermediaries between the VPs and social enterprises whose principal role is to bridge the information gap between the parties. In this case, these are often incubators, university research centers or organizations launched by universities to create opportunities for investors and beneficiary enterprises to meet and become acquainted (venture competitions).

There are few differences with the traditional model at the teaming and fund-raising stages. The exception is the underlying orientation of investment strategies, since VPs and VCs operate on the basis of structurally different objectives. According to Pepin (2003) enterprises participate in foundations that operate as VPs on the basis of measurable objectives for social and financial returns.[5] There is an underlying divergence between the objectives of profit maximization by traditional venture capitalists and of maximizing the social return objectives by the venture philanthropist.

For VPs the deal flow management phase, namely the stage devoted to scouting for investment projects, does not present any particular methodological difficulties. The most attractive pools for identifying projects are international venture competitions and sector conferences. The main difference with respect to the traditional model regards portfolio composition choices. First Letts, Ryan and Grossman (1997) and then others[6] have argued for VPs to adopt risk management techniques in selecting the composition of their portfolios in order to balance risk. Traditional foundations have little incentive to adopt such techniques because they are not under pressure to generate financial returns for their 'stakeholders'. Letts, Ryan and Grossman argue that: 'Foundations generally face little risk when making grants. Far from worrying about losing money, foundations are more likely to worry about not spending enough' (1997, p. 4). The introduction of risk balancing criteria based on the preliminary analysis of social and financial performance would improve the efficiency of the process. It should be noted that some foundations are adopting control techniques typically used by VCs. One example is the practice of tying the compensation and career prospects of program officers to the performance of the projects/enterprises financed.

The investing phase is characterized by the choice of the decision-making criteria to be adopted in selecting projects. They may regard, for example, the presence of product or process innovations, the extent of the social impact, the potential for change in the target sector, and so on. The information needed to reach a decision can be gathered through requests for additional information over and above that initially provided by the applicant.[7] This phase is similar to the traditional due diligence process.

As regards the decision on how much to invest, in the traditional model there is normally a strong commitment between the VC and the enterprise, in which the investor provides a majority of the capital required. In addition, the investor often helps the company raise additional funds in the market. In the case of the relationship between a foundation and an SEV, the funding provided is usually only partial and subsequent fund-raising is normally carried out independently (Letts et al., 1997; Drucker, 2000).

The managing stage primarily involves capacity building. The team created for the project works with the social enterprise as a partner, focusing on the integration of strategic, organizational and managerial skills. The sustainability of the enterprise is tested and the foundation for its long-term success and access to additional financing is laid. It is often necessary to add to or diversify the initial team with external human resources, since foundations are not established as investment companies and therefore do not possess the skills needed to manage and develop the deal. Accordingly, the VP outsources the skills it needs to build the team created ad hoc for each project.

To summarize, each initiative undertaken is followed by the creation of a working group that focuses on capacity building at the beneficiary enterprise. In addition to the entrepreneur, the team is composed of permanent members (the staff of the foundation and other specific human resources), some pro-bono partners of the foundation and appropriate professional resources. This team collaborates to develop leadership and management capabilities, the financial sustainability of the enterprise, strategic planning and the capacity to interact with the market for financial resources.

An additional critical element of the managing stage that the venture philanthropy has to address is the extent of the relationship to be created with the enterprise. This sets venture philanthropy clearly apart from all other forms of financing that social enterprises have traditionally tapped. Foundations involved in such financing operations adopt a new form of interaction with the beneficiary organization. They range from being simple observers to actual partners in the development of management and strategic capabilities. Adopting the terminology of the traditional investment model, they move from a hands-off to a hands-on approach. The practices that can be adopted to implement this new conception of the relationship differ. For example, they can involve providing support in financial planning, mentoring or taking a position on the board.

Finally, a number of complexities emerge when we examine the problem of developing an exit strategy, that is, the harvesting stage. These include, for example, the difficulty of clearly establishing the moment in which a social organization has achieved its mission and is ready to face the long term. Another issue is the criterion to adopt in deciding when the target is ready to leave the relationship with the venture philanthropist in order to access scale-up financing. Two well-established venture philanthropists – the Roberts Enterprise Development Fund (REDF) and Social Venture Partners (SVP) – have defined the following characteristics for determining readiness for harvesting:

- good leadership and management capacities within the market, together with an ability for strategic planning and responding effectively to market developments;
- sound organizational infrastructure;
- capacity to set short-term objectives on a consistent basis and keep track of goals reached;
- positive social outcomes and clear progress towards fulfilling their mission;
- a clear vision of the future and possible scenarios.

Should the VP decide to disinvest, it needs to establish an exit strategy. The following are examples of some of the available options (Alter et al., 2001):

- access new funders: the strategy essentially involves a new investor 'taking over' the investment in a social enterprise. The latter would normally have developed an adequate level of capacity building but not yet achieved its final objective, and therefore needs additional financing before consolidating its position. It therefore does not represent a definitive exit from the enterprise;
- build earned income opportunities: this is not a final exit strategy either. The venture philanthropist supports the social enterprise in creating opportunities to diversify the services or goods it produces in order to increase income;
- strengthen social purpose enterprise activity: this can be defined as a definitive exit strategy in relation to the state of development and self-sufficiency achieved by the social enterprise. It consists in supporting the enterprise in monitoring the market and identifying unsatisfied needs on which it can focus a market-based business;
- merge with a for-profit or non-profit organization: this is a final exit strategy and involves supporting the original enterprise in merging with another organization in the same market;
- spin-off program into new non-profit organization: this is another definitive exit option in which the venture philanthropist helps the social organization in formally spinning off the program from a parent organization. The new organization has a different mission from that of the parent, its own governance bodies, financial base and specific objectives.

In concluding our examination of the parallels, we take the perspective of the enterprise intent on completing the preparatory activities prior to contacting the investor. In the traditional model, this was the preparing stage. As we noted, other intermediaries (the enablers) are involved in bringing the enterprise to investors. In the case of SE this function is normally performed by the foundations themselves, which interact with the entrepreneur from the earliest stages of the entrepreneurial process. Nevertheless, numerous other players have emerged, such as university research centers, international venture competitions and specialized incubators ('social incubators'). These initiatives and organizations lay the foundation for the creation of the physical and virtual premises starting from which innovative ideas can be developed and set the stage for initial contacts with potential partners and other practitioners. Box 4.1 describes one successful social entrepreneurship enabler.

BOX 4.1 The Global Social Venture Competition

The Global Social Venture Competition began in 1999 as an initiative of the Haas School of Business. In 2001, the Columbia Business School and the Goldman Sachs Foundation formed a partnership with Haas to extend the scope of the competition to create an international platform for promoting social entrepreneurial ventures.

The purpose of the GSVC is to support the creation and growth of successful social enterprises around the world. Such ventures are defined as enterprises that have both financial and social goals integral to their purpose. In their role as enablers, they use the competition to elevate the visibility of the field and the quality and quantity of new ventures. This role in driving the development of the sector is pursued through close partnerships with business schools, MBA students, the academic world and profit-seeking enterprises, all with the aim of creating a mix of synergies and reciprocal know-how essential to bridging the knowledge gap.

http://www.socialvc.com

4.4 CONCLUSIONS

Starting with the differences between the VCP model and traditional foundations (see Table 4.1) outlined in the previous sections, we have proposed a venture philanthropy model potentially capable of bridging the gap between the two worlds. This process is still developing in practice.

Table 4.1 Differences between venture capital and the traditional foundation model (adapted from Drucker, 2000)

Key practices and stages of the process	Venture capital process	Traditional foundations
Risk management (*deal flow management*)	High risk. Capital lost if project fails.	Low risk for foundations, high risk for SEVs. Fund must be spent in any case.
Amount of funding (*investing*)	Substantial commitment aimed at contributing capital in several stages and providing support in the search for additional financing.	Partial commitment. SEVs responsible for carrying out subsequent fund-raising independently.
Length of relationship (*Harvesting*)	5-7 years, linked to success of enterprise.	1-3 years, based on arbitrary criteria.
Terms of engagement (*Managing*)	Strong partnership and often pervasive influence in decision-making, partly related to small size portfolio.	Low direct involvement in management owing to the difficulties posed by the large number of projects under way.
Organizational capacity building (*Managing*)	Financing and contribution of resources aimed at successful implementation of business plan.	Financing and contribution of resources mainly aimed at covering infrastructure costs and/or general expenses.
Performance measures (*Fund raising, Deal flow management, Managing*)	Risks and returns clearly defined.	No monitoring of performance indicators.
Exit strategy (*Harvesting*)	Definition of a clear exit strategy.	No pressure to define exit strategies.

The key contribution of venture capital to bridging philanthropic giving and investments in SEVs rests on measuring performance. Relations between traditional venture capitalists and start-ups are constructed on a foundation of financial data that can serve as performance measures for both parties.

They need to be monitored over the course of the project.

As noted earlier, this is a more complex task in the case of a social enterprise. The VP has to develop formal instruments to measure both the financial sustainability of the investment and its social return.[8] This is essential for the proper operation of the complex system of interests that underlie the process of equity financing.

Other distinctive features of VPs in their relationships with social enterprises can be summarized as follows (Emerson, 1998):

- constant attention and support for capacity building at the social enterprise, the development of its organizational and managerial capacities in the various areas of operations. From the construction of a sound organizational infrastructure based on qualified staff and a clear division of duties to the development of the capacity for objective-oriented thinking and responding effectively to the expectations of the different stakeholders, the definition of business strategies and the building of a network of relationships with the community;
- a partnership approach to managing relations with the entrepreneur from a long-term perspective, providing support over the entire start-up phase;
- collaboration in defining an appropriate exit strategy by developing indicators that measure the strength of the enterprise and its ability to survive in the long term.

Social venture capital is thus a way for the world of foundations to reinvent itself. It clearly highlights the key to developing a successful social enterprise: a highly innovative entrepreneurial idea. This requirement is compatible with the intention of the enterprise to access new sources of financing, with a good chance of stable, enduring success.

One exogenous condition for these opportunities to materialize is the existence of a financing market capable of absorbing the demand from social enterprises. Venture philanthropy could act as a catalyst for change, opening the way for new financial approaches able to replicate its adaptability.

NOTES

1. For example, in accordance with the objective of maximizing its social return, the social enterprise is more likely to invest any surplus in its social mission rather than consider it a direct return on the investment in equity capital.
2. Take, for example, the increasingly important role of corporations in equity investment or the change in dynamics after the bursting of the high-tech bubble, which shifted the focus from Internet technologies to other sectors (energy, nanotechnology, etc.).
3. For a more detailed description, see Marino (2005).
4. The provision of financing by an individual philanthropist or, to adapt the traditional terminology, a social business angel, is still rare.
5. According to the author, the former would be the prerogative of the North American model.
6. See, for example, Drucker (2000).
7. From http://wwwfondazionedynamo.org.
8. See chapter 3 for a summary of the main approaches to measuring the performance of a social enterprise venture.

5. Exploiting the view: venture philanthropy models across practice

Clodia Vurro

5.1 STATE OF THE ART IN VENTURE PHILANTHROPY PRACTICE: AN OVERVIEW

In July of 2000, *Time* magazine's cover story on the 'New Philanthropists' (Greenfeld, 2000) focused on the 'multi-millionaires of the technology boom.' It explained that:

> Many of today's tech millionaires and billionaires are applying to philanthropy the lessons they have learned as entrepreneurs [...] One solution has been the founding of venture philanthropies which use the same aggressive methods as venture capital firms, whose money typically comes with technological expertise and experience at running lean, efficient organizations. This new breed of philanthropist scrutinizes each charitable cause like a potential business investment, seeking maximum return in terms of social impact – for example, by counting the number of children taught to read or the number inoculated against malaria.

Since the Roberts Enterprise Development Fund (San Francisco, USA), the Robin Hood Foundation (New York, USA), Ashoka (Arlington, USA), and Social Venture Partners (Seattle, Washington) – the earliest and most successful pioneers of a new wave of philanthropy – appeared in the early '90s, venture philanthropy (VP) has developed significantly, entering the popular lexicon definitely around 2000 with notable press coverage in *Time*, *Fortune*, and on web sites around the world. In 2002 *Business Week* (cover story) explained that 'the new philanthropy displays an impatient disdain for the cautious and unimaginative check writing that dominated charitable giving for decades'. And, as it further clarified, the main distinguishing points of this new approach to giving are:

> It's more ambitious: Today's philanthropists are tackling giant issues, from remaking American education to curing cancer. It's more strategic: Donors are taking the same systematic approach they used to compete in business, laying out detailed plans that get at the heart of systematic problems, not just symptoms. It's more global: Just as business doesn't stop at national borders, neither does charitable giving. Donors from William H. Gates III to George Soros have sweeping international agendas. It demands results: The new philanthropists attach a lot of strings. Recipients are often required to meet milestones goals, to invite foundation members onto their boards, and to produce measurable results – or risk losing their funding.

The number of funds and supportive organizations are growing rapidly, and the phenomenon is no longer specifically American. The principles and the philosophy behind VP are crossing their original geographical boundaries, finding their apex in the formation of the European Venture Philanthropy Association (EVPA), founded in 2004 by philanthropists from the European private equity community. Its purpose is to promote VP in Europe and to provide its members with the services needed to learn from good practice elsewhere as well as from one another. The EVPA is also planning its own seed fund to help launch new VP operations (www.evpa.eu.com). Compared to the scale and scope of VP in the US, however, ferment today in Europe is restricted to a small number of dedicated funds.

Despite the growing interest in and expectations of the potential of VP for the overall development of the social sector and for scaling the impact of social entrepreneurship (SE), current coverage has also blurred the general understanding of what VP is and what it hopes to achieve.

In very general terms, the VP approach borrows principles from the practice of venture capitalists in the business world, but its primary focus and intent are on increasing organizational capacity of social entrepreneurial ventures (SEVs). In other words, putting together the risk-taking characteristic of the business sector and the innovative fostering of social change intrinsic to the SE concept, VP rests on the premise that the best investments in solving social problems require more than money. In other words, the extent to which social entrepreneurial ventures develop their growth aptitude also depends on a supportive environment. It is in this context that VP plays a relevant role, providing grants but above all strategic assistance in a number of ways.

From a survey conducted by Morino Institute and Community Wealth Ventures (2001) on the practices of the major VP organizations in the US, the following main areas of contribution to grant recipients emerge:

- addressing organizational issues;
- helping to attract and retain key management and board members;
- assisting in the development of product and distribution channels;
- helping leverage partnerships through their strategic relationships with other organizations and with other organizations in which they've invested;
- creating and executing development/expansion strategies;
- developing financial plans, improving funds development, helping to establish new revenue sources, and creating syndicated funding by bringing together other venture philanthropy investors and foundations;
- helping management leverage strategic benefits ranging from management development to the application of technology to strengthen the organization and magnify its effectiveness; and
- providing access to industry and subject matter experts and knowledgeable advisors.

It is clear from the list above how different VP is from traditional philanthropic giving. It represents a renewed approach to financing the social sector, applying strategic investment management practices to support 'strong' social entrepreneurial organizations in need of help to grow. Time is definitely up for traditional, weak nonprofit organizations needing to be rescued.

Moreover, while at its earliest beginnings VP was more directly associated with that movement of enterprising nonprofits, supporting their lack of business skills, now the expression enterprising is more frequently used in conjunction with SE. In other words, SEVs represent the counterpart of innovative business start-ups, and are 'fundable' in venture capital parlance because they know perfectly what they want to accomplish and have a clear and concrete view of how to realize their vision, rather than being guided by an abstract ideal of societal well-being and social outcomes.

To consider the comparability between traditional venture capital and the VP approach from a different viewpoint, VP organizations and venture capital funds share some features: both base their bottom line on the selection of valuable fund recipients, in terms of success, longevity, and day-to-day efficiency. Additionally both are answerable to those who provide financial resources for the performance of the fund. Finally, like venture capitalists, venture philanthropists expect results and accountability from the organizations they support (Letts et al., 1997).

These similarities demonstrate how it is possible to apply processes and practices typical of the business world to philanthropic organizations, even if limited to the objectives and missions that for VP are necessarily different, resting on a different set of investment opportunities and expectations.

Having a definition of VP certainly helps to raise awareness, distinguish among different approaches, and classify extant innovative financing practices. However, in that the phenomenon is now evolving out of the incubation phase into mature and increasingly accepted practices, an upward trend in defining consolidated standards is remote. At this level financing models, selection criteria, or funding strategies vary considerably across organizations, ranging from different levels of engagement in grant-making to strategic assistance. Perhaps the most critical area now concerns the utilization of criteria for assessing success. There is still very little agreement about measurement and comparability of results and return on investment.

The dimensions along which VP varies (and these dimensions map out the research agenda) from its traditional counterpart follow:

- venture philanthropy model: these range from multi-donor funds that adhere closely to the philosophies and practices of venture capitalists, to the foundations of wealthy individuals that, while new, actually operate in a fashion more similar to traditional grant-makers. This dimension of variance also includes the scope and scale of strategic assistance, skills and resource transfer to grant recipients, and also the specific field(s) toward which investments are addressed;

- selection criteria and portfolio composition: whatever the criteria for screening potential grant recipients are, it is at this level that the difference between nonprofit-based VP and SEV-based VP emerges most clearly. In general the need for strong leadership and entrepreneurial orientation, together with the capacity to scale typically guide the choice of nonprofits in portfolio composition. The same selection criteria are adopted by VP organizations looking for potential recipients that adhere to the SE concept. But in this case they are accompanied by a more focused evaluation of the extent to which the entrepreneurial idea is innovative and has potential for 'irreversible social change';
- fund performance measurement: the last dimension of variance concerns the measurement of performance. As mentioned above this represents the critical region of venture philanthropy, in that consolidated practices are still lacking. Measurement is not only referred to aggregate fund performance but is much more complicated in terms of evaluating portfolio organization results.

The reminder of this chapter exploits the view on VP models in practice, seeking explanatory examples that typify the above-mentioned dimensions of variance. Appendix 5.I exemplifies VP models applied by three acknowledged venture philanthropists. Their interpretation of their relationship with the funded organizations diverges. But regardless of the specific differences, all three stress their focus on social change and social innovation as the only possible way to break traditions in the social sectors and in the way organizations deal with social problems. After working closely with leading social entrepreneurs, all pursue, in varying ways, three major interrelated objectives:

- to enhance the legitimacy and credibility of SE and SE organizations. This objective is strictly linked to the orientation of funds toward the measurable results that characterize funded organizations. Such credibility is not exclusively linked to the economic and financial results of both the grant recipients and the fund per se, but depends on the longevity of the organizations, that is, their ability to survive in the long run and expand their initial level of influence. Additionally the credibility/legitimacy objective is pursued through a selective portfolio composition. Schwab Foundation, for example, works especially on developing standard measurement tools to monitor the differences among various entrepreneurial activities. The members of the foundation are subjected to an annual re-certification process;

- to provide the opportunity for networking among social entrepreneurs as well as with other individuals and organizations who can mobilize support for their initiatives. This is why network creation and the provision of opportunities to exchange ideas, best practices, and information characterize all three VP models;

- to provide financial and other resources. While Echoing Green and Ashoka provide financial support to their recipients, the Schwab model relies exclusively on technical and professional assistance and accountability for outcomes. In other words, the foundation's contribution to the financial sustainability of SEVs is achieved through a matching strategy, between SE and resource-providers.

Figure 5.1 summarizes a general process of investing in a SEV. Regardless of the details of each fund, generally charitable giving from one or more than one donor converges into a VP fund that in turn invests in SEVs, both in terms of financial support and in transferring technical and professional skills. As a result, financed SEVs can produce an innovation (that is, new product or service, new method of organizing, and so on) that initiates social change. Within this process the measurability of results and self-sufficiency remains constant.

Acumen Fund is now one of the leading examples of how social problems can be addressed through philanthropic investment. Box 5.1 briefly describes the main characteristics of the Acumen Fund's approach.

BOX 5.1 Acumen Fund

According to its mission statement: 'Acumen Fund is a non-profit global venture fund serving the 4 billion people living on less than $4 a day. Our aim is to create a blueprint for building financially sustainable and scalable organizations that deliver affordable, critical goods and services which elevate the lives of the poor. We adhere to a disciplined process in selecting and managing our philanthropic investments as well as in measuring the end result.'

This fund was incorporated on April 1, 2001, thanks to seed capital from the Rockefeller Foundation, Cisco Systems Foundation, and three other individual philanthropists (that is, the donors). To date, Acumen investing strategy has focused on three different areas: first, the identification and support of innovators with a social mission represents the basic criterion in portfolio composition. Second, the investment activity is supported by the creation of an active global community of individual philanthropists, foundations, and corporations that share the desire to enhance their engagement in global social issues. Additionally, Acumen focuses on thematic portfolios in order to maximize the transfer of shared learning between portfolio investors facing similar challenges. At the same time, it minimizes overall risk by varying the degrees of risk and social return within the portfolio. Third, measurement and reporting of progress and impact are pursued regularly. Acumen's approach to measurement is systematic and concerns three levels of measurement: at the investment, portfolio, and Acumen fund level. In order to achieve comparability and consistency, the measurement process is based on a set of indicators that have been developed through the support of McKinsey. While these measurement indicators are primarily used to guide investments and business processes, the assessments and results are made available also to partners and advisors in a semi-annual investment report.

Acumen has three portfolios, with eleven investments:

- the Health Technology Changing Lives portfolio supports innovative healthcare technologies that improve the quality of lives in South Asia and Africa. These initiatives alter market dynamics by reducing the cost of treatments and increasing access to previously unavailable products and services;
- the Housing and Finance portfolio invests in scalable enterprises focused on expanding economic opportunity

in the Muslim world. The aim is to strengthen and scale enterprises capable of bridging the gap in access to technology, capital, and markets;
* the Water Innovations portfolio, which was launched in December 2003, invests capital and management support in financially sustainable and scalable enterprises that make safe and sufficient water accessible to the poor. We seek to improve water access and water quality through affordable technologies in filtration, purification, testing, storage, and delivery.

Acumen Fund provides successful examples of how to improve societal well-being by combining traditional business practices with social-purpose activities. They consider as fundamental to their success the ability to identify and support promising innovations and leaders within the chosen areas of portfolio concentration. 'As with venture capital, this may entail vetting hundreds of proposals to distill just a few we may fund. It also requires an extensive network of philanthropists, innovators, business people and community leaders on the ground. The capacity to draw upon the international reach and informed depth of our portfolio managers and advisory panels enables us to identify, screen and select opportunities that can optimize our impact on a pressing global issue.'

Acumen Fund
http://www.acumenfund.org

5.2 VENTURE PHILANTHROPY MODELS

As anticipated in the introduction, VP organizations vary in the way they establish relationships with funded organizations. The International Venture Philanthropy Forum (http://forum.nesst. org/venture.asp) classifies VP practices across three main models.
The first one includes organizations that provide financial and capacity-building resources directly to individual visionary leaders, who can address a social problem in an effective and innovative way. Ashoka and Echoing Green (Appendix 5.1) exemplify this model in that they focus their selective attention on

entrepreneurs whose traits are consistent with those of socially innovative entrepreneurs as described in chapter 1.

The second model refers to those organizations that provide capital and technical assistance to for-profit enterprises generally owned and operated by nonprofit-affiliated organizations to generate income and provide employment opportunities for marginalized groups. Roberts Enterprise Development Funds is an example. The last model consists of organizations that invest in nonprofit organizations in order to support them in the process of hiring and training managers.

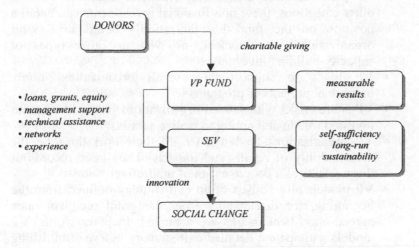

Figure 5.1 The process of investing in SEVs through philanthropy

However, distinctions between the last two models are decreasing. VP organizations are placing more emphasis on innovation in selecting among potential recipients, rather than focusing only on nonprofits.

According to the definition of SE provided in this book, VP models directed towards SE are a sub-set of the VP general approach. In particular, the first and the second model seem to be more aligned with that aspect of innovation concerned with improving societal well-being and initiating social change that characterizes the entrepreneurial model of SEVs (that is, their entreprenuerial model is consistent with the concept of SE).

Regardless of the differences across models, due to the diversity of the target-organizations, VP models share the following features:

- VP organizations provide longer-term, multi-year investments in SEVs or nonprofits as opposed to single-year grant awards;
- VP overturns the grant-making approach, instead embracing an investment approach tailored to the specific characteristics of the grant recipients;
- VP provides more than simply financial resources. Among other categories, these non-financial investments can entail a position on the funded organization's board to support organizational development, as well as other types of capacity-building investments;
- VP tends to support the overall organization, rarely individual projects or programs;
- VP shares risks with funded organizations in that it takes an invested role in attempting to realize success;
- VP organizations tend to base all their operations on the measurability of results and impacts. They keep records of these results as a concrete sign of their effectiveness;
- VP models also consist of an exit strategy defined from the beginning, for disengaging from the grant recipient once agreed-upon benchmarks are achieved. In other words, VP models anticipate a detailed exit-strategy before establishing a funding relationship with a nonprofit or alternatively a SEV. Such a strategy should identify those sources of financing that could be used at the end of the relationship with the VP in order to allow grant recipients to survive in the long run.

According to the criteria explained above, the traditional financing relation between the funding foundation and the funded nonprofit is overturned. Foundations in fact have always tried to minimize their intervention within the funded organization's field of action (Letts et al., 1997). This attitude has limited their ability to acquire information on the characteristics of the financed project, including in terms of potential success or failure. Rarely foundations have hired external consultants to solve simple organizational problems or exigencies, but nothing more than this.

On the other hand, this kind of relationship has discouraged the financed organizations from revealing their problems. As a result the efficiency and effectiveness of the funded projects have been impaired.

Since the VP approach is based on the provision of financial capital but also on skill and technical resource transfer, risk and problems of funded organizations are shared with foundations. The reciprocal knowledge is enhanced, at the same time increasing the opportunity to collaboratively address problems and thus enable success.

There can be cases in which, in an attempt to strengthen the engagement with funded organizations, venture philanthropists enlarge their model to activities complementary to the venture fund. A successful example of such an approach is that of NESsT (USA), an 'international, nonprofit, nongovernmental organization dedicated to finding lasting solutions to systemic poverty and social injustice through the development of social enterprises – mission-driven businesses that increase the financial sustainability and social change impact of civil society' (http://www.nesst.org). Box 5.2 summarizes the main features of the extended model of interaction with social entrepreneurial ventures promoted by NESsT.

BOX 5.2 Nonprofit Enterprise and Self Sustainability Team
        (NESsT)

The NESsT model is articulated in different action fields:

- *NESsT Venture Fund*: the investment strategy of the NESsT Venture Fund (NVF) responds directly to the key challenges entrepreneurs face in building the capacity and profitability of their social enterprises. The NVF strategy combines the provision of capacity-building support and financial capital investments to social enterprises. The strategy refers to main areas of intervention: one side includes capacity building, that is, the provision of multi-year, targeted and tailored capacity-building and consultation support to build their expertise, skills, and knowledge of enterprise development and management. The other side concerns the financial

---

support and consists in the provision of a multi-year, targeted, and tailored package of financing to a portfolio of social entrepreneurs to capitalize their start-up and growth;
- NESsT University: this acts as an incubator for social entrepreneurial opportunities through the provision of basic skills and professionalism in dealing with social problems. Programs stress in particular accountability in the SE field;
- NESsT Consulting: since 1997, NESsT has offered a variety of consulting services to nonprofit organizations, donors, and international organizations, on a variety of topics, such as self-sustainability, feasibility studies, and so on;
- NESsT Marketplace: increasingly VPs tend to associate the enhancement of SEVs' visibility with the traditional areas of intervention (financial support and technical/professional support). In the NESsT's model this activity is interpreted thorough NESsT Marketplace, which represents a global, on-line shopping portal designed to enable social enterprises to reach a wider consumer market for selling their products and services.

NESsT
http://www.nesst.org

A further aspect of the current VP models that emerge from practice is the composition of the team to support the grant-recipient in the start-up phase. One of the main characteristics of social problems is that they are community-based. SEVs therefore need to know well their community of reference in order to tailor products, services, and modes of organizing to the specific characteristics of the served market. As a result, SEVs are hardly comparable and require a variety of different and site-specific skills. This is why, in providing support to socially innovative entrepreneurs, VP organizations seek flexibility in the composition of the supporting teams.

An example of this approach is provided in Box 5.3. It concerns an Italian foundation – Fondazione Dynamo – established in 2003 with the goal of improving philanthropy in Italy.

5.3 FONDAZIONE DYNAMO, PHILANTHROPY ENGINE

Founded by INTEK SpA, holding quoted in the Milan stock Exchange, Fondazione Dynamo – Philanthropy Engine – is a recognised Partnership Foundation. Dynamo intends to contribute to philanthropic development in Italy, through the financial, technical and managerial support and promotion of new social ventures able to operate according to efficiency, autonomy and sustainability criteria. According to the Foundation approach: 'Venture Philanthropy is the application of the Venture Capital model to the non-profit sector: a managerial and financial investment that helps a non-profit organisation define its own strategic plan and implement it by strengthening the entire organisational structure in order to maximize results of social interest.'

In transforming entrepreneurial ideas into self-sufficient projects to initiate social change, Fondazione Dynamo works through a three-stage approach:

- identification of the potential project: the screening criteria focus mainly on the innovative attribute of the project, on the measurability of expected outcomes, on the social impact expected by the project in terms of changing patterns of interaction within a specific field of intervention and the possibilities to scale the innovation;
- shared identification of further significant parameters and indicators in order to enhance the ability to evaluate the project's potential;
- systematic outsourcing of all activities whose purpose is to create and manage SEVs through partnerships with companies with high professional standing. The project team relies on a limited staff that is enlarged when necessary to encompass field-specific competencies. These supplementary hirings further build capacity in the areas of instruction in leadership and management abilities, financial self-sufficiency, strategic planning, and the relationship with the market.

Fondazione Dynamo
http://www.fondazionedynamo.org

5.3 SELECTION CRITERIA AND PORTFOLIO COMPOSITION

For a long time foundations have allocated grants to nonprofits without considering the risks associated with failure. In traditional financing models within the social sectors, whether or not grant recipients succeed in pursuing their social mission is of little importance to foundation operations. In other words, unlike venture capital funds, foundations can grow and operate regardless of the performance of the nonprofit organizations to which they give funds.

VP overturns this logic, basing its managerial philosophy on a more 'engaged giving' – that is, giving to invested SEVs the necessary bundle of organizational skills necessary for growth and survival in the long run.

As a consequence, VP organizations tend to establish lasting relationships with organizations able to demonstrate longevity and a certain degree of predictability of results, with a view towards the feasibility of the specific social entrepreneurial project concerned (Morino Institute et al., 2001).

This is why VP organizations tend to make explicit the criteria for the selection of a grant recipient.

As anticipated in previous sections, the transfer of skills and resources is becoming easier and easier through ready access to a network of consistent SE organizations and other supportive actors.

Selection criteria are generally focused on those areas that define the SE field:

- entrepreneurial orientation, at both the individual and organizational levels. In the first case the main concern is initiative of the entrepreneur, commitment to the specific field in which the entrepreneurial project applies, problem-solving ability, and personal integrity. At the organizational level, the concerns are innovativeness and self-sufficiency demonstrated in prior experiences;
- sustainability of the project: in terms of well-defined objectives and mission and feasibility of the project;
- impact on social change: the accent here is mainly on the scalability of the project across geographical boundaries.

Also the relevance of the social problems can be considered in evaluating rival projects.

When the VP organizations focus their activities on a specific field of intervention or on a specific geographic region, they first spend time and resources on educating themselves about site/community-specific problems. Their purpose is to select the SEVs or entrepreneurs most qualified to deal with the community in which they are going to operate.

This is the process followed by another Italian foundation active in promoting philanthropy as a strategic investment activity: Fondazione Oltre. Box 5.4 explains the foundation's model.

BOX 5.4 Fondazione Oltre

Oltre is a private foundation, founded in 2002 by Luciano Balbo, a successful entrepreneur in private equity. It aims to achieve an effective and professional approach to philanthropy, based on the active involvement of donors in the strategic development of funded organizations. The objective relies on the enhancement of societal well-being, lasting in time.

Fondazione Oltre is committed to those features that make philanthropic organizations consistent with the VP approach. But since Fondazione Oltre is focused on social exclusion in the Milan-based area, its selection activity is based on studying other organizational models for dealing with social exclusion and on the drivers, critical issues, and challenges of the social problems to be faced. In this way Fondazione Oltre can not only select among potential problems that characterize the community in question, but also catalyze the interests of social actors who specialize in relevant areas. For this reason Oltre represents a model in its sector, for those who intend to develop innovative entrepreneurial projects and initiate social change. Thanks to this approach Oltre has also built a strong network that can support actual and potential social entrepreneurs and nonprofits in tackling social exclusion.

Fondazione Oltre, (http://www.fondazioneoltre.it)

5.4 MEASURING FUND PERFORMANCE

The last main dimension of variance concerns the methods and procedures for measuring performance. For a description of the main instruments that apply to the measurement process, see Chapter 3.

For the scope of this chapter, it is important to note the great variability in the methods and tools used, as well as the extent to which measurement is applied. This still represents an important criterion in VP models, emphasizing the differences among portfolios and assessing the real potential and impact of VP in supporting SE.

However, relevant to the issue of variability, the most experienced foundations tend to equate social and economic measurements with the longevity of the financed projects or entrepreneurs. The longevity factor is applied to areas such as the ratio of projects or entrepreneurs who reach self-sufficiency; the ratio of entrepreneurs who continue to lead the original venture; or the ratio of entrepreneurs who lead the sector that their organizations consider important.

Of additional interest is the impact a VP organization believes its activity has beyond the results of a specific SEV. The development of models that become leading reference points in a sector, the changed laws and policies in different countries, the creation of social movements, and so on are also considered as relevant factors in assessing fund performance and effectiveness.

5.5 VENTURE PHILANTHROPY: THE PATH AHEAD

The comparison among best practices and consolidated experiences in the field of VP demonstrates how this new approach to financing is now at the forefront of innovation and creativity within the social sector, in terms of ground-breaking potential and supportive contribution to the enhancement of societal well-being in initiating social change.

Although widespread attitudes toward VPs both inside and outside organizations are largely optimistic, the relationship between SEVs and VPs is still problematic. In view of the fact that organizations consistent with SE are recent and not always widely acknowledged, it is difficult to clearly distinguish between SEVs and nonprofits. The lack of an overall system to define SE and set clear boundaries across different approaches to social problems, makes it difficult to promote SEVs. Although misunderstanding and/or misinterpretation constitutes a significant barrier within the industry, it is certainly not the only one faced by VP and socially innovative entrepreneurs. The most prominent barriers to the development of VP practices are listed below:

- lack of a proper network: usually entrepreneurs and venture capital firms are matched via active networks. The lack of a good network can certainly impede the beginning of a financial relationship within the SE frame;
- different meaning for 'societal well-being' and 'social change': given the ambiguity of the social dimension and the difficulty of expressing in concrete and measurable terms the extent to which SEVs can contribute to social change, perceptions differ as to what constitutes an innovative entrepreneurial action;
- lack of an adequate business plan: VPs stress the importance for SE start-ups of an adequate business plan, that is, one with a complete and consistent business concept, and essential and relevant data. Clearly assessment of the adequacy of a business plan is influenced by the widespread debate as to what constitutes SE and social change;
- VP finance timing: as explained in the introduction to this chapter, venture capital and venture philanthropy are associated in that both involve risks, even if in different action fields (for example, an innovation in social sector for a VP). Thus the stage of development of the social start-up is important in determining whether it is included in a VP portfolio. From the point of view of venture capitalists, in fact, start-ups at a very early stage of development represent too high a risk. In that many of the VP organizations are themselves quite new, they might well favour entrepreneurial projects or SEVs that are relatively mature, in comparison with good business ideas that still need to be incubated. Such a situation could generate a gap in financing, which, given the newness of the SE phenomenon, is not totally filled by other types of investors, such as angel investors – that is, private investors who provide capital directly to start-up companies at a very early stage of development;

- lack of expertise and skills: previous research on the state-of-
  the-art in venture philanthropy (Morino Institute and
  Community Wealth Ventures, 2001) has emphasized that
  funding organizations tend to be focused on a specific and
  univocal field of intervention, such as youth or education, job
  training, or technology-oriented projects. Additionally, it is
  widespread practice to focus on a specific geographical
  region, thus selecting projects and entrepreneurial
  organizations that insist on that region. This practice can
  create field-specific expertise and financing models hardly
  replicable across countries and fields of action.

There is no doubt concerning the ground-breaking potential of
venture philanthropy. Many of the problems faced by VP
organizations and many of the barriers to the development of the
sector will be solved in time as the field becomes mature in terms
of consolidated practices and proved successes and as the
communities and society at large learn about SE and the
opportunities within it.

APPENDIX 5.1

Echoing Green Foundation	Ashoka	Schwab Foundation
GEOGRAPHICAL REGION		
New York, USA	Arlington, USA	Cologny/Geneva, Switzerland
WEB SITE ADDRESS		
http://www.echoinggreen.org	http://www.ashoka.org	http://www.schwabfound.org
FOUNDER		
senior leadership of *General Atlantic*, LLC and *The Atlantic Philanthropies* (APS)	Bill Drayton	Klaus and Hilde Schwab
KICK-OFF		
1987	1980	1998
WHO THEY ARE		
Echoing Green provides first-stage funding and support to visionary leaders with bold ideas for social change. As an angel investor in the social sector, Echoing Green identifies, funds and supports the world's most exceptional emerging leaders and the organizations they launch. These social entrepreneurs and their organizations work to close deeply-rooted social, economic and political inequities to ensure equal access and help all individuals reach their potential.	Ashoka is a global non-profit organization that invests in social entrepreneurs around the world. Ashoka pioneered the 'social venture capital' approach in international development. Ashoka's mission is to shape a citizen sector that is entrepreneurial, productive and globally integrated, and to develop the profession of social entrepreneurship around the world.	The Schwab Foundation provides a global platform to promote social entrepreneurship as a key element to advance societies and address social problems in an innovative and effective manner. It aims: • To be the foremost organization for identifying, selecting and highlighting accomplished social entrepreneurs ; • To be a driving force that builds a global community of outstanding social entrepreneurs and others interested in promoting social entrepreneurship;

| | | • To be the preferred partner for companies and social investors seeking to support social entrepreneurs around the world.
• To be a global standard bearer for excellence in social entrepreneurship and innovation for the public good. |

INVESTMENT STRATEGY

| Echoing Green believes the same energy and creativity that characterize commercial entrepreneurship can foster new solutions in the social sector. That is why Echoing Green takes risks on undiscovered leaders when others won't. Echoing Green is a leading global social venture fund that invests in new organizations at their earliest stages. | Ashoka identifies and invests in leading social entrepreneurs, that is extraordinary individuals with unprecedented ideas for change in their communities – supporting them, their ideas and institutions through all phases of their careers. | The Schwab Foundation does not give grants. Rather, it invests its limited resources in creating unprecedented opportunities where social entrepreneurs who have successfully implemented and scaled their transformational idea, can further the legitimacy of their work, have access to usually inaccessible networks, and in consequence, mobilize the financial and in-kind resources that enable them to continue to strengthen and expand. |

VP MODEL

| • *Identify Visionaries*: Through a highly competitive selection process, Echoing Green identifies talented yet unproven social entrepreneurs.
• *Invest in Innovation*: Each year, they invest at least $1 | Ashoka pursues a 'venture capital' approach to financing social change. Ashoka intervenes at the point in the entrepreneur's work when the risk is greatest, when almost no other support is | The model is based on the following initiatives and activities:
• The Social Entrepreneurs' Summit to connect people and share knowledge.
• Participation in the Annual Meeting of the World Economic Forum at Davos, |

million to help Echoing Green Fellows transform innovative ideas into action.
• *Provide Hands-on Support*: they provide technical assistance and consulting to help new leaders build organizations, increase their organizations' capacity and manage growth. They also facilitate peer-to-peer learning to enhance leadership skills and ensure organizational sustainability.
• *Connect People*: They harness the experience and expertise of their global network of social entrepreneurs to share best practices and ensure success.

available, and when a modest investment can generate large-scale social returns. The Ashoka stipend serves as a full time salary for the social entrepreneur, freeing him or her to focus exclusively on his/her new idea while establishing an institutional base from which to operate. Ashoka leverages its investment by making available a range of value-added service (e.g., contacts and information, collaboration among the Fellows, and so on).

and at the Forum's Regional Meetings.
• Mobilizing in-kind and financial resources not through grant making.
• Maintaining standards:
• Raising awareness of social entrepreneurship.

SKILLS AND RESOURCE TRANSFER

• *Financial support*: individual and partnership fellowships;
• *Technical assistance*: focus on conferences and network creation;
• *Accountability to outcomes*: programs, projected outcomes and measurement tools are developed cooperatively.

• *Financial support*: a living stipend typically for three years, depending on individual need and local salary standards.
• *Technical and professional assistance*: network creation

• *Technical and professional assistance*: network creation
• *Accountability to outcomes*: programs, projected outcomes and measurement tools are developed cooperatively

---

SELECTION CRITERIA AND PORTFOLIO COMPOSITION

Applicant is an emerging social entrepreneur:
• Demonstrated

Ashoka implements a rigorous selection process for identifying

The Schwab Foundation applies the following criteria in selecting members of the

entrepreneurial characteristics
• Demonstrated leadership potential
• Strong passion and commitment for the program area in which they plan to work
• Intelligence and problem solving skills
• Practical skills (e.g., strategic, organizational)
• Personal integrity
Applicant's plan will result in a sustainable organization:
• Clear and compelling mission and objectives
• Sound strategy and plan for program development and delivery
• Plan for evaluating success and performance
• Plan for financial sustainability and growth
• Existing support network
Applicant can clearly articulate their vision for social change:
• Seriousness of the social problem they will address
• Innovative idea and approach
• Potential for tangible

and electing the most innovative social entrepreneurs, with the greatest probability of achieving large-scale social impact. Selection criteria are:
• The New Idea
• Creativity
• Entrepreneurial Quality
• Social Impact of Ideas
• Ethical Fiber
Ashoka receives nominations from local groups of Nominators, such as journalists, academics, social entrepreneurs (including Ashoka Fellows), and individuals well-placed in the non-profit and social innovation communities. The Ashoka Country Director and selection team in that country conducts a first interview and site visit. Candidates who 'pass' then undergo a second interview by an international senior staff member, who forwards the most promising candidates to the Ashoka

network:
• *Innovation*: the candidate has brought about social change by transforming traditional practice.
• *Reach and Scope*: the social entrepreneur's initiative has spread beyond its initial context and has been adapted successfully to other settings.
• *Replicability*: aspects of the initiative can be transferred to other regions and are scalable.
• *Sustainability*: the candidate has generated the social conditions and/or institutions needed to sustain the initiative and is dedicating all of his/her time to it.
• *Direct positive social impact*: the candidate has founded, developed and implemented the entrepreneurial initiative directly, together with poor or marginalized beneficiaries and stakeholders. Impact manifests itself in quantifiable results and testimonials and is well documented.

	Selection Panel. Based on	
impact to the beneficiary population • Potential for replication and growth • Potential for effecting systemic change (e.g., policy change, societal change, influence in their field)	extensive interviews and background checks the local panel selects Ashoka Fellows, who must then be approved by the organization's international board to become Ashoka Fellows.	• *Role model*: the candidate is an individual who can serve as a role model for future social entrepreneurs and the general public. • *Mutual value-added*: candidates must demonstrate an interest in building a network of outstanding social entrepreneurs that stimulates and supports its participants actively to help one another.
FUND IMPACTS		
• investments for over $22 million in seed and start-up grants • more than 380 social entrepreneurs • organizations launched in 30 countries on 5 continents	• over 1,500 Ashoka Fellows in 53 countries since 1981; • Ashoka Fellows work in the 6 broad fields of learning/education, environment, health, human rights, civic participation, economic development; • approximately 150 new Fellows are elected each year.	• the Schwab network includes 84 social entrepreneurs.
PERFORMANCE MEASUREMENT		
• Return on investment • Longevity • Developed new models of addressing particular social issues • Opened offices in multiple cities	Since 1997, Ashoka has implemented a process to measure the impact of Ashoka Fellows around the world. This annual Measuring	Schwab performance depend on the extent to which the following objectives are reached: • Legitimacy and credibility or social entrepreneurs • Opportunities for

• Changed laws and policies • Created new products and services that otherwise would not exist • Sparked movements in the public sector	Effectiveness study examines the progress of Ashoka Fellows and their projects at regular intervals after their stipend periods have expired.	networking among social entrepreneurs as well as with other individuals/organizations who can mobilize support for their initiatives. • Financial and/or in-kind resources

6. Organizing a social enterprise

Barbara Imperatori and Dino Ruta

6.1 INTRODUCTION

In the last few years, researchers have focused on different and relevant topics relating to Social Entrepreneurship (SE), in order to develop a theoretical framework (Leadbeater, 1997; Emerson and Twersky, 1996; Borzaga and Defourny, 2004; Dees, Emerson and Economy, 2001; Mair and Marti, 2004). The authors highlight the social relevance of the emerging ventures, strategic opportunities, critical role of the social entrepreneur and financial challenges, but only a few of them discuss the organizational dimension that drives a social enterprise toward success.

The aim of this contribution is to point out peculiarities and organizational challenges that characterize the process of implementation and development of a Social Enterprise. We consider the organizational problems that social entrepreneurs face in order to design a sustainable configuration over time.

Our main purpose is to provide indications for the organizational design, but we also underline the cognitive effectiveness – from a heuristic point of view – of the emerging new organizational configuration.

In section 6.2, we discuss the rationality beyond human behaviors from an individual to an organizational perspective, as a precondition to design an effective organizational solution.

In section 6.3, we present in detail the six main dimensions (social entrepreneur; strategy and environment; organizational structure; coordination and integration mechanisms; reward systems; people practices) that are strictly interdependent and need to be aligned in order to create a sustainable competitive advantage in a social enterprise.

Section 6.4 discusses some challenges and limitations as practical implications for SE development.

6.2 SE AS A COGNITIVE FRAME FOR THE ORGANIZATIONAL ACTION

Over the last twenty years, we have witnessed a flourishing literature, belonging to different disciplines, that questioned the supremacy of the classical economic behavioral paradigm (Sen, 1987; Frank, 1987; Lindenberg, 1990; Zamagni, 1995; McFadden, 1999) suggesting that individuals could also pursue objectives different from self-interest. These objectives are endogenous to the prevailing model and also depend on cultural and cognitive factors. This is the birth of the relational paradigm that integrates the rational paradigm *stricto sensu.*

By adopting a relational, socio-normative perspective, it is possible to explain different phenomena apparently conflicting with behavioral models described in the economic theory (Tvesky and Kahneman, 1981; McFadden, 1999), such as, for example, the beginning of a new entrepreneurial adventure leading to a Social Enterprise.

The relational paradigm goes beyond the idea of intention in the action typical of the economic rationality (that is, individuals act according to an optimizing logic), explaining that human beings are influenced by the social context that shapes their perceptions and influences preferences (Argyle and Henderson, 1985; Elster, 1989; Zamagni, 2000).

The acknowledgement of the social dimension of the human action is therefore not simply a behavioral model inspired by feelings such as philanthropy and love for others, neither is it a residual or a strange way of interaction; rather it is something more precious: an heuristic model, that allows individuals and society to develop, moving towards higher levels of knowledge and progress (Habermas, 1981).

When the social-oriented individual behavior is comprised within the organization, it is possible to combine efficiency and social impact by the interaction of different people having both economic and social purposes. Moving from the individual to the organizational level we find some ingredients that, properly combined, specify and characterize a social enterprise.

The following dimensions have been explored in more detail in the previous chapters. Here, we consider only the main features that are instructive for our model and discussion.

- entrepreneurial attitude: a social enterprise is the result of an entrepreneurial impulse to social innovation that takes shape and develops thanks to the 'social entrepreneur' (Shane, 2000);
- well-being enhancement: it is driven by a social objective that leads to the creation of a social value that is measurable and available for the whole society without exclusions, with the final purpose of producing a relevant social change across time. Societal welfare is the first objective for social entrepreneurs, who may enhance societal well-being rather than maximize their personal welfare (Dees, 1998a; MacMillan and McGrath, 2000);
- innovation: a social enterprise is the result of an initial innovation process linked to the recognition of a social gap. The sustainability of the social enterprise is achieved by a continuous innovation process in the social field (Dorado and Haettich, 2004);
- orientation to the market and to economic value: a social enterprise is characterized by a business and market orientation that guarantees the generation of an economic value: producing societal welfare in a profitable way (Laville and Nyssens, 2004).

A social enterprise faces an organizational problem that can be summarized in the following aspects:

- both human and financial resources can be found in traditional and non-traditional markets, where rules and assumptions can differ in terms of evaluation of exchanged resources: volunteers vs. employees, purchasing vs. donations, and so on;
- different actors have different competencies, in some cases they are different with respect to their knowledge and to their preferences about the output and resource allocation (social effectiveness vs. efficiency);
- it is a dynamic problem in which elements and context conditions can change over time and modify the social impact and economic results.

Some elements belong to the concept of enterprise itself, some others are more specific when related to social impacts. The balance between social and economic dimensions should be dynamic and perceived as fair. The social dimension is first of all central for the founder (or founders) who decides to pursue a social benefit otherwise not produced; the business dimension is the engine of organizational action that supports the social orientation of the entrepreneur. When one of these two dimensions becomes overwhelming, the balance of social enterprise is in danger. The social dimension pushes towards the constant search for the 'social gap', independently from the economic and financial equilibrium, while the business dimension pushes towards efficiency. This balance is often threatened by the choices that from time to time are taken by the decision makers whether they are entrepreneurs (social oriented) or workers (social or business oriented) that enter the company as collaborators. We could say that social entrepreneurs find in the social domain a factor that does not enhance motivation *per se*, but if not present, creates un-satisfaction (that is, hygienic factors, Hertzberg, 1966).

It's more likely that workers perceive the social dimension as a motivational factor conditioning their own actions and their behaviors. It is relevant, in an organizational perspective, to understand how to hold social entrepreneurs, workers (full-time, part-time, volunteers, and so on) and the business and the social dimensions together.

6.3 DESIGNING A SOCIAL ENTERPRISE

The aim of this part is to further understand the Social Enterprise structure that results from the entrepreneurial idea of the social entrepreneur. How is the social dimension tied to the business dimension and how do entrepreneurs move from the initial idea to the product/service assuring sustainability over time?

Designing an organization means designing those mechanisms and structures that are able to lead and align people's behavior with the organizational goals. In the following part we analyze those organizational solutions for the social entrepreneurship that can create the conditions to balance social and business dimensions, aligning the entrepreneur's social mind-set to the rest of the organization. We then present the organizational dimensions that characterize social enterprises (see Figure 6.1).

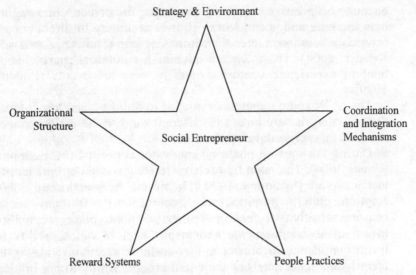

Figure 6.1 The organizational dimensions

6.3.1 The Social Entrepreneur

A social enterprise starts thanks to a social entrepreneur. According to Drucker (1986), an entrepreneur is focused on vision and opportunity, creates an entrepreneurial orientation and develops continuous innovative ideas. The heart of entrepreneurship is an opportunity-seeking orientation regardless of existing resources (Stevenson and Jarillo, 1990).

In this context, social entrepreneurs are different from traditional economic entrepreneurs, because they have a desire to enhance societal well-being in a sustainable way, to initiate change in society (Drayton, 2002).

Social entrepreneurial thinking requires a cognitive focus on social potential of an opportunity that must be perceived as both suitable and feasible, not only in a strictly financial sense, but also in term of consistency with the entrepreneurs' cognitive orientation. Perception of self-effectiveness is in fact a substantial antecedent of perceived opportunity (Weick, 1989; Krueger, 1993).

Additionally, social entrepreneurs are leaders that have to be able to mobilize people through the combination of social and business perspectives. A leader in a social enterprise has to encourage a positive change by provoking the debate, encouraging new thinking and social learning. It is necessary to direct people towards a solution, rather than imposing one (Heifetz, Kania and Kramer, 2004). These leaders have high emotional energy. They tend to experience venture events as personal events (Prabhu, 1999).

The skills and competences needed to build up and to exploit a Social Enterprise are linked in different ways to the various stages of social enterprise development.

During the start-up phase an innovator is needed (McBeth and Rimac, 2004). The main traits characterizing social entrepreneurial leadership are (Swammy, 1990; Thompson, Alvy and Lees, 2000; Johnson, 2003): ambitiousness, courage to withstand social censure; sensitivity to feeling of others; ability to persevere; ability to articulate, communicate and inspire a clear vision; ability to instill confidence in others; ability to think creatively; ability to identify and meet needs of the client groups; ability to put in long hours of work; ability to convince and empower others to turn the vision into reality. These skills and abilities are mostly common also to other entrepreneurs, but what is different is the mental and cognitive orientation to solve or alleviate a social problem. The profit maximization is viewed as a means to the more relevant social end (Johnson, 2003).

While in the earlier development stage, a social enterprise needs an entrepreneur that is first of all an innovator; when it starts to consolidate, a manager is needed, a manager who is focused on the formal and organizational processes necessary to sustain the growth of the social enterprise (Rimac and Armstrong, 2005).

6.3.2 Strategy and Environment

A SE is characterized by the virtuous circle that originates among innovation, societal welfare, and economic value in a recursive way.

Our thesis is that, firstly, this is guaranteed by the mind-set of the people that create and then participate in a Social Enterprise. This mind-set is a relevant precondition to all the decision processes and therefore to individual and organizational performance.

From an organizational point of view, this means that a 'strategic intent' is needed, that is, the ability to construct an organizational opportunity (Hamel and Prahalad, 1989).

According to Ajzen (1991), a decision maker should perceive the course of action as (a) within his/her competence and control (feasible, self-efficacy and collective efficacy), (b) personally desirable and (c) consonant with social norm.

It is necessary to establish an organization that supports these three dimensions, by the creation of a 'nutrient-rich' environment (Shapiro, 1982).

The mind-set we refer to is first of all the 'cognitive place' where the societal welfare and the business innovation dimensions find a synthesis.

The individual decides and acts following a rational model that is however limited, in line with the model of 'administrative man' proposed by Simon (1947), because of human nature itself. Those limitations are at the origin of some systematic biases (Grandori 1999), as they activate framing processes that generate a selective attention; some objectives are perceived as central, while others remain in the background and therefore are considered, maybe unconsciously, less relevant in a given moment (Festinger, 1957). In this sense, we say that people adopt a reference frame in defining a problem; this frame inevitably influences the decision process in terms of identification and evaluation of possible alternatives.

In this sense, social entrepreneurship can be interpreted as a cognitive framework, that is, an interpretative approach or a cognitive space social entrepreneurs, and managers, use to identify problems and generate possible actions. Through this approach, they move from the acknowledgement of a gap in the social performance and create an entrepreneurial opportunity (Krueger, 1993). SE is therefore a lens that drives firms' decisions and people's actions, always referring to the balance process as it is perceived by individuals.

A frame is a point of view; it allows some heuristic rules that unconsciously guide the unstructured decision process (March and Simon, 1958). This, for instance, could explain the way some social entrepreneurs are not aware about their social role, but they decide and act in a way that is naturally linked to a cognitive paradigm, where the two dimensions – social and business – stay naturally together. Heuristic rules and cognitive styles can be reinforced and shared at organizational level enacting a collective framing process that transforms an entrepreneurial idea into a common shared value, a sort of cultural guideline for the entire organization. In this sense we referred to SE as a cognitive place that is enforced by the social entrepreneur and by the entire organizational solution.

In fact, it is a task of the organization to prevent its natural decaying at the individual level, by sustaining this mind-set within the organization. In this sense, the organization compensates individual rationality, emphasizing specialization – also from a cognitive point of view – and at the same time assuring the integration of the action by means of specific organizational design rules.

6.3.3 Organizational Structure

The choice between functional specialization (competences) and the ability to manage interdependencies (integration) has always represented a critical issue in the organization design (Lawrence and Lorsch, 1967; Galbraith, 1977).

When one dimension is preferred to the other, the organization inevitably communicates and assumes an orientation that allows the achievement of an objective in the place of another. The organizational solution depends on the complexity of the activities that should be carried out. Lawrence and Lorsch (1967) define complexity of a task as a function of its clarity, of its difficulty and of the time required in order to observe the results or the actions that need to be taken. Additionally, complexity depends on interdependence of the activities involved. The interdependence reaches its maximum when reciprocal interdependence and environmental dynamism are present.

A first principle of aggregation is the one of interdependencies that emphasizes the coordination economies among activities. Those are implemented by using different competencies, but are linked together through intense information flows, which are necessary in order to reach the final output (Gerwin and Christoffel, 1974).

Another principle of integration, alternative to the one of interdependencies, concerns technical and orientation similarities. Activities that are different in terms of subject, time horizon and objectives can require similar techniques, that is, the same work practices. Technical similarities emphasize learning opportunities and, as a consequence, the dynamic development of competencies over time.

The other relevant dimension is the one related to orientation; the focus moves from the characteristics of the activities to the attitudes that should be possessed by those that have to implement some activities (Grandori, 1999). Orientation can be 'specialistic' or 'generalistic', towards short or long term, towards optimization or innovation. These different orientations are interrelated if we consider that innovation-oriented activities also have a specialistic focus on the medium and long run.

What we would like to underline in this contribution is linked to the social orientation that presents its specific characteristics, even if we associated it to innovation (social innovative entrepreneurship). The social dimension represents the ultimate orientation of some activities that, independently from their time horizon, from the orientation towards innovation or specialization, characterize the social enterprise as it is. These activities should be aggregated among them and separated from those that are not socially-oriented.

From a methodological point of view, the analysis of the activities and the definition of the structure also have the aim of individuating the phases of the value chain in which the social value is generated. These phases represent the core competence (Prahalad and Hamel, 1990) of the social enterprise, that is, the organizational place where the social prevails over the business dimension. These activities require learning and innovation orientations. The opposite is not true; this means that activities that are learning and innovation oriented may not have a social orientation.

6.3.4 Integration and Coordination Mechanisms

In a social enterprise technical specialization represents a first important driver for the aggregation of the activities and the identification of organizational units (Rimac and Amstrong, 2005). Additionally to differentiating activities, it is necessary, at least at a first organizational level, to define coordination mechanisms aimed at preserving the unity of the firm (Lawrence and Lorsch, 1967). Coordination mechanisms support the information flow among activities that reside in separated units. They can be defined as integration mechanisms when they generate the process by which the efforts of the different sub-systems are conducted to the unit, allowing the company to carry out its collective task. In other words, integration is something more than simple coordination, since it also includes the cultural dimension of the organizational action.

Indeed, another way to look at the same phenomenon is to correlate the environmental and task complexity. When the two variables are low, the organization uses its own resources for generation; in the opposite case, when the variables are both high, the organization needs to dedicate resources to the integration as a consequence of the increased integration need deriving from the increase of the different organizational sub-systems (differentiation). This represents the case for a social enterprise, where organizational units are very different among them as a consequence of their high technical specialization and of their orientation (Bergquist, 1992). Organizational impasse is generated in presence of activities that are different in terms of clarity, difficulty and time horizon, when the need for integration absorbs resources and requires priority in terms of focus and investments.

A social enterprise presents a high need for integration. If it is not properly addressed, organizations become like a group of independent and autonomous decision makers, each one with his own objective in mind, and this can create problems and dysfunctions.

The complexity paradigm postulates that in the presence of a high integration need, organizational solutions with a high investment on costs, time and space should be implemented. A low need for integration can be met by behavioral rules or formal documents. With an increase of the need for integration, procedures, plans and programs, hierarchical superiors, committee task forces, linking points at a managerial-level, integrator roles, and integration mechanisms can be designed (Lawrence and Lorsch, 1967). As can be easily noted, there is a measurable increased investment in resources for integration:

- by the time spent in defining rules, procedures and plans;
- by the time spent by single persons: coordinators;
- in temporary groups that are activated: committees and task forces;

- in the formalization of new roles like linking points or integrators;
- in the new mechanisms: simple or integrating;

A social entrepreneur is the first integrator of a company, especially if this is small in size. His/her role as an entrepreneur and founder allows him/her to manage and balance different needs of the sub-environment. However, if complexity is higher, integration mechanisms inevitably involve different people. Plans, rules, programs are not enough to regulate individual perspectives and interests that are very different from one another. The group therefore takes the place of the social entrepreneur in space, contingencies or time and becomes the organizational actor capable of diffusing the SE frame. This frame is institutionalized in decision routines that reinforce the unity and the alignment among specialized units and between the executives and the rest of the organization.

When rules are too rigid, orientation linked to production, and efficiency substituted for social innovation, SE can divert from its objective. A SE should have a strong orientation to innovation, and its organizational model should be based on a strong unifying culture and present loosely coupled coordination mechanisms.

6.3.5 Reward Systems

Reward systems present a double purpose: on the one hand they have an insuring role for workers, on the other they stimulate and drive them towards a high performance, in line with company objectives (Stajkovic and Luthans, 2001). The insurance side is provided by the fixed compensation, while the incentive power is guaranteed by other compensation forms.

A social enterprise can rely on a total compensation mix including fixed and variable reward, but also on some other non-monetary elements like the opportunity to identify oneself with the social mission of the firm, the social value of its activities, the quality of the working environment, the fulfilling of the affiliation need in order to attract, motivate and retain people (Greening and Turban, 2000). The non-monetary elements of the compensation mix represent a very powerful tool in order to customize the job offer on the specific needs of different people.

Social enterprises have at their disposal many of these elements. However, social enterprises should not neglect monetary rewards, as these still remain among the main instruments to compete on the job market. Considering all employees as volunteers could generate a lack of motivation among the workers due to a perception of unfairness. This could generate higher turnover rates and undermine the quality of performance.

Therefore, with regard to the wage level, a social enterprise should be in line with the market level, while its specificities allow it to propose a wider compensation mix that is able to meet the social needs of workers. A slightly smaller entry-salary could be applied in order to verify the intrinsic motivation of the employee to the social mission of the firm. Finally, rewards play an important role in order to direct the employee's behavior towards the social purposes of the organization. Therefore, incentive systems should always combine the social and professional dimensions of the individuals.

6.3.6 People Practices

One of the best indicators of the future success of a social enterprise lies in the organization's ability to attract, retain and develop people with the right skill set to work in and manage the social enterprise.

According to Ajzen's model of intention (1991), in order to sustain the course of action each individual has to perceive each task as (a) within his/her competence and control (feasible, self-efficacy and collective efficacy), (b) personally desirable and (c) consonant with social norm.

The concept of human resources (HR) is often linked to the formalization of specific processes like performance evaluation, selection, competence mapping, which should more properly be defined as functional HR. Strategic HR has, instead, a wider logic that considers corporate strategy, desired behaviors and processes that should be activated in order to lead people's behaviors. Talking about HR therefore means studying all those aspects that are explicitly and intentionally defined in order to influence organizational behavior, supporting people's performance and reinforcing their psychological contract with the company (Rousseau, 1998).

A theoretical model which links results (goals) to people profiles is the one that underlies the workforce scorecard (Huselid, Becker and Beatty, 2005) and that captures four relevant dimensions:

- mind-set: did people understand and assimilate corporate strategy? Is it the right one to support the execution?;
- skills: do people, and particularly those covering key positions, have the necessary skills in order to execute strategy?;
- behaviors: do top managers and the rest of the workforce have a behavior that is consistent with the goals to be achieved? Have critical positions been assigned to excellent people?;
- result: did the workforce achieve its business objectives?

Organizational culture determines skills; skills affect behaviors; behaviors determine success. This is the causal relation model of the variables we analyzed. Obviously the planning process has the opposite direction, as the starting point is represented by results, from which the appropriate behaviors are defined and then the necessary skills and culture are pointed out in order to execute strategy. The approach is contingent, strategy leads the organization, but only thanks to a strict interdependence that links implementing capacities with the actual capabilities of the workforce.

The need for differentiation and integration, in presence of a strong role of the social entrepreneur, leads to a people management strategy characterized by a shared culture that is strong and clear; this is the basis upon which different paths of growth for competences and behavior set roots. This leads to rejecting the concept of 'hybrid' regarding the competencies to be held. It is in fact more appropriate to emphasize specialization relying on organizational mechanisms in order to make different people work together effectively.

The only 'hybrid' element could be represented at a higher level, by the social entrepreneur, who is able to synthesize the social and the economic dimensions and understand their delicate balance in every decision. As we move down the hierarchy, the double dimension is lost. Moreover, if we consider that the social entrepreneur chooses his/her own collaborators relying more on cooptation than on selection, the hiring process of other employees will be inevitably directed to select specialized personnel.

Indeed, the design of human resource management (HRM) processes is not only limited to the social or economic dimensions, but is also related to the value of the competencies that are held by the people and their uniqueness with respect to the market (Lepak and Snell, 1999). The more the human capital that generates value for the SE is unique and of high value, the more the organization will directly invest in it. This differs significantly from transactional strategies (low value, low uniqueness), partnership strategies (low value, high uniqueness) or market acquisition strategies (high value, low uniqueness).

6.4 ORGANIZATIONAL CHALLENGES AND CONCLUSIONS

Our analysis mainly focuses on the acknowledgement of the organizational specificities of a social enterprise in the beginning of the entrepreneurial project and in its consolidation, in a static logic. We can now try to point out some organizational challenges that the social entrepreneur will be required to interpret in a context of dynamic management, typical of a social enterprise.

With regard to this aspect, the challenge resides not simply in the transformation of the entrepreneurial intuition into economic results, but essentially in its sustainability over time, through an ongoing process of social innovation and change.

In particular, the first organizational challenge that should be managed by a social entrepreneur is linked to the growth of the social enterprise. We already pointed out that the number and the nature of the activities carried out by the entrepreneur change with the expansion of the firm, as many of them are assigned to co-workers. This usually implies a higher separation of the social enterprise from the entrepreneur, accompanied by a higher technical specialization, a higher degree of formalization and a lower centralization.

These are problems that are typical of the organizational development of every company. However, in the case of a social enterprise they are amplified, given the double nature of organizational objectives (social and business) and the strong social characterization that usually represents a shared trait of identification of the first group of founders. It is often difficult for this group – and for the social entrepreneur – to recognize and integrate more stringent economic and specialization aspects in their managerial style. Those could lead to a loss of identity and motivation in the founders and generate difficulties in the acceptance of a shared model by the newcomers.

A second organizational challenge, strictly linked to the organizational size, is the replication of the organizational model. Among the objectives of a social enterprise there is continuous innovation that is, in the end, a contribution to the general development of society. However, this objective can clash with the establishment of the organizational model among people.

This establishment makes the organizational solution not easily transferable, exportable and replicable. At the same time it can undermine the legitimacy of the model over the long run, whether it is a winning model or not. In the absence of contamination and of diffusion of the organizational model, in fact, it can always be interpreted as an exceptional – favorable – combination of events that cannot be replicated. A sort of exception linked to particular people and places.

The replication of organizational solutions is, in fact, a process by which organizations re-use the knowledge they produced (Winter, 1995), by the creation of some 'replications' that are a series of local routines similar to the ones of origin (Winter and Szulanski, 2001). Replication strategy includes different phases. 'To replicate', in fact, means (Bradach, 1998): discovering and refining a business model; choosing the 'necessary' components for the replication of the model in another geographical area; developing the capacity of transferring knowledge; keeping the model working once it has been replicated.

The biggest challenge in the replication process of a social enterprise is probably connected with the necessary identification and codification of the first one, the so-called 'template'. The template can include information that might be relevant, necessary, useless or not replicable, but still represents the starting point (Winter and Szulanski, 2001).

The social enterprise, where the entrepreneurial adventure starts, is the template of the replication process and for this reason it has to be codified and studied. This implies that it has to be made independent from the people that ensure its vitality and its action. Therefore, specificities should be transformed into organizational routines; unfortunately, the codification process could find some limitations in the social nature of the Social Enterprise and in the relevance of its idiosyncratic competences, first of all the ones of the social entrepreneur.

At this point, a first consideration about the role of the organization design emerges: the organizational solution is a way to combine activities with different nature, to produce social and economic values; but it is also a way to enable diffusion and legitimating of the business social model. The more the organizational investment in codifying, formalizing, structuring activities, the easier the knowledge transfer and the model replication will be. Of course, some activities are not structured, but it is necessary to codify all those that are predictable, in order to enhance organizational sustainability (Simon, 1947).

The third organizational challenge that a Social Enterprise has to face in its evolution, is the one linked to the succession of the social entrepreneur. It is always critical for a company to survive after its founder, but this is much more critical for a social enterprise, in that it is particularly difficult to distinguish between the company and the entrepreneur. The central and unique character of the leader, as we discussed before, is a distinctive trait and success factor of the SE, which therefore risks a loss of tension and legitimatization if the entrepreneur leaves the business.

The only possible solution to this challenge is the design of an organization that can substitute or support its founder with its mechanisms, culture and routines.

Overall, much depends on how well the social entrepreneur is able to build an organization aimed at generating, developing and consolidating its own social value. The risk lies in basing the success of the enterprise exclusively on the entrepreneur and on the entrepreneurial spirit of his/her older collaborators. Difficulties, as the change in people and in environmental conditions, make sustainability complicated. The key to this problem is in structure and organizational mechanisms. The organizational paradigm has a relevant role in a social enterprise that has a strong social character that has to be separated from its founder. This means that it should be independent from people, but included in the organizational code, this being the main factor that assures the survival and the stability of the organizational and cognitive frame based on innovation, social welfare and economic profitability. The cognitive framework consists in the alignment of consists in the alignment of the mind-set between entrepreneurs and co-workers, and is the critical point in determining organizational culture and action. The organizational glue is therefore determined by the vision that all the participants of the venture have regarding the individual and social welfare that the organization generates (mind-set). Consistently with this mind-set, the integration of competencies, behaviors and individual results will determine organizational performance.

In conclusion, this chapter focuses on the role of organizational design and considers SE as a cognitive framework where heterogeneous components live together. Its principles suggest differentiating based on a social enterprise orientation and its technical specificities, with the ultimate goal to integrate the different pieces in a whole entity through appropriate integration mechanisms.

7. 'LocalFeed': societal wealth generation in Southern Africa

James D. Thompson and Ian C. MacMillian

7.1 SOCIAL WEALTH GENERATION

Governments and philanthropists in the United States and other rich nations spend billions of dollars each year supporting philanthropic causes that attend to the manifold social problems of the world. Some of their efforts – cumulatively on the order of hundreds of millions of dollars each year – go toward supporting start-up firms and small entrepreneurial businesses, a strategy linked to the belief that the creation and growth of new enterprises fuels the growth of the economy, particularly through employment. To date, however, few people have considered the role that entrepreneurial activity can play beyond improving employment. Our research suggests that entrepreneurship can serve as a weapon to attack social problems, the benefits of which extend beyond simple job creation. Some such benefits are described below. Furthermore, the outcomes of our projects suggest that entrepreneurship can create a 'virtuous cycle': the greater the profits made, the greater the incentive for the entrepreneur to grow the business; and the more the societal problem is solved.

7.1.2 Societal Wealth Impacts of Entrepreneurial Action

Productivity enhancement: Many entrepreneurial efforts result in significant enhancement of productivity, often starting at the regional level and then extending to the national level. The creation of Sun Microsystems, for instance, massively increased the productivity of engineers, scientists, project managers and researchers, first in the United States, then globally.

National competitiveness: At an aggregate level, the cumulative effects of entrepreneurial activity add to a nation's ability to compete with other nations.

Quality of life: Many entrepreneurs, particularly in the US, are seizing upon opportunities to create business ventures that focus on improving the population's quality of life. This enhancement of quality of life manifests itself in several major forms:

- enhanced national health in the form of better ways to treat, diagnose and prevent illness via products that promote improved wellness and life extension and vastly superior devices for the physically and mentally disadvantaged;
- improvements in quality of work life created by the development of new products and equipment that increase worker safety as well as allow employees more flexibility to work out of their homes or from remote locations;
- enhanced national education, training and learning using technologies that dramatically improve the quality of the workforce, with concomitant gains in national productivity;
- enhanced efficiency of government services in which entrepreneurial providers of information and telecommunication systems dramatically increase the quality and availability of services;
- improvements in national nutrition whereby new enterprises enhance the quality, availability and quantity of food for poorly nourished segments of the population;
- personal wealth generation leading to philanthropy. Entrepreneurial success often positively influences societies by creating philanthropists, whose huge infusions of philanthropic funds into areas like the arts (Guggenheim/Getty museums); medical research (Mayo clinic, Bill and Melinda Gates Foundation); and social welfare (Turner Foundation) provide critical resources that the public sector either cannot provide or cannot adequately support.

7.2 SOCIETAL WEALTH GENERATION VIA EXPLORATORY ENTREPRENEURIAL PHILANTHROPY

Coupling this last societal wealth benefit (philanthropy) with the other benefits of entrepreneurial activity creates an opportunity to deploy entrepreneurship research in a radically new way. We can deploy philanthropic seed funds to create 'exploratory enterprises' to conceive of, plan for, and create enterprises that are designed to profitably attack social problems. In doing so, Societal Wealth Enterprises can serve as an alternative to current ineffective and sometimes enormously wasteful public sector initiatives. In some cases only a fraction of food sent to aid drought-devastated countries actually reaches the children who most need it.

Our basic thesis is that many social problems, if looked at through an entrepreneurial lens, create opportunity for someone to launch a business that generates profits by alleviating the social problem. In essence, it is a shift in activity from the public domain – governments and non-governmental organizations – to the private domain – businesses and private individuals. This sets in motion a virtuous cycle: the entrepreneur is incentivized to generate more profits and in so doing, the more profits made, the more the problem is alleviated.

Oftentimes this process is obstructed by two major obstacles: low profitability and the resultant lack of seed funding. This is where the entrepreneurial philanthropist first comes in. If philanthropists endow the seed funding for Societal Wealth Enterprises, in many economies, particularly developing ones, it should be possible to attract local entrepreneurs who are quite happy to live with the smaller profit streams eschewed by their counterparts in more wealthy economies. Evidence of 'micro innovation' and 'macro results' is offered by Chapman Wood and Hamel in discussion of the World Bank's Innovation Market (Chapman and Hamel, 2002).

A powerful appeal to the philanthropists is that their contributions have a chance to remove problems rather than to simply alleviate them, and the associated recurrent 'annual tin cup' dependencies. By dependencies we mean the fact that a philanthropic program that 'fills the tin cup' and does not reduce the problem simply creates a sustained dependence on the part of the recipients, who have to keep coming back.

Ideally, the second impact of Exploratory Entrepreneurial Philanthropy lies in replicability – the injection of seed funds, if successful, plants the seed for follow-on entrepreneurial initiatives.

Like all entrepreneurial efforts, however, success is not guaranteed. In fact the cynic might argue that if there were an obvious entrepreneurial solution, some entrepreneur would already have found it! This is where the third component of Exploratory Entrepreneurial Philanthropy kicks in. Our position is that we may be able to mobilize the talents of universities and business to undertake a new mode of research via entrepreneurial exploration, whereby we conceive of, design and plan Societal Wealth Enterprises and then recruit local entrepreneurs to launch and manage them. The profits they can make, though small by developed economy standards, can be perfectly adequate by the local entrepreneur's standards.

Exploratory Entrepreneurial Philanthropy is already being undertaken by the Snider Entrepreneurial Research Center (SERC) at the University of Pennsylvania's Wharton School of Business. We have four major programs underway in the areas of nutrition, healthcare and education. The Program has identified needs within each domain, conceived of possible social entrepreneurial solutions, developed business plans and then seeded the formation of a pilot business to implement the solution as a social exploration. The underpinning of each program is what we call a 'wedge' strategy. We start with a small, easily accepted and implemented initiative as the wedge to engage the entrepreneur; then unfold the full opportunity by discovery. The emergent pilot business is developed, and re-directed if necessary, throughout the learning process.

One such project, LocalFeed, is described in the case study below. In the spirit of using case studies to help advance theory, the objectives of this case study are:

- to affirm extant theory by describing what we found that we expected to find;
- to articulate what we expected to find but did not, which suggests places for adaptation of theory to the local situation;
- to present what was found that was not expected, which allows us to extend theory to take into account the unexpected.

7.3 'LOCALFEED': ANIMAL FEED PRODUCTION

LocalFeed is a Southern African producer and distributor of animal feeds founded by an individual who for the purposes of the case we will call Greg in late 2000.[1] Specifically, the company produces high quality feed mixes for poultry, cattle, and pigs in a region populated predominantly by small-scale and subsistence producers.

In many parts of the world the protein sources of choice in the human diet are derived from animal products. In Southern Africa the major sources of such nutrition are poultry, beef, pork and milk. Due to high cost and scarcity, meat is consumed less frequently in poorer environments, such as many rural areas, when compared with wealthier urban settings. Plant products rich in protein, for example groundnuts, are a common substitute where available.

Most meat products sold in retail stores are procured from large-scale livestock production enterprises such as commercial farmers and feedlots. These enterprises utilize large volumes of nutritional inputs in the form of animal feeds, which constitute up to 70 percent of the total Cost of Goods Sold (COGS) of the meat. The production of feed for poultry and livestock requires access to, and the purchase of, seasonally generated agricultural commodities such as corn; and the nutritional expertise to formulate feed mixes with appropriate combinations of protein, carbohydrates, fats, and minerals. Furthermore, a particular animal type may require up to five different feed mixes during its life-cycle, each mix delivered according to life-cycle stage. In the production of poultry broilers (chickens grown for meat consumption), for example, if a high-fat, high-energy mix developed for larger, high-growth birds were to be fed to very young chicks, the chicks would die of diarrhoea as a result of the inability to digest the fats contained within the mix. The feed formulation business is further complicated by differences in digestive tracts and physiology between species. While certain minerals and agricultural inputs provide outstanding nutrition for one species, they can be toxic to another. Finally the problem of compiling the lowest cost mix is compounded by frequent changes in the prices and availability of ingredients, and exchange rate volatility for imported nutrients.

7.3.1 The Entrepreneur and the Opportunity

The case started with our interest in deploying linear programming technology to calculate optimal feed mixes for animal feeds as a route to delivering lower cost feeds for livestock production. The University of Pennsylvania Veterinary School runs a very sophisticated program for US producers of livestock and we posited the possibility of adapting this program in areas where there is considerable malnutrition. Greg was the seed for the societal entrepreneurship venture, in a region of sub-Saharan Africa that had suffered massive economic decline and disinvestment for almost two decades and was characterized by an unemployment rate in excess of 50 percent.

As a former medium-size poultry and pork producer, Greg had observed that the existing suppliers of feed mixes produced what he believed to be low quality products, with a resultant lower yield in animal production output. Furthermore, he believed the incumbent producers of feeds to be oligopolistic, over-priced, and indifferent to the potential of two under-served market segments, namely subsistence farmers and small-scale commercial producers of poultry. Having recently exited a venture, he was interested in exploring the feed mix industry with a view to entering the industry. The concept was simple – to enter the industry with lower cost, higher quality feeds targeted at small-scale and subsistence producers of poultry. Discussions with Greg made it clear that an attractive market opportunity might exist. What was encouraging was that Greg had a history of starting small businesses with few resources and growing them into profitable enterprises without infusions of significant capital.

In order to frame the proposed venture, identify key assumptions, and determine an effective learning path we constructed a Discovery Driven Plan (DDP) (McGrath and MacMillan, 1995). DDP is a fast, efficient, means of assessing the feasibility of an idea. A DDP provides a simple, but powerful, means of communicating to a prospective entrepreneur what they need to deliver in order reach their desired profits and profitability goals. Given the high degree of uncertainty of the proposed venture, and the lack of market data, it appropriately afforded the entrepreneur that ability to assign ranges of possible values as assumptions rather than the inaccurate prediction of specific values in a traditional financial model. By running a sensitivity analysis thereafter, the most critical assumptions were identified and a 'learning plan' designed to gather more accurate data as quickly, and cheaply, as possible.

In 2000 more than 90 percent of poultry producers in this region grew between 50 and 200 broiler chickens per six week cycle. By comparison, a large producer in a country like South Africa might produce in the order of 300 000 birds per six week cycle. In this particular region, however, the three largest poultry producers had an estimated output of 6 000 birds per cycle. The data on numbers of small-scale producers and potential feed sales volume did not exist. In order to get a sense of what the figure might be we established the number of chicks sold to the region by the national breeder. This figure was approximately 50 000 per week. Using a rough estimate of the average small-scale producer volume of 20 broilers per week the market was approximated at between 1 500 and 2 500 potential customers. What was not clear, however, was how many actually purchased, or would purchase, commercially formulated feeds versus home-grown and mixed feeds. Greg's position on this was he would learn the approximate value of the assumption as early as possible by including consumer questionnaires to be handed out during a series of local educational seminars that he was going to launch for small-scale farmers in a number of rural locations.

In discussion of the competitive landscape we were made cognizant of the fact that the direct competition, comprised primarily of three large national and international incumbents, had a precedent of competitive intolerance. Accordingly, we challenged Greg to spend his imagination (rather than capital) in order to gain market validation prior to (A) the purchase of assets, and (B) further investment of our time or resources.

Furthermore, we proposed the following:

- no product would be distributed or sold on credit terms. All sales would be cash-on-delivery. Aside from the mitigation of credit risk, this policy would support liquidity and force the product to withstand the market test on price and quality, rather than on ease of purchase. If the quality and price were right, the customer would pay cash;
- he should not approach any large customers of feeds such as the larger commercial farmers. In this way he might stay below the radar long enough to delay the inevitable

competitive response, until such time as he was in a position to weather it.

7.3.2 The Launch

Local legal, political, and competitive considerations made it most appropriate for the entity to be created as an independent business unit within an established firm, via an agreeable arrangement with management. In the event of successful launch it would be spun-out as an independent company. It was started with six employees, six shovels, a concrete mixing floor, a storage shed, a telephone, and a small infusion of funds for working capital and the purchase of raw materials. All ingredients were mixed, bagged and loaded for dispatch by hand.

Greg designed a sales strategy that proved to be particularly effective. He elected to focus first on poultry feeds as this was the area of greatest demand and shortest animal production cycle. The market was broken down into areas around key towns and villages. He first identified a distributor in an area, and then advertised an education and sales seminar to be held close-by. Furthermore, he instructed his salesman to identify well known small-scale producers in each area. These farmers were paid personal visits, something formerly unheard of, but exceptionally well received. They were invited to bring interested friends.

The education and sales seminars comprised of three presentations. The first was a presentation of basic poultry costings, expected returns, and simple accounting methods, delivered by Greg. The second session was delivered by a veterinarian on disease prevention, identification and response. The third was delivered by a representative of one of the large chick hatcheries on the different types of bird, their costs, and respective life-cycles.

At the end of each seminar participants were informed of the distributor location and that feed prices were available at a slightly lower cost than competitive products. Existing producers were encouraged to test the new feeds; non-producers were encouraged to begin an experimental poultry production trial.

7.3.3 Early Growth: Reaching a 'Ceiling'

After twelve months LocalFeed was selling 140 tons of products per month to approximately 120 customers. A typical customer was an unemployed family growing between 50 and 200 broilers per month that had attended one of the education seminars. Greg demonstrated during the seminars that should a family produce, and sell, 200 broilers per month they had the potential to earn approximately $222. When compared with a minimum wage of $1.00 per day this was not an unattractive proposition, particularly when viewed against an unemployment rate above 50 percent. Market feedback was increasingly positive and Greg had begun salvaging junk-yard equipment that could be re-built to assist with increasing production demand. The venture employed 16 workers.

At eighteen months the venture was selling 230 tons of products per month and had grown to 28 employees. The customer base had grown proportionately. Although LocalFeed was well established in the chosen niches, Greg was concerned that they seemed unable to break through a 'ceiling' in sales of 300 tons per month, and that he may have overestimated the size of the market.

We utilized the Attribute Mapping tool (McGrath and MacMillan, 2000) to design a basic customer interview, and a key sales employee was dispatched to interview thirty customers across the sales region. The representative returned with positive feedback on product performance, availability, and price relative to competitors. However, the most useful information received was in response to the question 'What do you currently tolerate about our product but would prefer to do without?' The most surprising answer was that LocaFeed's products had a shelf life of six weeks versus the three months of the competition. This was previously unrecognized to the LocalFeed team, as was its importance due to the six week production cycle of a broiler.

When probed as to why this was a problem when in fact distribution points were readily accessible, the real insight was gained. Customers in this market segment were primarily small-scale producers who did not have their own transport, and relied on third party transport, for which they paid dearly. For many this was a delivery scheduled once per six week cycle when they would purchase a batch of chicks and the calculated feed requirement. As a precaution against early spoiling of the product, due to it perhaps having been in the distribution depot for one to two weeks, they were purchasing a 'safety net' of longer life product from competing firms; even though convinced the product yield was lower.

Correcting the problem required minor modifications in formulation at almost no extra cost. The sales person was dispatched the following week to thank those customers who had offered the information, and to inform all customers that the product shelf life had been enhanced. The result was an immediate increase in sales; three months later the sales ceiling was broken.

7.3.4 Product Optimization: Focus on Key Cost and Production

In its first two years of operations the company gained control of approximately 25 percent of the local market. Although the young business was considered relatively successful Greg was concerned that the profit margin fluctuated between a low three and five percent. He had also received information that the rapid growth of LocalFeed had attracted the attention of the larger, more established competitors. The word on the street was that the competition was considering a significant across-the-board price cut in an attempt to force LocalFeed out of the market.

In June of 2003, we initiated the next phase of our engagement with LocalFeed, a now successful small regional producer and distributor of animal feeds. The purpose of the engagement was to identify cost reduction possibilities and other parameters with which to improve LocalFeed's ability to compete during a protracted price war, should it develop.

One of the key contributions we believed we could make was to use University of Pennsylvania Vet School expertise and very smart University of Pennsylvania undergrads[2] to build a simple, but effective, linear program to minimize the Cost of Goods Sold without compromising the quality of product. Early in the review it became evident that the opportunity to contribute was larger than we had recognized. The company had begun by offering six products. It was now offering 26. Due to the increase in recipe formulation complexity, management was reluctant to re-formulate as frequently as prices changed, and were using the same recipes for up to four weeks. With growth, what had begun as a few hours work, and a call to a nutritional consultant for an acceptable fee, was now a task that was taking up almost 20 percent of Greg's time. He believed the business unable to afford expensive multi-product formulation software applications and was not convinced he had the skills to use such tools.

We revised the DDP and produced an update more representative of reality in that it incorporated data and information not previously available to us. The purpose of the exercise was to:

- determine the operational requirements that would need to be met in order to achieve the goals of management (based on competitive expectations);
- run a sensitivity analysis, to determine the relative contributions to model variance of each of the assumptions we would be required to make;
- identify the future key cost and profit drivers of the business.

Of particular interest here was the fact the sensitivity analysis produced valuable insights that were specific to the local environment. First, due to revised theft and loss provisions, the shrinkage assumption migrated to the top of the sensitivity analysis chart as the greatest contributor to variance. When product prices are inelastic; margins are in the order of 3 to 5 percent; Cost of Goods Sold in excess of 70 percent; and a provision for shrinkage between 5 and 10 percent (in extreme cases 15 to 20 percent); the ability to effectively manage inventory losses has a profound effect on profitability.

Second, LocalFeed had extended credit terms to a number of distributors and was dismayed to see the implications of the decision. Receivables had sky-rocketed and bad debts had followed suit. As a result there were large associated costs, and a cash flow pinch.

Our recommendations were as follows:

- embark on an aggressive collections initiative to drastically reduce receivables;
- we would build and deploy a product optimization program as soon as possible;
- we would evaluate how we might construct a simple set of Excel-based management tools with which to manage inventory, plan production, and purchase raw materials.

7.3.4.1 Product optimizer

This optimization software was designed in collaboration with the University of Pennsylvania's School of Veterinary Medicine,[3] and was delivered to LocalFeed in August 2003. The optimizer we developed is an MS Excel-based linear program, running in Visual Basic (VBA). Use of the program requires only limited knowledge of Excel, and no knowledge of VBA. The program is configured to simultaneously optimize up to 46 recipes, based on as many as 249 ingredients (50 ingredients are presently loaded into the system, and the user has the option to add up to 199 more). The user is able to update price, availability, and nutritional content information for each of the ingredients and feed formulas. The program provides summary outputs to aid in cost tracking, margin analysis, production management, materials ordering, and package labeling. (See Figure 7.1).

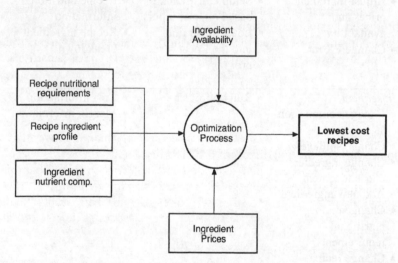

Figure 7.1 Lowest cost feed formulation

Tables 7.1 and 7.2 give a more detailed look at the scope of the program. The feed production module was delivered in August 2003 and in use by the following month. At that time there were stronger market signals of an impending effort by the major competitors to displace LocalFeed by instituting a 20 percent reduction in selling prices. Based on simulated raw material cost savings, considerably reduced levels of receivables, new inventory control systems to be implemented, and the ability to accurately respond to a volatile Foreign Exchange rate, Greg pre-empted the move by implementing an across-the-board, 20 percent sales price reduction. Sales immediately climbed. Within a month all competitors had matched the new price levels. LocalFeed's operating profit margins held constant due to the effects of superior formulation; and then began to climb as lower levels of inventory, bad debts, shrinkage, and interest on bank loans were reflected in monthly financials.

Table 7.1 The scope of the program

INPUT	PROCESS	OUTPUT
• Adjust ingredient prices and availability • Change FX rate	• Setup constraints based on user inputs • Load constraints into the linear program	• Recipe nutritional information • Recipe ingredient breakdown
Infrequent • Change commission % • Change spillage % • Change ingredient nutrient content • Add new ingredient • Change recipe nutritional requirements • Change recipe selling price	• Run optimizer	• Cost information • Margin information

7.3.5 Management Controls

The production management software was provided to LocalFeed as an update to the existing Excel program in February 2004. The software allows the user to translate the optimizer results into production plans quickly and effectively, while also integrating various inventory tracking functions. Production planner outputs include manufacturing summaries for use on the production floor, cost information, raw material requirements, and customized nutritional labels for packaging.

Table 7.2 Details on the scope of the program

INPUT	PROCESS	OUTPUT
• Select desired production amount • Record receipt of raw materials • Record shipment of finished goods • Record receipt of returned goods	• Load formulas from the optimizer • Calculate production requirements • Copy relevant info to summary outputs • Adjust inventory to account for production • Adjust inventory for new receipts or shipments	• Raw material ordering requirements • Production summaries by feed type • Cost/margin data by recipe and for batch • Nutritional content labels • Inventory receipt/shipping records
Independent Routine • Update inventory levels to match stock check	• Compare book levels to actual inventory	• Detailed spillage report

This addition to the product optimization tool was particularly difficult to deploy as there were a number of employees who were reluctant to accept such an accurate inventory management procedure. It took approximately four weeks of continual struggle to reconcile raw material inventories with invoiced production, and the rolling weekly production plan. However, once implemented the system proved invaluable for loss control. The combined financial effects of these, and the tools above, are discussed beneath in the results section (see Figure 7.2).

7.4 PROJECT TIMELINE

Although continuous, the project can be broken down into six phases, the first four of which were sequential and completed as of October 2005. (See Table 7.3).

7.5 NEXT STEPS

Profit optimization: LocalFeed was less interested in this aspect than cost control during the early chase for market share. Given that the enterprise is reaching capacity, they may soon be required to choose among combinations of products, or volume sales of each, rather than producing all orders due to availability of excess capacity. At writing we are planning a profit optimization model which will take into account not only sales prices, product sales volumes, and associated costs, but also the profitability of various customer profiles. Anticipated deployment is early 2006.

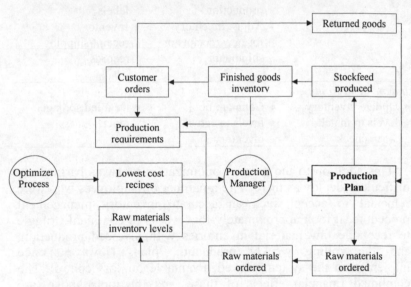

Figure 7.2 Production management

Table 7.3 Timeline

DATE	PHASE	DESCRIPTION
November 2000	I The start	Entrepreneur recognizes opportunity and negotiates deal with corporate partner. Discovery Driven Plan (DDP)
... – August 2002	II Early growth – reaching a 'ceiling'	Building a customer base: education seminars, distribution strategy, market research
... – August 2003	III Product optimization – focus on what matters most	Linear program for product formulation
... – February 2004	IV Production management – internal focus	Inventory management, production planning, raw materials procurement
January – April 2006	V Profit optimization	Next step: build the analysis tool with which to determine the optimal product-volume mix
January 2006 – ...	VI Regional roll-out	In parallel with Phase V, entrepreneur is seeking out opportunities to replicate the model elsewhere in region. This will be followed by roll out in other countries.

Regional roll-out: One of the key mandates of our program is that initiatives should be spun out to other locations once the pilot model has been shaken down and debugged. To this end, Greg is actively seeking out further opportunities in the greater region of Sub-Saharan Africa. We are currently evaluating enquiries from other parts of the developing world.

It is our hope that we are able to use Greg's expertise to establish similar plants, with comparable, if not greater, regional impact on human and animal nutrition.

7.6 IMPACT TO DATE

At the time of writing the LocalFeed project has both internal and external impact.

7.6.1 Internal

The most recent financial year saw LocalFeed provide employment for sixty people and produce a Net Income of US$ 500 000.00.

Operating profits have increased by 15 to 20 percent.

Automated formulation and record keeping functions have proven a significant timesaver for management – estimated at a minimum 25 percent of Greg's time.

Monthly income and cash flow streams have smoothed such that it is now considerably easier to access short-term finance for seasonal raw material purchases.

7.6.2 External: Benefits beyond Direct Employment Creation

When asked about LocalFeed's greatest achievement Greg's response is quick and direct: 'Our greatest achievement is unemployment reduction precipitated by hundreds of micro-businesses. We have 600 customers earning a better living, approximately one third of whom had never produced poultry, eggs or other livestock products, prior to attending our seminars. Furthermore, between 10 and 15 percent of our clients have grown to production units of 1 000 to 4 000 broilers per month. They are employing family members, and others, to work with them; or in some cases, where they have jobs, to manage the units while they are away at work.'

The LocalFeed team is now advocating to their customers the value of diversification in order to counter market demand fluctuation. A number of their customers have begun successfully producing broilers, layers and pork. 100 layers provide income generation potential of an additional $55.00 per month.

Product price levels, for higher quality feeds, remain reduced for the entire region of operation – farmers and producers in the area can now obtain feed at 20 plus percent lower price, whether it be from Greg or from other producers.

New competition is entering the region due to the major increase in demand for feeds precipitated by the availability of lower cost feeds. This has a multiplier effect on food production.

Animal yield and health has increased to the degree that the rate of growth increase allows an additional production cycle per annum through the same poultry facility, increasing customer Return on Assets (ROA).

7.6.3 Second-Order Effects

In response to shortfalls in government funding, the regional department of correctional services has begun to undertake its own initiatives in providing food for prisoners. Having successfully experimented with the production of broilers they have established larger production units which are operated by prisoners. Surplus poultry is sold on local markets for funds to plant and grow vegetables. In turn, further surplus funds are being used to purchase egg laying poultry. One prison has its own a broiler unit, vegetable crop and egg production facility catering for the nutritional needs of prisoners.

More recently a regional department of military service has adopted a similar program to that of the correctional services department.

At the time of writing, the authors are informed that a number of churches are attempting to develop community-based agricultural production programs in remote areas.

The National Poultry Association is considering the establishment of poultry processing plants for small-scale producers in the region in which LocalFeed operates, as well as others. Greg has been approached to serve as an advisor to members of the national committee and to take up a Board seat on the regional committee. The purpose of the initiative is to provide a means of processing and distribution to producers who are unable to sell their output locally.

Due to the significant increase in demand for poultry chicks in the LocalFeed area, national breeders are seeking to invest in new poultry breeding facilities. Their position is that they are no longer able to service the region from current facilities, and require decentralized production capacity to meet increasing levels of decentralized demand. This is an indication of increased levels of poultry consumption attracting production investment to support demand.

7.7 AFFIRMATION THEORY

Social entrepreneurship theory would lead one to expect a number of factors which might influence the success or failure of a project such as this. Many such factors have been identified during the course of consulting to small and medium enterprises (SMEs) by the Wharton Small Business Development Center and the Graduate School of Business, University of Cape Town. The Supporting Emerging Enterprises (S.E.E.) model was developed over a number of years, working with hundreds of SMEs, and provides a useful framework for conducting early investigations in the consulting process, gaining understanding of the key issues facing management, and presenting findings and recommendations in an acceptable manner. The most relevant of these to this case are discussed below:

- selecting the entrepreneur: possibly the single most important decision one can make is with whom to partner, work, or support. The private equity mantra of investing in the management team first holds true. A Societal Wealth initiative requires a greater degree of commitment, tenacity and perseverance than that demanded by a regular start-up;
- understanding the entrepreneur: it was established early that Greg was ambitious, and eager to build a large, profitable business. If this had not been the case we would have assumed the risk of producing growth-oriented goals, methods, and objectives that would have suffered the fate of

non-implementation due to incongruence of motivations. Another consideration to bear in mind is that the entrepreneur does not know what they don't know. On more than one occasion this affected the response times to our requests for data and information. We had obviously not communicated clearly enough the importance to him of what we wanted to develop. He had also never seen or used a linear program, so had no way of making his own judgment on consequence;

- understanding the environment: it is common practice to do market, legal, business and government assessment prior to investing in a new environment. What is important is to understand the behaviour of prospective consumers within the above-mentioned environment – and how that behaviour will affect the proposed business and revenue model. For example, due to the nature of process and timing, legal action may be the course of last recourse in the event of dispute, and even this may be futile;

- working at a distance and preparation: though significant communications advances have been made during the last five years they are not yet reliable in Southern Africa (South Africa excluded for the most part), particularly in rural settings. For example, it is not uncommon to have 'email down' for a week at a time in some areas. Even cellular services can be subject to frequent break-down. This project demonstrated clearly that there is no substitute for 'face time'. Besides getting to know someone better by having spent time at their location, the mere fact that one has made the effort to travel from a distance can make all the difference in the world to establishing legitimacy;

- realistic expectations: not all cultures work on the same clock. Not all people have similar ambitions or equivalent abilities. Not all environments are conducive to speedy process. It is therefore important to set, and agree on, expectations as early as possible. This prevents mutual frustrations as the project unfolds.

7.8 ADAPTATION OF THEORY

Establishing legitimacy and trust: The place where we most underestimated the challenge was in creating local legitimacy. For many entrepreneurs the engagement of a new venture is a deeply personal commitment, and they can be deeply suspicious of the intentions of outsiders and foreigners wishing to participate in their domain.

In many environments the rule of survival applies, and financial disclosures are produced according to the nature of the asker – if they exist at all. Sometimes they are purposely obscure or obscured. Building early trust is paramount if one hopes to get the real data. Developing a strategy for legitimacy can be as important to future success as any other key success factor.

7.9 EXTENSION TO THEORY

Early expectations of the project were modest when compared with what has been affected by LocalFeed during the last 24 months. The program began as business consulting assistance for a societal wealth start-up, with a view to replication elsewhere in the region, should it succeed. In addition to having met, and surpassed our expectations, it has provided us with additional insights into the assessment of Societal Wealth Generation potential, and strategy for program growth and impact.

Such observations are outlined below in the hope they might provide others with an expanded consideration set when seeking out and evaluating opportunities:

- 'wedge' strategy: neither we, nor the potential entrepreneur, are necessarily aware of the complete opportunity set that might emerge from the proposed venture. This case study demonstrated that one method of overcoming this short-coming is to start with a small, easily accepted and implemented initiative as the wedge to engage the entrepreneur; then unfold the full opportunity by discovery. This case has proved consistent with our other initiatives, thus validating the point;
- funding–opportunity asymmetry: the 'wedge' is the first step of the as-yet-unknown project or business development pathway. The need to let the business development pathway unfold poses two challenges in gaining access to funding. The first of these challenges is that a project such as this would have failed a conventional assessment by a traditional

funding source. There was no market data to support the feasibility of the LocalFeed concept, and it was less than plausible that such a market could be created in what was perceived as an impoverished region; second, due to the dual nature of their business proposition societal wealth start-ups run the risk of being viewed as 'neither fish nor fowl'. They are neither non-profit organizations, nor purely for-profit entities. Because they are for-profit they are unable to access traditional non-profit funding sources. The societal wealth component of their business proposition causes traditional for-profit funding sources to be wary, since they promise low profits, and run the risk of profit dilution in the name of societal contribution. It is here that Entrepreneurial Philanthropy has the potential to make a meaningful contribution through the provision of seed funding and support services. It is also a niche that more development initiatives might begin to consider with renewed interest and a creative mindset;

- context-driven assumption volatility: Our first attempts at determining the key cost and profit drivers of an animal feed production unit were based off US examples. As a result we failed initially to recognize the magnitude of influence of assumptions regarding shrinkage, receivables management (extremely risky in certain environments), a volatile foreign exchange rate, and the seasonal working capital requirements of raw material purchases in a region with relatively low levels of storage capacity;

- embedding a Pacemaker: The creation of LocalFeed has benefited not only its stakeholders, but has forced incumbent competitors to either meet new metrics of performance, or forfeit their position in the region. In this case they have chosen to stay and compete by producing higher quality products at lower prices. Furthermore, due to the increase in poultry demand and production, there are new entrants in the market, competing at improved standards. The resultant benefit to the local society is far greater than that directly achieved by LocalFeed alone. The opportunity to set a new pace is now a key factor in evaluating the potential impact of new programs as we move forward into other areas. It is here that first world technology, applied appropriately, presents enormous potential in the attempt to address some of society's great problems;

- creating a virtuous cycle: as profits and profitability increase, management is increasingly incentivized to expand capacity and advance efficiency. It is important to recognize that the societal problems of nutrition and unemployment are confronted and improved at a relative rate. At writing the authors are informed that LocalFeed has approved a major capital equipment purchase which will allow the business to extend its current product lines, and expand into two new markets. This investment is likely to fuel further reductions in unemployment, and increases in nutrition availability and so the cycle continues.

NOTES

1. For the purposes of confidentiality the identities of business, region, and founder have been disguised.
2. Our thanks go to the UPenn undergraduates who assisted in the research of the animal feed market, and in particular, to Christopher Wilfong for his outstanding contribution to the project as a whole, and more specifically, in the construction of the linear program and management tools.
3. The authors would like to note the significant contribution made by the UPenn Vet School, and in particular thank Dr. David Galligan and Dr. James Ferguson for their insight, assistance, and most of all, patience with our barely minimal knowledge of animal nutrition.

8. Sustainable tourism in Turkey: Çıralı case study

Ulku Oktem and Ferit Karakaya

8.1 INTRODUCTION

As stated in the United Nations Commission on Sustainable Development (UN-CSD) decision, tourism is now one of the world's largest industries and one of its fastest growing economic sectors. Current performance and the projections for tourism and the increasing reliance of many developing countries on this sector as a major employer and contributor to local and national economies highlights the need to pay special attention to the relationship between tourism development and environmental conservation (United Nations, 1999). Undoubtedly, tourism is inseparable from the natural environment and has varying degrees of both negative and positive impacts on economic, social, and environmental characteristics and riches of a region. As stated by the Secretary General to the United Nations:

> Ironically, damage to the environment threatens the very viability of the tourism industry because it depends heavily on the natural environment – its beaches and mountains, rivers, forests and biodiversity – as a basic resource (United Nations, 1999).

The World Conservation Strategy (WCS) developed by the United Nations Environment Programme (UNEP) and World Conservation Union (IUCN) in 1980, defines Sustainable Development as 'improving the quality of human life whilst living within the capacity of supporting ecosystems' (WWF, 2001, 2003a). Since then, as the Brundtland Commission has produced the widely accepted definition for the concept in 1987, a strong and clear mandate for Sustainable Development has materialized through the Earth Summit in Rio de Janeiro (1992), and finally in the World Summit on Sustainable Development (WSSD) in Johannesburg (2002).

A thorough scanning of documents produced by all related institutions, public or private, and studies by different academics (Eagles, McCool and Haynes, 2002; Harris, Griffin and Williams, 2002; Ritchie and Crouch, 2003) will show that there is a general agreement on the fact that tourism needs to be a sustainable industry. It must be recognized that Sustainable Tourism Development is a subset of Sustainable Development. It is established that Sustainable Development, and hence Sustainable Tourism Development, has three properties of equal weight, Environmental Sustainability, Social Equity, and Economic Viability:

- the Environmental dimension of sustainable development means maintaining the long-term integrity of the planet's life support systems and environmental infrastructure. This requires investment in maintaining the natural environment to ensure the continuity of ecological processes and the quality of associated environmental goods and services upon which all life depends;
- the Social dimension emphasizes the manner in which resources, wealth, and opportunity are shared to ensure all citizens have access to minimum standards of human rights, security, and social benefits and through sustainable business practices their lifestyle continuously improves;
- the Economic component of Sustainable Development requires that growth be pursued in a way that brings economic benefits to the society at large and does not endanger its natural and man-made capital stocks.

At the World Summit on Sustainable Development (WSSD), it is stated that:

> In all these three areas tourism can make a substantive contribution, provided adequate attention is given to it by governments, the private sector, local communities as main actors, and the international system of development agencies (World Tourism Organization - WTO, 2002).

Since the Rio Earth Summit, sustainability has become the central issue in tourism development policies throughout the world. The systematic planning approach in tourism has become a standard and a widely accepted procedure (WTO, 2001). Similarly, the European Union (EU) states,

The council considers support for a viable tourism sector which respects the environment and local, social and cultural traditions, as an important contribution to sustainable development (EU, 1998). According to the World Conservation Union (IUCN), Sustainable tourism represents one of a suite of regimes under which the biological and cultural resources of a country may be used in a sustainable manner (IUCN, 1999).

Finally, the plan of implementation included in the WSSD final report reads:

Promote sustainable tourism development in order to increase the benefits from tourism resources in host communities while maintaining the cultural and environmental integrity and enhancing the protection of ecologically sensitive areas and natural heritages (WTO, 2003a).

As the examples above demonstrate, the mandate on Sustainable Development clearly encompasses tourism development as a whole, and not in the form of trendy 'alternative tourism' schemes.

8.2 PRIORITY ISSUES IN SUSTAINABLE TOURISM DEVELOPMENT

Clearly, there is a need to consider the importance of tourism and develop plans, with reference to, for example, Agenda 21.[1] The Travel Industry, like any other, uses resources, generates waste and creates environmental, cultural and social benefits while incurring certain costs in the process. Mostly due to the magnitude and irreversible nature of damages, a particular concern is the degradation of biodiversity and fragile ecosystems, such as coral reefs, mountains, coastal areas and wetlands. The World Tourism Organization (WTO) identified ten issues (Table 8.1), as top priority, key elements necessary to focus on for achieving sustainability in the operations of the Travel Industry.

Table 8.1 Top ten issues for achieving sustainability in the travel industry

---

1) Waste Minimization

---

2) Energy Conservation and Management

---

3) Management of Fresh Water Resources

---

4) Water Management

---

5) Hazardous Substances

---

6) Transport

---

7) Use Planning and Management

---

8) Involvement, Education and Training of Staff, Customers, and Communities in Sustainability Issues

---

10) Design for Sustainability

---

11) Partnership for Sustainable Development

Source: Yunis, 2003

8.3 FROM 'TOURISM VS. CONSERVATION' TO 'TOURISM AND CONSERVATION'

The notion of Sustainable Tourism Development, urging conservation of natural resources and cultural values with particular emphasis on planning and management, has been changing the nature of the often challenging relationship between tourism and the natural environment; more clearly, between the proponents of environmental conservation and the members of the travel industry along with governments that allowed its uncontrolled rapid growth.

In the past, until about a decade ago, the gap between the above mentioned groups had been widening due to the well meaning yet naïve rhetoric of the conservationists, pointing fingers at 'tourism' as the root cause for environmental and cultural degradation. The problem of holding 'tourism', a non-entity, responsible is also present in the literature. Page and Dowling (2002) are not alone when they state, 'the natural environment is harmed by tourism'. This notion has been so prevalent and been adopted so freely by so many authors, that unfortunately it has been serving to deepen the conflict which was also recognized by Page and Dowling in the following way: 'conflict is understood to mean that the tourism-environment relationship is not compatible and that tourism is the cause of conflict'.

Consequently, the solutions provided put the burdens of stewardship, education and clean-up on the same abstract target: 'tourism'. These groups have failed to understand and appreciate the heterogeneous and the complex structure of the Travel Industry, and more importantly, failed to recognize that the occurrence of negative impacts was primarily due to mismanagement and lack of proper planning. This was recognized by some scholars like Briassoulis and Van der Straaten who emphasized the importance of planning and the wide range of interrelated activities that needed to be covered (Briassoulis and Van der Straaten, 2000).

As a response to the conservationists' allegations, the Travel Industry, in a rather politically correct way, drafted documents like 'Agenda 21 for the Travel Industry' (UNEP, 2002), the 'Blueprint for New Tourism', and established bodies like the 'Tour Operators Initiative' and World Travel and Tourism Research Center to 'monitor, assess, and communicate the environmental practices of the travel and tourism industry' (Go and Mautinho, 2000).

Although 'tourism' (the Travel Industry) defended itself quite well by admitting some responsibility and making promises to change, the travel organizations pointed the finger at the state of the world, and the barriers against free trade and globalization. All of which has changed almost nothing in practice and in reality.

The real shift towards 'sustainable tourism', if any, came with the very recognition of proper planning and management of natural resources as the key and the essential element to achieve sustainability and to bridge this gap in understanding and practices between different players. Almost all projects in the past decade, whether by the World Bank, the UN system or the Global Environment Facility (GEF), focus heavily on participatory management plans regardless of the project objectives. This is a clear indication of sustainability becoming the new paradigm and bridging the gaps between interests of different groups.

The issue of tourism in protected areas and in fragile ecosystems is a very important one since it provides almost a perfect venue to demonstrate that tourism and conservation can and should coexist. Many protected areas have a great potential as a tourism product. When planned and managed firmly and rigorously, tourism can both provide the necessary funds to maintain the proper management of a protected area, and allow access to more people, increasing awareness and appreciation. As it is pointed out by UNEP, 'Tourism activity in a national park or any other protected area can serve as a self-financing mechanism and therefore as a tool of conservation' (UNEP Protected Area Management, Tourism in Protected Areas).

Whenever tourism and conservation of natural environments are used in the same context, almost without exception, the term 'ecotourism' comes into play. Among many definitions of ecotourism with the common denominator being the 'intent of the traveller to experience nature', the definition by the Ecotourism Association of Australia and NEAP appears to be credible and realistic: 'Ecotourism is ecologically sustainable tourism with a primary focus on experiencing natural areas that fosters environmental and cultural understanding, appreciation and conservation'. The issue is more pragmatically stated by the World Tourism Organization in the following statement:

> The valorisation of natural parks or protected areas, via a profitable activity
> for local communities such as tourism, also serves to ensure a better
> cooperation between farmers and the authorities ecotourism is used as a tool
> for nature conservation (WTO, 2001).

During the late '80s and early '90s, the proponents of ecotourism reported impressive growth rates of 20 – 40 percent; as Page and Dowling state, even the World Tourism Organization reported that ecotourism was 20 percent of the global market in 1998 (Page and Dowling, 2002). However, Fennel also points out that, the WTO reported that ecotourism constituted only 2 – 4 percent of global tourism (Fennel, 2004), during the launch of the International Year of Ecotourism in 2002. Despite the conflicting numbers from different interest groups, there is no doubt that ecotourism and nature tourism experienced a significant growth.

However, the fact remains that the 'superb' growth of ecotourism is still dwarfed by the 7 percent growth of tourism considering that this smaller percentage increase still translates to a larger actual number when one recognizes that 763 million people travelled as tourists in 2004 (World Tourism Organization News Release, 3 October 2005). Due to the incoherence in the definition, hence the difficulty in measuring ecotourism, it is suggested that ecotourism accounts for 1.5 – 2.5 percent of all tourism (Fennel, 2004). Therefore, expecting ecotourism, as defined above, to expand and take over the Travel Industry, bringing a solution to its current problems, would be unrealistic. In his statement at the launch ceremony of the 'year of ecotourism' in New York, the Secretary General of the World Tourism Organization stated 'Obviously, the concept of sustainable development applied to tourism cannot be reduced to ecotourism, which is just one of its components' (WTO, 2002).

Ecotourism can be a powerful tool to demonstrate the successful coexistence of tourism and conservation as long as it is functional within the framework of sustainable development and part of a sustainable tourism development strategy. The fact still remains that the issue of Sustainable Tourism Development cannot be separated from the tension between biodiversity and globalization (WWF, 2001, 2003a); only time will show whether the notion of sustainability will become strong enough to bridge that gap.

8.4 THE MEDITERRANEAN BASIN AND SUSTAINABLE TOURISM DEVELOPMENT

Sir David Attenborough states that the Mediterranean 'is the oldest humanized landscape in the world. Nowhere has mankind had a greater effect on his environment, or left more continuous, detailed and abundant evidence of his activities' (Attenborough, 1987).

All conservation organizations agree on the fact that the Mediterranean region is one of the most significant biodiversity hot spots, second only to the Tropical Andes, with over 50 percent of 25 thousand vascular plant species and 20 percent of marine species being endemic to the Mediterranean Sea and its surroundings (WWF, 2004c). The geographic features of the region may explain the high levels of biodiversity. The

Mediterranean is the largest among the world regions, characterized by the Mediterranean Climate: prolonged dry summer seasons and wet and mild winters. The topographical heterogeneity on the land mass creates the conditions for the large diversity of ecosystems and habitat types for natural life, with notable species including the Monk Seal, three species of marine turtles including *caretta caretta*, the Fin Whale, Anatolian Leopard, Iberian Lynx, and Barbary Deer. The Mediterranean region also provides a resting ground since it is on the main migratory routes connecting Africa, Europe and Asia.

This unique ecosystem of the Mediterranean basin has been under increasing pressure on many fronts as elucidated in Table 8.2.

Table 8.2 Recent changes to Mediterranean ecosystem

• Population over 425 million of which 150 million live on the coast
• 170 million visitors per year
• 48% of urban centers lack sewage treatment
• 80% of wastewater discharged, is untreated
• Each person generates 254 kg of solid waste per year with a grwth rate of 3% per year
• Of close to 40 million tones of municipal waste per plastic accounts for the 75% of the waste on the sea surface and the sea bed
• Some 60 oil refineries dump about 20 000 tones of oil per year
• 28% of the world's sea-borne oil traffic transits the Med with some 200 000 crossings per year
• 30% of all sea-borne trade either originates from or directed to the ports in the Med of which 50% of the cargo is considered dangerous
• Mediterranean Sea is semi-enclosed with Gibraltar strait 14 km wide, and Suez Canal a few meters wide; the renewal of Mediterranean waters will take 80 to 150 years

Source: UNEP MAP, 2005

8.4.1 Mediterranean Gap Analysis by WWF

Through its national organizations in Italy, Spain, Greece, France and Turkey, the WWF network has been active in the Mediterranean region for more than 30 years. In order to assist in coordination and policy development, as well as to better focus on the conservation effort, WWF International established the Mediterranean Program Office in 1992. The goal is stated as 'to conserve the natural wealth of the Mediterranean and to promote the sustainable use of natural resources for the benefit of all' (WWF, 2003b). WWF Mediterranean Program Office has been directly involved in the coordination of 30 projects in 6 programs in Algeria, Croatia, Lebanon, Libya, Morocco, Portugal and Tunisia, while assisting national organizations in the Mediterranean (ibid).

The objective of the Mediterranean Marine Gap Analysis was to assess holistically the marine and coastal features of the entire Mediterranean basin and to identify the most important unprotected coastal areas. This was the first time a study on such a scale was conducted. Thirteen locations of high ecological value were identified as priority areas in need of conservation and/or improved management.

The Gap Analysis not only indicated the areas that sustained heavy damage; such as the Italian Adriatic coast, the Spanish Coast from Barcelona to Valencia, and the coast between Syria and the mouth of Nile, but also pointed out the opportunity areas such as southern Turkey and the coast of Cyrenaica in Libya for monk seals and loggerhead turtles respectively.

8.4.2 The Mediterranean Action Plan

The Mediterranean Action Plan (MAP), of the United Nations Environment Program (UNEP) is a regional cooperative effort through which 21 contracting parties to the Barcelona Convention seek to meet the challenges of protecting the marine and coastal environment while boosting regional and national plans to achieve sustainable development.

UNEP-MAP concerns itself with pollution generated on land through various economic activities and attempts to provide solutions thorough integrated coastal zone planning and natural resource management. In 1995, MAP has revised the Barcelona

Convention, incorporating the Rio Declaration Principles, and created the Mediterranean Commission on Sustainable Development (MCSD), which demonstrated the commitment of contracting parties, that is, 20 countries of the Barcelona Convention, the European Community, and 15 relevant organizations, to work towards integrating environment and development in the region (UNEP-MAP, 2004).

8.4.3 Sustainable Tourism Development Efforts in the Mediterranean

The Mediterranean is the world's leading holiday destination, accounting for 30 percent of international arrivals and 25 percent of receipts from international tourism. The number of tourists in Mediterranean countries is expected to reach between 440 and 655 million in 2025 (with 235 to 355 million on the coastal region), almost double the 1990 numbers (260 million, with 135 million on the coastal region) (WWF, 2004c). Turkey is considered to be third in the world in annualized real growth with 9.2 percent (World Travel and Tourism Council, 2003).Tourism also has both direct and indirect influence on employment in the region. Table 8.3 shows examples of its significant impact on these economic factors.

The Mediterranean Commission on Sustainable Development (MCSD) has developed the Mediterranean Strategy for Sustainable Development (MSSD), which defines 7 interdependent and interactive priority fields. Table 8.4 illustrates the 'objectives toward sustainable tourism development in the Mediterranean' derived from these priority areas.

Within 10 years from the establishment of the MCSD, the objectives, priorities, and metrics identified for sustainable tourism development, helped demonstrate the shortcomings of the collective effort in several fronts, such as in governance, in commitment, and in application.

Damaging impacts of tourist activity on the natural environment and on the social character of a destination, mainly, occur due to the lack of (or poor) public policy, management and public/private partnership. In the case of the Mediterranean region these issues manifested as needs for:

- better planning;
- improved infrastructure;
- inclusion and empowerment of local populations;
- increased capacity, all of which coupled with access to capital and technology.

Table 8.3 Impact of tourism on the Mediterranean economy

• In Greece tourism accounts for 10% of total employment
• In Malta tourism accounts for 30% of total employment
• In Italy, more than 2 million people have been employed in tourism related jobs, in 1999
• In Tunisia, in 2000, tourism industry created 355 500 new jobs, providing new employment opportunities to about 10% of the total active population
• In Croatia, tourism is expected to employ 427 000 people by 2013 (40% of total employment)
• In Turkey there were 1.4 million people employed by the tourism industry in 2000 and this number is expected to increase to 2.12 million (8% of total employment) at the end of 2010
• In the Mediterranean tourism sector represents on average more than 15% of exports of goods and services

Source: WWF, 2004b

Sustainable Tourism Development is a new management concept in which current practices are replaced with new ones based on principles of sustainable developments. A major obstacle to abandoning the status quo and transitioning into sustainable practices is the question of financial costs of adopting sustainability principles. One can easily draw a parallel between this concept and a similar misconception the western world experienced earlier. Before the 1980s when Japan proved to the world otherwise, it was assumed that production of higher quality product was always costlier. Similarly, now, the people who need to abandon the status-quo and adopt sustainability principles are concerned about possible increase in costs. This misperception has

been elaborately addressed in the following statement by the Tour
Operators Initiative (TOI) and Conservation International:

> From a financial standpoint, improved sustainability can lower costs through
> greater operating efficiency, reduced waste generation, and reduced
> consumption of energy and water. Sustainable practices can also lead to
> increased revenue and shareholder value by generating more repeat business
> and attracting new business from customers who value good environmental
> and social performance. A strong positive reputation as a company that cares
> about sustainability issues, coupled with improvements to the quality of the
> tourism experience provided to clients, can result in increased customer
> satisfaction and loyalty, strengthened brand value, enhanced publicity and
> marketing opportunities, and better acceptance by local communities in
> destinations (TOI, 2004).

Table 8.4 Objectives toward sustainable tourism in the Mediterranean

• Reduce the adverse territorial and environmental impacts of tourism, especially in existing coastal tourist areas.
• Promote sustainable tourism, which in turn reinforces social cohesion and cultural and economic development, enhances Mediterranean diversity and specificities and strengthens synergies with other economic sectors, especially agriculture.
• Increase the added value of tourism for local communities and actors in developing countries.
• Improve governance for sustainable tourism.

Source: UNEP.MAP, 2005

Although the claims in the above statement need to be tested
scientifically a more compelling argument which would appeal to
even some sceptics of Sustainable Tourism Development is clearly
expressed in the following statement by the TOI:

> Good performance and a high quality, sustainable product can also help a tour
> operator reduce the risk of conflict or problems with suppliers, governments,
> staff, and local communities, and improve its status which may mean
> enhanced access to key business resources such as capital, improved
> relationship with governments, and a motivated loyal staff (TOI, 2004).

Through the international mandate provided by the UNCSD and Johannesburg declarations, and considering the willingness of the travel industry to become sustainable, one might talk about what it would take to 'modify' the Travel Industry to bring about Sustainable Tourism. What would the performance metrics for sustainable tourism practice look like? How can one achieve the criteria set in these metrics? The base-line answer is to have a collective effort to minimize, and where possible eliminate, the negative impacts caused by uncontrolled tourism development. Unfortunately, the consensus on the above statement, the good intentions of travel industry, and enormous amount of documentation produced by many organizations, failed to eliminate, even to reduce, the adverse effect of uncontrolled tourism. The universal means to achieve this goal are yet to be developed. Past experiences indicate that the Travel Industry alone cannot achieve sustainability. Close collaboration between the public and private sectors and guidance as well as expertise provided by non-profit organizations are needed to materialize Sustainable Tourism.

8.5 THE ÇIRALI PROJECT

The rest of this chapter is dedicated to a 'Sutainable Tourism Project' effort to demonstrate accomplishments one can expect as well as the challenges one must consider when undertaking such projects. The Çıralı project, conducted by WWF Turkey and the European Union Life Programme and covering the period between 1997 and 2000, was awarded the UN Habitat Dubai International Award for Best Practices in Improving the Living Environment in 2000 (Dubai Award List, 2002). The main objective of the project was stated as 'To promote environmentally and socially sound development through integrated planning, traditional and alternative economic activities and biodiversity conservation' Çıralı is located Southwest of Kemer, Antalya within the provincial boundaries of Ulupınar Village of the city of Antalya. Çıralı was established during the 1930s when the wetlands and forest areas were transformed into farmland by the local population. The population of Çıralı is 550 and there are about 260 residences. In line with the massive tourism development in

Antalya, land in Çıralı has been subject to increasing demand. The historical aspect of Çıralı goes many centuries back in time since it is minutes away from the ancient city of Olympos and the 'eternal flames of Lycia'.

Olympos is known as one of six cities in the Lycian League with the privilege of three votes. Even though the exact date of establishment is unknown, the coins produced by the city date from between 168 and 178 BC. Destroyed by the Roman invasion, Olympos has gained importance again with the close attention of Emperor Hadrian. The ruins today are the result of scientific excavations conducted in the early 1990s.

Yanartaş (Burning rock) is the location of the mythological story of the Bellerophontes and the monster Chimaera. The eternal flames of Chimaera, also known as the 'ever burning fire of Lycia', is located close to the ancient ruins of Olympos. Only a few ruins with scriptures remain from the temple that was built in the name of Hephaistos in the Roman period, but the fire is still alive and burning.

The most important aspects of the natural environment of Çıralı are marine turtles and the beach, marine and forest eco-systems, and flora and fauna. In 1988 Tekirova beach, also located close to Antalya, was identified as one of the 17 important nesting sites for marine turtles in the southern Turkish coast. Since it has been opened to tourism development it lost this privileged status and the next best option for the marine turtles was determined to be the Çıralı beach. With 3.2 kilometers in length, a wet area distance of 2.3 meters and semi-wet area distance of 10 plus meters, Çıralı beach hosts an average of 33.2 turtle nests a year which all belong to *caretta caretta*, a threatened species.

In terms of Fauna, Çıralı hosts 18 species and 1 sub-species that are endemic. The Çıralı ecosystem is also significant since it hosts a number of species that are protected under the Bern Convention such as the *Chamaeleo Chamaeleon*. As for the flora, other than 865 different taxons, official reports speculate about 6 new plant species (WWF, 2001).

The lack of natural water sources, which can be a significant problem for many destinations in the Mediterranean, is hardly the case in Çıralı which has about 700 water wells. Due to high underground water levels villagers opened these wells for irrigation. The mountains surrounding Çıralı host many active springs, while the rivers Ulupınar and Yanar, in their journey to the Mediterranean, complement this generosity of nature.

In coastal settlements like Çıralı, coastal waters are under a constant threat due to human activity. Even though the very geological make up of Çıralı beach has distinct advantages in preventing pollution from building up, the limits to this natural 'self cleaning' function require stewardship at the very least.

8.5.1 Legal and Protection Statutes

In Turkey a protected area, referred to as a 'SIT' area, is defined by the 'Law for the Protection of cultural and natural entities' of 1983, as 'Settlements and the ruins of such that were produced by previous and historical civilizations, that reflect the social, economical, architectural, and similar characteristics of their periods, areas where significant historical events have taken place, and areas that need to be protected due to the determination of significant natural qualities.' There are degrees of association of a location's characteristics with the defined SIT qualification; 1st degree association being the strongest.

Çıralı and environs hold varying degrees of protected area statutes: the coastline and the beach are 1st degree natural SIT areas, the section located at the south of Çıralı next to the ancient ruins of Olympos is 1st and 2nd degree archaeological SIT area, and the inner parts behind the coastline is a 3rd degree natural SIT area. Çıralı is also included in the 'South Antalya Tourism Region' as declared by the Ministry of Culture and Tourism in 1995.

Çıralı is under the jurisdiction of various governmental bodies due to the wide range of activities it encompasses. Although most of Çıralı's 'protected region' status is clearly defined through Turkish laws and international agreements that Turkey has signed, the status of some of the local areas is uncertain and depends on the interpretation of the Turkish 'Law of Forest', that also defines areas to be protected with respect to land ownership. Currently there is a dispute on the ownership and land rights of a large piece of land awaiting final decisions through the legal system. The main issue is the legal status of construction and use of land by the local population. A number of federal governmental bodies view most of the construction activities that took place after the SIT declaration as illegal and have been filing lawsuits against the local population as well as local governments.

There are two levels of local government or administration units for Çıralı. The first one is the Village of Ulupınar and the second is Special Administrative Unit of the city of Antalya. However, there is yet another legal administrative entity that Çıralı falls under: the 'Union of Tourism and Infrastructure Development of Southern Antalya'. This institution is established based on the Law of Local Administration and is delegated certain powers of the municipalities. The character of this institution can be summarized as a network of local municipalities.

8.5.2 Tourism in Çıralı

Traditionally most visitors came to Çıralı for short trips, such as one or two day excursions, rather than long stay. Even though the pristine landscape, a long and calm beach, and close proximity to the ancient ruins of Olympos attracted a number of distant Turkish and foreign visitors, the character of the Çıralı tourism has not changed over the years. In addition to its attractive characteristics mentioned above a rather interesting aspect of the ecosystem in Çıralı is that mosquitoes are hardly present, even though there are suitable habitats. This significantly adds to its appeal since neighboring towns endure mosquitoes in the summer months.

Of the 550 residents, Çıralı's working population is almost equally distributed between two main economic activities: tourism and agriculture. The employment distribution, 33 percent in tourism, 21 percent in agriculture, and 46 percent engaged both in tourism and agriculture, has remained the same for the past few years. Starting in the 1980s tourism has gained importance throughout most of Turkey leading to construction of more tourist accommodations. In Çıralı the number of such establishments, mainly bed and breakfast operations and small family-run hotels have increased from 50 units in 1995 to 535 units in 2000. Most of these mom-and-pop establishments operate in structures which are either in legal dispute with or simply classified as 'illegal' by the different departments of the federal government. These tourist accommodations continue operating because of lenient enforcement of laws and regulations due to several reasons, such as: (a) to prevent hardship to locals who have income from these facilities, and (b) lack of funds to purchase and destroy the existing ('illegal') constructions while providing alternative, more suitable locations. Officially accepting these operations would legalize this 'illegal' practice encouraging expansion of the number of such facilities.

8.5.3 Project Planning and Implementation

Upon losing most of the natural treasures in the Belek and Tekirova regions of the Mediterranean, the WWF focused on protection and development of Çıralı, starting in 1997 and by partnering with the Turkish Government and the local population for development of a conservation program. Following a lengthy process of focusing on and understanding of the concerns related to Çıralı, shown in Figure 8.1, and considering a wide range of issues, the main objective of the WWF effort was determined to be the preparation and implementation of a 'management plan' which would also include a legally acceptable 'Protective Construction Plan'. The scope of the management plan included the following issues:

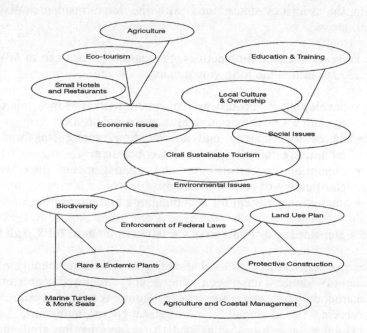

Figure 8.1 Issues and concerns related to Çıralı Sustainable Tourism

- protection of natural and archaeological values;
- diversification of economic activities in harmony with the natural environment;
- betterment of social services;
- harmonization of land use activities and construction with the natural environment;
- ensuring participation of local population in the decision making process;
- conservation of traditional values;
- establishing coordination among related institutions;
- monitoring the socio-economical and ecological impacts of progress.

So, the main objective of the management plan was delineated as 'To achieve sustainable development in Çıralı; the management plan will point out the necessary actions and put forward viable means in assistance to the authorized institutions in accordance with the priorities determined with the local residents'(WWF, 2001).

To reach the stated objectives, the team of experts from WWF decided to utilize the following means:

- developing a 'Protective Construction Plan' for Çıralı that complies with the existing laws and regulations;
- increasing capacity and coordination among stakeholders including establishing a Çıralı Cooperative;
- obtaining consensus on the management plan with clarification of responsibilities;
- instituting a system for accountability and monitoring.

8.5.4 Developing a 'Protective Construction Plan' for Çıralı

The most critical as well as challenging aspect of the management plan, no doubt, has been the legally required 'protective construction plan' whose fundamental goal has been determined as conserving the character of Çıralı through (a) maintaining and developing agricultural areas and (b) preserving the concept of mom-and-pop establishments. The Ministry of Culture and Tourism engaged WWF to undertake this effort. The final product that WWF has developed had the following major characteristics:

- the plan took the current status of existing buildings and operations as is, without questioning their legal status, and constructed forward looking development recommendations based on this foundation;
- the plan, which was a forward looking statement, was in total compliance with the Coastal Law and the protection statutes.
- proper infrastructure development has been emphasized and integrated into the implementation strategy;
- tourism areas and acceptable limits for increase in capacity have been carefully determined;
- agricultural areas have been conserved.

8.5.5 Increasing Capacity and Coordination among Stakeholders

Ecotourism and organic agriculture have been selected for diversification of economic activities, in line with conserving the character of Çıralı:

- ecotourism has been selected as the most suitable form of tourism given the massive tourism pressure, particularly in Antalya, and the traditional ways and means Çıralı has been catering to visitors. For the promotion of Çıralı as an ecotourism destination, trekking and hiking paths have been designed into the plan;
- switching to organic agriculture has been recommended since it would not only satisfy the goals of conservation but also would create a niche and a competitive edge for Çıralı. It was noted that to be able to accomplish this switch the farmers had to keep the ground free of all chemicals for a two year period to meet both national and international standards.

8.5.6 Obtaining Consensus on the Management Plan with Clarification of Responsibilities

The implementation of the protective construction plan and the efforts towards the development of the economic activities required an organization to implement and monitor the activities as a whole. The management plan has suggested two feasible models. The first option, setting up a department within the 'Union of

Tourism and Infrastructure Development of Southern Antalya' has been rejected by all stakeholders due to the consensus on the second option, the integrated management model, establishing a 'local coordination council' where all stakeholders are represented and share responsibilities.

The Council developed a Coastal Management Plan for Çıralı which has the following goals and objectives:

- to support social and environmental development through holistic planning and participation of all stakeholders;
- to conserve the nesting grounds of the critically endangered marine turtle *caretta caretta*;
- to diversify economic activities with the local residents, while conserving natural, cultural, and traditional values, towards achieving sustainable development;
- to promote the application of coastal management plans in similar areas and to announce results;
- to take necessary actions for capacity increase and raising awareness.

A 3 year action plan has been developed to reach the objectives outlined above.

8.5.7 Instituting a System for Accountability and Monitoring

One of the most important responsibilities assigned to the local coordination council was establishment of accountability and development of a monitoring system. Delegating this task to the Council, which represents all stakeholders, was in line with the bottom-up approach of the project. Implicit in this assignment was the development of a control system, including a performance matrix, for various planned activities. Measuring progress, clearly stating accountabilities of different players, and establishing a monitoring process were all identified as essential elements of the follow-up system. Although this mandate is elucidated in the plans the failure of attempts for its implementation to date remains the weakest part of the project.

8.5.8 Conclusion

Çıralı is a milestone towards achieving sustainable tourism not only in Turkey but also in the Mediterranean basin. Most of the accomplishments as well as challenges faced during this project are first time experiences of dealing with conflicting objectives similar to those faced by many communities in the Mediterranean Basin which are trying to understand and implement sustainable tourism principles. A very important outcome of this project is the lessons learned by everyone involved. These learning experiences will help the future projects in this very important field. The key to the success of this participatory process, initiated by WWF, has been the authorization of WWF, by the Turkish Ministry of Culture and Tourism, to develop the 'protective construction plan'. This plan, which became the backbone of the development process, is still the main guiding document that is being referred to both in improving on the original accomplishments and in attempts to resolve the roadblocks.

8.5.8.1 Accomplishments

The most impressive accomplishment of this project was the great extent to which the local community embraced various issues, most notably protection of the sea turtles. More specifically, the following achievements can be highlighted for this project:

- a physical plan for the areas is completed with a good co-ordination with the Ministries of Culture, Tourism, and Forestry;
- a co-operative has been founded and some organic agriculture activities started;
- local community has been educated through courses on environmental protection, eco-tourism, organic agriculture and use of computers;
- successful beach management practices have been introduced and embraced by the locals as well as the tourists, increasing the number of sea turtle nests and the hatchlings;
- a local environmental protection organization has been established in Çıralı;
- the First Çıralı Sea Turtles Festival was organized in May 2000 to inform the public about the project, to raise the

awareness of nature conservation and sustainable tourism, to publicize eco-tourism and organic agriculture, and to provide a market for the sale of local products. More than 2000 people attended the activities and the three day festival had wide coverage in national newspapers and television programs.

8.6 CHALLENGES

Most of the problems encountered in a large scale, multi stakeholder sustainable tourism project stem from four groups of challenges:

- legal challenges;
- financial challenges;
- market challenges;
- social challenges.

Although often these challenges are strongly interrelated and difficult to address in isolation, we attempt to highlight the key issues associated with each concern.

8.6.1 Legal Challenges

Legal challenges are probably the most complex issues since they include both local and national laws and regulations. In addition, some countries sign on to international agreements which are not always in total alignment with the local practices. In the case of Çıralı establishing legal entities, licensing, providing subsidies and tax breaks are all part of the multifaceted legal issues that have to be addressed. A number of these issues are still not resolved and await reconciliation between different stakeholders including government offices. Examples of the specific legal challenges facing Çıralı project are given below:

- laws are not crisp and clear, leading to multiple interpretations. Governments, local and national, can interpret land protection laws differently. Since modification of laws can only be done through the parliament, when different agencies have dissimilar interpretation of the same law, the issue ultimately goes to court, where resolving such problems takes a very long time hampering the potential progress;

- the area can be under the jurisdiction of multiple public entities. In the case of Çıralı, the municipality and its associated economic activities, such as forestry, agriculture and water, are under different jurisdiction. Therefore conflicts arising from this state of multi-jurisdiction usually require court rulings to determine who has the authority over others. Again, this is a time-consuming activity delaying progress;
- complex legal issues: lack of adequate law enforcement, lack of constructive interpretation, and/or specific laws. Supporting a region's development in a sustainable format through legal mechanisms is essential if the effort is to succeed. But, unless the laws encourage sustainable tourism development, bring accountability to the proper authorities, and are enforced constructively, they themselves can become obstacles. In the case of Çıralı, there is a lack of enforcement of some of the favourable laws and enforcement of others which are not necessarily favourable for capacity expansion and do not bring accountability to the right entities;
- licensing, subsidizing and providing tax incentives. Most of the time regulatory support is needed to facilitate successful implementation of desired outcomes. For example, depending on the situation, one or more of the following actions may be needed to achieve sustainability, and implementation of these ideas may require either modification of a law or institution of a new regulation: new entities may need to be established, conversion to a more sustainable practice may need to be subsidized (at least during the transition period), tax incentives can help businesses or individuals to adopt new practices.

8.6.2 Financial Challenges

Financing a multi stakeholder large sustainable tourism project would have its own complexities and multifaceted challenges. First of all there needs to be a close collaboration and partnership between public and private entities to jointly address most issues. The following are examples of situations where close public/private collaboration would be necessary for a successful outcome:

- development of infrastructure: transportation, land utilization, energy supply, use of water resources, waste management, etc.;
- investment, subsidies and tax incentives for capacity increase as well as modification of existing capacity to comply with sustainable practices. For example, in Çıralı it would be highly desirable to provide financial incentives to construct residences, guest houses and restaurants in the legally assigned sites and per sustainable building codes. It would be even more desirable to provide financial assistance to the owners of existing buildings in the disputed areas and to relocate these facilities as well as restore the full natural state of the region. Also, a two-year transition period (this period of no cultivating required to eliminate chemicals from the soil) required by national and international standards would ideally be subsidized and used for developing the necessary mechanism for managing the processes such as inventory, packaging, marketing, and exporting; that is, the establishment of a professionally managed cooperative;
- assessment and monitoring: Every sustainable tourism project must weave assessment and monitoring into its fabric starting from the very early stages. Since these activities also require financial support but do not provide a visible outcome such as building roadways or residences, usually they are the first items to be dropped from the budget. In the case of Çıralı lack of accountability, assessment and monitoring is slowing the progress.

There are other financial needs, such as educating the community and training contractors who will actually do the local planning and building.

8.6.3 Market Challenges

Market realities and competition must be understood very well for a successful sustainable tourism implementation. The growth in this piece of the pie is behind the growth in the 'alleged' supply. For example, an area that stands out with its natural resources, outstanding scenery, favourable climate and/or diverse plant and animal population will face pressure from the travel industry as well as from the local community to immediately maximize its financial potential without much consideration of the impact on the very environment that is attracting customers to that particular location. Therefore, a sustainable tourism project must recognize these market forces and ensure that the actions taken by various parties help preserve all natural resources of the area while giving them improved earning potential.

In Çıralı, when the local community recognized the tourism potential and its increased economic value they constructed small hotels and guest houses on some of the protected area. Now, the new plan must take these market forces into consideration and not only enable people to improve their economic status through tourism but also provide other incentives consistent with a sustainable environment, such as organic agriculture, to improve their earning potential.

8.6.4 Social Challenges

Educating the local community to raise awareness is essential to establish a successful sustainable tourism. The urge and push for capacity increase require an informed group of local people who not only have the right perspective themselves but also guard the areas against other interest groups who potentially can damage the environment.

In Çıralı educating the local community was the most triumphant part of the project. Protection of the sea turtles especially has been taken very seriously by people of all ages. They not only protect the turtles' nests, eggs, babies, etc. but also participate in the assessment of changes in the turtle population. Balancing short term interests and needs of the local community with longer term sustainable practices must be carefully revaluated. Implementation of limitations and restrictions imposed on the local residents by protected area statutes, such as not being able to renovate or enlarge their residences and being allowed only limited economic activities are challenges still faced by Çıralı project realization.

8.7 LESSONS LEARNED FROM THE ÇIRALI PROJECT

The effort as a whole was commendable. The Turkish government's awareness of the need for sustainable tourism in the Mediterranean region was essential and facilitated the project. The commitment and passion of the WWF is exemplary; the fact that a project officer lived in Çıralı for more than three years is a clear sign for this statement.

Obtaining the authorization to develop a legal requirement, within the jurisdiction of a powerful governmental body should be considered a victory for public/NGO partnership.

The most impressive achievement clearly lies in the extent to which the capacity of local residents has been carried through transfer of know-how, and assistance in organizing to perform various tasks ranging from daily measurements on the nesting grounds to growing avocados.

However, there are a number of issues beyond the capabilities and good intentions of all parties involved:

- since 1999, the plan still awaits full approval due to the objections by the Ministry of Agriculture and the Ministry of Public Works and Settlement;
- the ecotourism approach was premature. There is no sign of a planned ecotourism development in Çıralı;
- managing organic agriculture still needs to satisfy the great expectations created in the course of the effort;
- enforcement and monitoring is inadequate due to larger socio-economical problems in Turkey.

The Çıralı case, with its shortcomings, as well as the successes, is clearly a landmark in the long and arduous process of sustainable development in the Mediterranean.

NOTE

1. One example is 'Agenda 21 for the Travel & Tourism Industry: Towards Environmentally Sustainable Development', an action plan launched in 1996 through the collaborative efforts of three International Organizations – the World Travel & Tourism Council, the World Tourism Organization, and the Earth Council.

9. San Patrignano: a sustainable model for social entrepreneurship

Francesco Perrini and Sandro Fazzolari

9.1 INTRODUCTION

The idea of social entrepreneurship combines the passion of a social mission with business-like discipline, innovation, determination, and so on. Social entrepreneurship can include innovative not-for-profit business ventures, for-profit community development banks as well as hybrid organizations such as homeless shelters that start businesses to train and employ their residents. Therefore the social entrepreneur looks for the most effective methods of serving and accomplishing a social mission.

San Patrignano is the largest drug rehabilitation community in the world and is located just outside of Italy's Adriatic resort town of Rimini. This Italian community continues the vision established by founder Vincenzo Muccioli on how to get people to stop drug abusing themselves, all the while becoming a famous case of social entrepreneurship.

To be more precise, San Patrignano uses an earned income strategy designed to directly address a specific social problem and simultaneously make a profit that it uses to refinance itself and maintain its independence. It has the art of simultaneously pursuing both a financial and a social return on investment: only through its continuous improvement on an economic front can it fund its size and growth. The community is fuelled by a global social mission that attempts to give human dignity back to people who seem to have lost it. The lack of separation between the economic and social domains characterizes San Patrignano as an outstanding example of social entrepreneurship. Or rather, San

Patrignano's experience demonstrates how an entrepreneurial approach, based on recuperating the individual, teams up well to establish one of the most successful communities for recuperating drug addicts and social outcasts in the world.

At the present time, San Patrignano manages 56 industry clusters, such as wine-making, high end furniture, artwork, woodworking, graphics, cheese making, horse and dog-breeding and many more.

The community achieved significantly higher drug recovery rates among its members than any of the so-called 'state of the art' institutions in this field anywhere. Teaching youngsters a trade, profession or skill that aims to solve the core problem of loss of dignity is the ad hoc method the community utilizes. It does not subscribe to any of the international methods that utilize medication to treat drug addiction, but rather maintains that understanding, reaching out and unconditionally loving the person behind the addiction is the key to understanding what caused this particular case of 'loss of dignity' in the first place.

Its financial independence confirms what choices worked and those that did not because it does not receive government support. Though it actively seeks support from private donors, 'Sanpa', as it is known, is truly independent due to its financial success. This success nurtures pride that helps guests create the self esteem they will need to reinsert themselves back into the communities that treated them like outcasts. It is a winning atmosphere that is essential to its success on both fronts.

San Patrignano could therefore be approached from many levels: economic, sociological, medical and psychological. In this chapter, our primary goal is not to recount the remarkable work that the community carries out on a daily basis but to look at the community as a social entrepreneurship experience. We will be exploring how an entrepreneurial venture, whose mission is the social well-being of marginalized people, can be so successful from both a social and economic perspective.

We briefly describe the structure and the history of the community. Then the chapter examines the entrepreneurial initiatives, the relations with the other communities and the sources of financing utilized.

Moreover, this chapter considers three important critical factors that make San Patrignano consistent with the paradigm of successful social entrepreneurial ventures and social entrepreneurship, in an attempt to add value to the previous literature:

- *Geography*: the cultural fact that Italy is home to the community has an influence on its methods (i.e., contextual factors);
- *Work skills*: the creation of both group and individual responsibility is correlated to the underlying result of over 40 patient-staffed cooperatives that make up the primary source of funding the community utilizes to provide its entirely free-of-charge treatment program (i.e., balancing social and economic dimension of business);
- *Restoring an individual's right to choose*: the belief that nobody wakes up one day and decides to slowly begin killing themselves by drug abuse is considered to be the source of social innovation and societal wealth generation.

After attempting to further elaborate these three elements and using the benefit of over a quarter century of hindsight, a model is developed and proposed for further study and analysis.

9.2 WHAT IS SAN PATRIGNANO? THE STRUCTURE

'Drug Addicts Regain Personal Dignity through Productive Labour'

The community of San Patrignano was created in 1978 with the aim of offering a solution to drug addiction in the Rimini area. It became a cooperative in October 1979, when Vincenzo Muccioli and a nucleus of friends founded the Cooperativa San Patrignano, a new reality inspired by the principles of community life and solidarity. The organizational complexity of the community has grown in parallel with its size and the articulation of a therapeutic approach.

However, the ultimate pathway to recovery remained unaltered:

- renunciation of drugs and importance of work and personal responsibility;
- welcoming and treating guests without any social, political, or religious distinctions;

- offering this service completely free of charge which includes all board and lodging fees;
- using occupational training;
- the development of preventive and family support activities;
- collecting economic resources for its own production activities as well as public and private contributions.

In other words, San Patrignano embodies something of an ideal in community life that embraces values many of us hold dear: equality, reciprocity, shared well-being, a solid work ethic and an appreciation for nature and the arts. It makes sense to most of us that the rewards of labor should be invested in the well-being of our families and our community. Indeed, most communities strive in many ways to achieve this through contributions to, and lobbying for, non-profit initiatives. Despite these efforts social problems persist and the segregation between wealth and poverty, health and despair, inclusion and outcasting in our communities seems to become increasingly severe.

We could start by describing the complexity of the community. San Patrignano is located northeast of Rome and close to the Adriatic Sea, set on the hills between the Republic of San Marino and the city of Rimini. San Patrignano is one of the world's most remarkable communities, which for the past twenty years has continuously achieved extraordinary results working with marginalized individuals. 'The centre of attention is the human being' (Vincenzo Muccioli, Founder of the San Patrignano Community).

The company structure currently consists of:

- Fondazione San Patrignano, which manages the immovable property. The value of its land and building exceeds 51.6 million Euros. Its machinery is worth about 41.5 million Euro;
- Three cooperatives that cover the more than 50 production sectors headed by three main operating centers;
- Libera Associazione, which manages the costs of the therapeutic process;
- Consorzio responsible for the joint administrative management of the partners.

To be more precise, the San Patrignano Model of Drug Rehabilitation is a model of social services outside of the framework of government bureaucracy and tax funding.

In the small community of San Patrignano, drug addicts come to learn self-respect, the ethics of responsibility, and the spirit of community. Over the last 25 years, almost 40,000 drug addicts have lived in this community, each of whom has been provided with a home, a 'personal tutor,' the opportunity to study and learn a profession, and the opportunity to regain personal dignity through productive labor; of these, 70% have been completely integrated into society after completing their program.

The rehabilitation program focuses on showing individuals that life's path can be based on dignity, honesty, responsibility and respect. The community is engaged in more than 50 production combinations that cover a surface area of 260 hectares. Its activities are grouped into production sectors that work for the community itself and the outside market as well. The products and services are used within the community (see Table 9.1) or sold: 60 per cent of the community's revenue comes from the sale of products made by the guests, and fall into these categories:

- craftwork. The various areas include decorations and ornamental items, ironwork, woodwork, weaving, furnishing and fitting;
- wines;
- cheeses;
- flowers and plants;
- animal breeding. Sensitivity to some animals has a profound therapeutic value because it contributes to overcoming the difficulties in interpersonal relationships;
- events organization;
- graphic arts.

Moreover, the community's internal activity includes education courses for children, dance and gymnastic courses as well as a sport centre.

Among the problems that affect the drug addict, drug use is the least relevant. The core of the problem is not drugs, nor the inability to abstain: it is the human being with his fears and the black holes that threaten to suck him in. That is why I do not like to say nor hear that ours is a community for drug addicts. Ours is a community for living, where you can begin in life again after years spent as a social outcast. Ours, if we really need a definition, is a community against social outcasting (Vincenzo Muccioli, Founder of the San Patrignano Community).

Table 9.1 List of sectors

Kindergarten (for kids under 3, the older ones go to the public school)	Bricklayer workshop
	Garage
	Blacksmith workshop
Study room (to prepare students - not only children, but also young guests - for exams in public schools)	Vegetable garden and greenhouse
	Gardening
	Creative Manufacturing
	Pig breeding
Dog Kennels and breeding	Horse breeding and stud
Wine cellar and vineyards	Cattle breeding and milking
Dairy	Editorial office
Switchboard	Audiovisual department
Medical Centre	Music room
Teenager House	Weaving workshop
Chemistry Laboratory for detergent production	Tractor drivers
	House keeping
Veterinary clinic	Accounting office
Co-generation power plant	Legal office
Kitchen	Technical department
Decorations	Purchase department
After-school activities	Sales office
Shop	Personnel department
Electricians	Admission office
Joinery	Public relations office
Bakery	Communications office
Graphic arts workshop	
Plumbers	
Laundry	
Meat working sector	
Feed production	

The San Patrignano Community is based on a belief that drug addiction recovery does not happen in a vacuum: guests experience success and struggle with hardships while relating to other people and learning to provide for themselves.

They learn the meaning of responsibility and develop the independence and dignity that work can bring.

Guests live in groups of about 10 to 12 (the same people they also work with), along with two tutors. In the first year of recovery, the therapeutic aspect of work is emphasized and after one year, individuals can choose the training opportunity that best fits their skills. After a year-and-a-half, guests can become tutors for new entrants.

Housing is provided, in the community for drug addicts with children. Over the last 10 years, a village of 60 small houses has been built for couples and families that reunite, and for the guests' families who have chosen full-time volunteer service. In San Patrignano's kindergarten, 60 children from drug-ravaged families are looked after by trained staffs who are assisted by young mothers undergoing recovery. Today, some 120 children under the age of 12 live in the community.

Once the drug recovery process is complete, individuals who do not want to leave the community can be hired for up to two years by the co-operative as part of their transition. If individuals still wish to remain in the community, they may do so as members of the community but cannot work at the co-operative. Of the almost 20,000 guests who have passed through the program over the last 25 years, only 100 have remained as staff. Guests who leave after two or more years are always welcomed back. Guests who leave early and do not complete their program are never allowed to return. This is a community based on a philosophy of commitment and respect for self and others, the program's success is based on how serious a commitment individuals make to themselves and the community as a whole.

It is possible to assert that the job assumes a priority role in the recovery process. To be more precise, the therapy coincides with the working activity residents choose for themselves. For this reason, strong attention to job quality and not only to quantity exists. To work for or within the community becomes a moment of personal growth, of assumption of responsibility, participation and identification with collective life. Of the importance of the work ethic towards one's dignity, founder Vincenzo Muccioli once said:

> Dignity is not conquered by requests or pretence, but by the sweat of the brow in laboring towards its reconstruction and defending it with one's own work (A pictorial visit of San Patrignano, 2003, www.sanpatrignano.org).

By way of conclusion, it is important to note that San Patrignano does not have a standard rehabilitation program and there is no 'normal time' within which the program is or must be concluded. Before being accepted into the community, many guests take part in a preparatory program conducted by local associations that assist people during their decision making process. They follow up the potential candidates by organizing meetings during which they offer human willingness tests and the consultancy necessary before entering the rehabilitation program. The newcomers immediately stop taking drugs and they are assigned to a production sector. Withdrawal symptoms are at times treated with some medication as deemed necessary by the medical staff on hand. But for the most part guests get through this difficult first period with the support of their tutors and the encouragement given to them by the community spirit. Those who wish to smoke cigarettes are furnished with ten cigarettes per day, no sharing or borrowing is allowed. This too is designed to make individuals responsible for managing one of the many daily tasks they will have to learn to deal with because cigarettes are distributed at breakfast for those who are showered and dressed on time. Daily tasks that most of us take for granted like getting changed and ready for breakfast are made into integral parts of the responsibility ethic. Other examples include the setting of the lunch and dinner tables, an exercise that requires mathematical precision, but is an effective measurement of the progress individuals are making.

Through this approach and the excellent organizational structure, San Patrignano has created remarkable social benefits realizing its mission and embracing social entrepreneurship. This successful experience has been replicated in two communities in Sweden, as well as in Los Angeles. Or rather, the success of the community can, perhaps, be best summarized in the words of Andrea Muccioli, son of the founder and current President of the San Patrignano Community:

> If we manage to build a relationship on love and trust, if we are able to look somebody in the eyes and have his problems, his struggles and his need for help mean all the world to us, then we are on the right path and we will be able to walk together (www.sanpatrignano.org).

Another aspect of Italy's heritage is worthy of note. The government has not been involved to any great extent in addressing the problem of drug addiction. This has left those who wish to deal with this problem to find their own innovative ways of financing and operating. Thus the emergent properties of this region helped to ensure the survival, and ongoing success, of San Patrignano. This factor has contributed to construct the entrepreneurial approach of the community and its independence in seeking resources.

9.3. SAN PATRIGNANO HISTORY

This section presents the more important stages of the community, evidencing the phases that have contributed to its development concerning the current social–economic approach and other critical factors (a detailed timeline is provided in Appendix 9.1).

What was an unthinkable project of Vincenzo Muccioli started to take shape in 1975, driven by his desire to understand the social roots of drug addiction. The period between 1975 and 1978 can therefore ideally be called 'the project' in which its founder began to speak with some drug addicts and decided to take them in by inviting them to his own weekend house near Rimini. The community was formally founded in 1979 with the establishment of the Cooperativa San Patrignano where most of the founding partners still have ties with the community.

From the beginning (see Annex 9.1 for timing details, at the end of the chapter), San Patrignano set itself the objective of being self financed in the conviction that asking for help or charity meant perpetuating the lack of dignity suffered by a drug addict.

By 1982 San Patrignano's guests numbered close to 200 and in 1985 the San Patrignano Foundation was established. Today, the community's guests average around 1,600 per year with approximately 600 new guests welcomed by the community each year. The average stay in the community is three years. In general, the number of guests continued to increase. This was paralleled not only by the necessary changes in the community's physical facilities, but also by the first organizational changes. The community began to give itself precise rules, define some crucial internal roles and organize its therapeutic and production process in a structured manner.

In 1994, three social co-operatives were created under the Foundation. These co-ops focus on integrating guests back into the workforce through skills development, and are one of the keys to the success of the program – 70 per cent of the addicts have been completely reintegrated into society after completion of their program in the community. And more than 50 per cent go on to find jobs in areas related to the professional training they received at San Patrignano.

By the beginning of 1995, the community guests were quite a mixed group, representative of Italian society as a whole. The age spread ranged from 13 to 53, with an average of 32. From 1 per cent to 3 per cent of the guests were non-Italians. Furthermore by 1995, the sad year that saw the death of founder Vincenzo Muccioli, the community had been operating for 16 years and some 10 000 former drug addicts had completed the rehabilitation program to go on to lead a normal life. His son Andrea Muccioli, upon unanimous decision of the entire community, took over as President after his father's death.

During these years, Andrea had started a series of new productive activities. These achieved international success. Moreover, the number of guests has varied between 1500 and 2000 at any one time.

In 1999 Andrea was pondering the future of San Patrignano. The community was becoming more involved in external activities, such as fundraising from private donors, starting and collaborating with other drug rehabilitation communities and influencing drug policy. He felt torn between these types of issues, his role as community leader and keeping track of San Patrignano's day to day operations. He needed to make a change. McKinsey & Company made a study. Its first recommendation was to separate the leadership role of the community and make Andrea Muccioli formally President, and at the same time, create a second role. Andrea had been introduced to Roberto de Micco, a 50 year old manager with a long career at IBM, who was also actively involved in community work. The new organization would permit Andrea to focus more on the real mission of San Patrignano, with activities and external relations related to issues of drug rehabilitation, prevention and reintroduction of guests into society. He could also pay much needed attention to new guests to ensure their effective integration into the community.

To be more precise, these years have seen the beginnings of establishing and consolidating the financial structure of the community with the aim of guaranteeing its long-term survival. For example, fund raising and marketing have been developed to support the central and characteristic activities of rehabilitation therapy. A commercial office has been set up to deal with marketing and strategic economic management of the different areas of production partially destined for the outside market.

During 2002/2003 San Patrignano, along with ten other important volunteer organizations, managed the National Campaign for the prevention of drug use sponsored by the President of the Council of Ministers – Office of the Government Commissary of Drug Control Policies and the Minister of Labor and Social Policy. Today San Patrignano leads the new National Campaign Against Drugs sponsored by the Presidency of the Council of Ministers and the Ministry of Welfare, titled 'Don't Kill Your Brain, (Contro la Droga Usa il Cervello)'.

9.4 GEOGRAPHY

The origins of San Patrignano – the time and place from which it emerged – are integral to how it developed. San Patrignano was founded in the 1970s when drug addiction escalated around the western world and was taking the lives of many of Italy's young people. The place is the region of Emilia Romagna, which encompasses the community of San Patrignano. As early as the 1970s Rimini had an obvious problem with young drug addicts in the streets. Vincenzo said about the piazza where he and his friends had met as youngsters:

> I passed that same piazza and would see the young people lying on their sides, weakened, emaciated, and dirty. They were there totally abandoned, and those that passed did not look at them, or they made deprecating comments. It was a sight that filled me with sadness that I could not get used to. I knew nothing about those young kids. And still I wanted to understand their choice and the reason why they had started with drugs.

However, the region's tradition is one of 'civil economy', a term coined in 1753 by one of Italy's first great economists, Antonio Genovesi. San Patrignano was founded on 'self respect and respect of others, the ethics of responsibility and serving others' (V. Muccioli), core principles that can be traced back to this 'long grand tradition'. The region of Emilia Romagna is seen as one of the greatest 'models of economic democracy'.

Quoting Michael Taylor in *Community Anarchy & Liberty* (1982):

> These early precedents are what made San Patrignano's cooperative 'business/therapy' model a natural fit. There is a history of reciprocity in the region. Reciprocity is made up of a series of acts each of which is short-run altruistic (benefiting others at a cost to the altruist) but which typically make every participant better off.

9.5 THE NEW SOCIAL ENTERPRISES AND THE NEW LEADERSHIP

At the present time, San Patrignano manages 56 industry clusters. That being so, this section describes the successful start-up of a number of business ventures in the Community under Andrea's leadership, which helped reduce its dependence on private donors using an entrepreneurial approach.

Andrea takes over the leadership and along with his younger brother Giacomo, makes a series of new decisions that basically exits the community from certain businesses and strengthens others in an effort to maximize the human capital the community has at its disposition. It goes without saying that the success from an economical front has to do with the free labor the community enjoys. It has also capitalized on certain economic phenomena that have effectively strengthened Italy as a whole in certain sectors. For example the wine industry in Italy has of late made remarkable progress surpassing France as the world's number one exporter to the US. From an economic point of view, the most important venture was the investment in wine production, a long term San Patrignano product. Andrea had matured the idea to leverage on this capacity by producing better quality wine that commanded a higher price. Therefore, new equipment had been installed and the first vines of quality stock had been planted in 1994. A world-class enologist generously agreed to become part of the project and quality grapes typical of the Romagna region, such as Sangiovese, were used to make the first new wines. Since then international vines such as Cabernet Sauvignon and Merlot were added along side white varietals such as Sauvignon Blanc. The production was called Terre del Cedro because the cedar is the community symbol. San Patrignano exports to Europe, Scandinavia, England, the US and Canada and the brand is known as representing high quality wine in the whole world.

By 1999 the wine producing and exporting venture alone was generating US$ 5 million per year, which was the total of all revenues in 1995. Moreover, a Terre del Cedro wine dedicated to founder Vincenzo Muccioli, called AVI, won a prize for best emerging wine from one of the most important Italian wine guides published by the Italian Sommelier's Association or AIS.

Another example, one that would be dear to the founder Vincenzo is the creation of the yearly Vincenzo Muccioli Challenge which has become one of the most important international show jumping competitions. Today, San Patrignano is on the world map for major equestrian events. The competition is organized and managed by community guests, under the leadership of Giacomo Muccioli and promoted by Franke Sloothaak (Olympic gold medal winner in show jumping). In addition, a series of smaller events are organized throughout the year. These initiatives are also profitable ventures that consistently earn money.

9.5.1 San Patrignano Branches

San Patrignano today has two branches that are spin offs or clones of the original model. In 1990 the Community founded a residential branch for drug rehabilitation at San Vito Pergine, in the mountains above Trento. It now hosts 120 young people. The spirit and principles that guide this facility and its educational path are the same as those of San Patrignano itself. There are two special initiatives make the San Vito Pergine experience unique, namely the Canine Training Facilities and Touring and Racing Bicycles. The first was founded in 1998 for training dogs capable of assisting the disabled. Dogs from municipal pounds are trained by members of the Community and are then given to people with different disabilities, through arrangements with institutional or not-for-profit associations working with the disabled. The second initiative exists since the founding of the Trento branch. It produces parts for touring and racing bicycles. The use of the newest materials and techniques is one reason this facility has established an enviable reputation in the field.

The branch at Sant'Agata Feltria, in the Marche region, was established at the end of the 1980s as a 'holiday home' for the children of San Patrignano. Now, it mainly hosts those who, due to health or other problems, need a retreat that features a close family environment. There are about 130 guests in this branch of the Community, which centers around a fully-renovated farmhouse, recently expanded, and surrounded by 100 hectares of pasture and chestnut groves.

The direct assistance of San Patrignano abbreviated the time necessary to adapt this location and facilitate its implementation. Or rather, the model was transmitted as a result of the physical transfer of people from the original community, who were entrusted with the responsibilities of supervision and coordination. The financing of these communities was also assisted by San Patrignano, which allowed them to overcome one crucial initial problem of finding sources of finance.

To be more precise, the main critical aspects of the phases of development were:

- identification of the people responsible for transmitting Vincenzo's vision of the community;
- the choice of charismatic leader;
- the implementation and adaptation of practices to a smaller community;
- managing dimensional growth;
- developing an individual identity;
- handling relationships with local authorities.

9.5.2 San Patrignano Founding Partner of Rainbow International Association against Drugs

San Patrignano's importance is also demonstrated by the founding of the Rainbow International Association against Drugs (an associative international network) in 1994, in which it is the leading community.

Rainbow yearly gathers at San Patrignano and the following communities participate: Botticella di Novafeltria, San Vito di Pergine, Lega Abruzzese Anti Droga, LAAD, Basta, DeHoop, Delancey Street Foundation and Vitanova. It is a purely voluntary and not-for-profit association. The goal is to serve as a reference point toward promoting national and international relationships between therapeutic communities, in order to encourage discussion, information exchange, and, in general, the investigation on addiction-related themes. These communities have declared that they have changed their organizational makeup due to getting to know the example of San Patrignano.

San Patrignano, Botticella, San Vito di Pergine and Delancey Street Foundation's models are called 'community models'. In this model, no clear distinction is made between working and rehabilitation insofar as the former is an integral part of the latter and lies at the beginning of pathways of not only occupational development. Moreover, there is a choice of autonomy with regards to seeking funds from the public sector or not.

The other communities are labeled 'institutional models' because they are similar to the public institutions that partially govern their functioning. They are closely tied to their home State and have some formalized procedures and limitations.

Therefore, the community can be defined as a nucleus, constituted from shared culture, principles and values, such as dignity, responsibility, solidarity, withdrawal, rules etc. It acts like a tool to integrate the organizations and that in and of itself aids in orienting the behavior of persons and other therapeutic communities.

9.6. FUND RAISING

How does San Patrignano financially support its growth? Which are its sources of financing? How has it supported its entrepreneurial mission and entrepreneurial activities?

San Patrignano does not let its own limited resources keep it from pursuing its vision. It is skilled at doing more with less and at attracting resources from others. It uses scarce resources efficiently and leverages them by drawing in partners and collaborating with corporations and other stakeholders. The community explores all options, from pure philanthropy to the commercial methods of business sectors. Thus San Patrignano develops strategies that are likely to support and reinforce its social mission. To be more precise, San Patrignano has always offered all its services free of charge. Thanks to the productive activities of its three social cooperatives, the community itself procures approximately 50% of the financial resources necessary to support community life. The community would in any case meet difficulties trying to become entirely self-sustaining, so Andrea decided to change the structure of fund raising. The President wanted to enter into the world of fund raising to put into place the basis for a wider pool of contributors upon which to draw upon. Today, the community relies on outside contributors and sponsors, such as private individuals and companies, for around 60% of its income. Among the more important supporters are some of the more illustrious entrepreneurs, like the Moratti Family, the journalist Enzo Biagi, the stylist Giorgio Armani, the Bracco Group, and so on.

Another fund raising initiative sees the possibility to buy San Patrignano Solidarity Shares. Buying one or more shares means providing a contribution of vital importance, year after year, to San Patrignano's mission. Shares have no economic or financial value, but have a deeper significance. Each share has a value of €50.00. Each shareholder is entitled to several benefits, including visits to the community, participation in the annual shareholders' meeting and a subscription to the community newsletter, which contains updates on all current projects.

Moreover, companies can add their logo to that of the community in relation to an event or advertising campaign. Otherwise, they may donate a portion of the sales of a predetermined product to San Patrignano. Sponsorship also permits one to associate a company's name to that of San Patrignano's activities in several ways:

- Institutional sponsor (collaboration on a specific project)
- Event sponsor (sports, cultural, scientific, etc. events)
- Technical sponsor (providing material and/or services for the community)

These new initiatives included co-marketing of the San Patrignano name with well-known Italian consumer products, i.e. mentioning in the commercials that a part of sales would be donated to the community. This method would reinforce the image of San Patrignano and also prove beneficial for the partner's image.

Therefore, it's possible to assert that San Patrignano is a model of social service which doesn't weigh on society or on private finances, but which rather becomes the protagonist of a virtuous circle which, on the one hand gives a free services to whomever needs it, and on the other, produces goods and economic resources whose results extend beyond the limits of the community.

9.7. LESSONS TO BE LEARNED

In the light of the community's success, San Patrignano has increased international interest as a therapeutic model. So many people and institutions have approached San Patrignano with the request to create a San Patrignano-like community in their home countries. Andrea described the effort required to recreate a community like San Patrignano: 'You need an enormous commitment from all the people involved. It's necessary to institute a very strong common identity. In fact, Sanpa-like communities have been reproduced in Sweden, Canada, Norway and Holland.' (Muccioli, 2006, interview)

By way of conclusion, we can affirm that San Patrignano is a corporation with a social mission, explicit and central. It is skilled in perceiving and assessing opportunities in order to create social benefits and societal wealth generation.

To be more precise, San Patrignano plays the role of change agent in the social sector, by:

- adopting a mission to create and sustain social value;
- recognizing and relentlessly pursuing new opportunities to serve this mission;
- engaging in a process of continuous innovation, adaptation and learning;
- acting boldly without being limited by resources in hand.

A mission of social improvement cannot be reduced to creating private benefits (financial returns or consumption benefits) for individuals. However, making a profit, creating wealth, or serving the needs of people with drug addiction problems may be part of San Patrignano's model, as long as profit is used towards helping reach out to those who need help and is not the gauge of value creation. Social impact and a long term social return on investment must be the objective of the community, in an effort to rid the world from this terrible plague.

Consideration of the San Patrignano experience provides a variety of lessons for social entrepreneurship.

The first is the necessity to create networks from varied sectors in the economy (in this case more than 50 production combinations) thereby creating a need for social entrepreneurship and creating a virtuous cycle. As profits and profitability increase, management is increasingly stimulated to expand capacity and advance efficiency. It is important to recognize that the main societal problems of San Patrignano are confronted and improved at a relative rate, keeping the recovery of guests as the primary objective, this obviously overtaking any economic goals in terms of importance.

The second is that social entrepreneurs need to develop relationships with persons who serve as managers who provide skills or resources vital to current task-handlers as well as those that will succeed them. The need exists to establish some processes to safeguard against the loss of skill in an effort to connect and provide a continuous exchange and updating of information as the yearly Rainbow conference aims to do. For example, that potential loss could be safeguarded against by promotion from within, staff consistency and informal local networks to be developed over time.

The third is geography that can represent a constraint on the scalability (replicability) as can the size of the social enterprise, determining the organizational problems to be solved. It is important to identify potential conflicts from the tension between internal and external concerns and to establish procedures to protect organizational goals. Not all countries work in the same way, respect the same scheduling or timing, hence what may take several years in one place may be accomplished in a relatively short period of time in others, is not always possible.

The fourth is related to funding. By creating incentives for local communities to cooperate in the funding of social entrepreneurial ventures like the bakery business (supplying bread to the local surrounding communities at lower prices) and the dog training sector (in which needy or elderly people are given the companion of a lifetime that has been specifically trained for the special task required) can have multiple effects, such as success in obtaining outside grants as well as indirect positive publicity for the main goals of San Patrignano or whatever the social venture may be called.

San Patrignano teaches us that the social entrepreneur can coexist with the real world economy. As long as the mission of the community or organization in question is held central to the existence of the enterprise then positive results really do have a fighting chance.

APPENDIX 9.1

- 1978 Vincenzo Muccioli together with a group of volunteers hosts the first group of young people in a house owned by his family in the hills above Rimini.
- 1982 San Patrignano hosts nearly 200 guests.
- 1985 The San Patrignano Foundation is created to collect the contributions of all the supporters of the community.
- 1986 San Patrignano is recognized as a professional training facility by the Emilia Romagna Region.
- 1987 The community opens a facility in the Marche Region, in Sant'Agata Feltria, which now hosts more than 100 people.
- 1990 The San Patrignano Foundation is recognized as a non-profit agency by the Italian State following Muccioli's family renouncing any claim to their real estate donated in favor of the community. The community is listed in the Regional Register as an auxiliary agency in the drug-addiction section. The community opens a facility in the Trentino Alto Adige Region, at San Vito Pergine, now hosting 100 people.
- 1993 The community's guests total 1600.
- 1994 Three social cooperatives are created to facilitate the reinstatement of guests of the community to the working world.
- 1995 Vincenzo Muccioli, founder of the community, dies.
- 1995 Together with seven large European and American communities, San Patrignano founds Rainbow International Association Against Drugs, a non-profit organization now comprised of 200 associations and rehabilitation facilities from all over the world fighting for the culture of life and against any form of drug legalization.
- 1997 San Patrignano is accredited as a Non-Governmental Organization (NGO) in special consultative status with the Economic and Social Council of the United Nations.
- 1998 Andrea Muccioli represents San Patrignano at the United Nations' General Assembly on the world drug problem.
- 1999 San Patrignano organizes and hosts Rainbow International's fifth annual Meeting.
- 2000 President of the Italian Republic Carlo Azeglio Ciampi and Nobel laureate Shimon Peres pay visit to the community.

- 2001 Archipelago Social Cooperative is founded in Riccione, in order to integrate young men and women who have completed their program of recovery into the work force and society as a whole.
- 2002 A new 100-bed residential structure, built expressly for minors with histories of social marginalization and drug abuse, is inaugurated.
- 2002/2003 San Patrignano, along with ten other important volunteer organizations, manages the National Campaign for the prevention of drug use sponsored by the President of the Council of Ministers, Office of the Government Commissary of Drug Control Policies and the Minister of Labor and Social Policy.
- 2003 The community celebrates its 25th anniversary.
- 2003 The association 'Friends of San Patrignano' is founded to support activities aimed at rehabilitating drug addicts and ensuring their social reintegration, as well as to raise awareness in the United States about the dangers of drug abuse.
- 2004 San Patrignano organizes the first edition of 'Squisito!' (Il Made in Italy nel Piatto), a food and wine festival.
- 2004/2005 San Patrignano leads the new National Campaign Against Drugs sponsored by the Presidency of the Council of Ministers and the Ministry of Welfare, titled "Don't Kill Your Brain – Contro la Droga Usa il Cervello".
- 2005 Tenth anniversary of the death of Vincenzo Muccioli
- 2005 San Patrignano equestrian centre hosts the FEI European Jumping Championship, attended by the top of the equestrian world.
- 2005 The Solomon R. Guggenheim Museum in New York hosts the first ever charitable event in the United States benefiting San Patrignano.

10. CaféDirect: fair trade as social entrepreneurship

Kai Hockerts

10.1 FAIR TRADE AT GLANCE

This chapter outlines the case study of CaféDirect (Hockerts, 2003), a social purpose business venture (Hockerts, 2005, 2006). Recent decades have seen an unprecedented increase in world trade, linking consumers in developed countries ever closer to producers in developing countries. Globalisation has brought wealth (through industrialisation) to numerous people in Asia. However, many regions in Africa and Latin America have been less fortunate. They are relying strongly on cash crops (that is, agricultural produce that is destined for export on the world-market rather than to be consumed locally) as their main source of income. As more and more developing countries have encouraged their farmers to switch from subsistence farming to the production of cash crops, production has soared and prices for cash crops have fallen to rock-bottom levels. The groups affected worst by this trend are the so called smallholders.

> Smallholders are farmers who've got a few hectares or a very small plot of land where they'll grow tea or coffee etc. Throughout Latin America and Africa there are many smallholders. They own a small plot of land and the family members often work on the land. It's usually quite difficult to get a good income (Wills, 2002, interview).

Fair trade has grown out of the development movement as a tool to help these disenfranchised producers by providing minimum prices, training, and long-term financing. In sharp difference from other developmental programmes (which are mostly financed by governmental donors and usually run on a large scale), fair trade is financed via the consumers in the developed world. Fair-trade products are sold at a price premium to finance the fair-trade process. It is important to realize that fair trade is not intended as just a charitable donation. Fair trade can thus be located somewhere between 'development through trade and trade development' (Tallontire, 2001a). Citing the definition for fair trade that CaféDirect adheres to Newman proposes the following distinction:

> Fair Trade is a trading partnership, based on dialogue, transparency and respect that seeks greater equity in international trade. It contributes to sustainable development by offering better trading conditions to, and securing the rights of, marginalized producers. Fair Trade organisations (backed by consumers) are engaged actively in supporting producers, awareness raising and in campaigning for changes in the rules and practice of conventional international trade (Newman, 2002).

The constitutive attributes of fair trade as defined in this chapter are accordingly:

- fair trade has a strong developmental motivation, wanting to help disenfranchised and self-employed smallholders to develop capabilities for accessing lucrative markets at prices that allow them a sustainable livelihood;
- its primary instrument is the manipulation of trading relationships through minimum prices, premiums, pre-financing, and training;
- fair trade is usually conducted by alternative trading organisations (ATOs), which have often been founded particularly for the purpose of fair trade.

The operational details differ from one ATO to another. However, most fair-trade schemes include the following elements (see for example Littrell and Dickson, 1999; Mayoux, 2001; Tallontire, 2001a):

- a minimum price, which will always be paid even if the world market price falls below this point;
- a price premium of a given percentage (10 percent in the case of CaféDirect, 5 percent for other Fair Trade companies),

which is paid when the world market price rises beyond the minimum price;
- pre-financing of 60 percent of the total order to allow the smallholders to buy fertilizer and seeds;
- training in quality control and marketing know-how to build the capacity to also trade on the world market independently of fair trade;
- ATOs trade rarely with the smallholders individually. Instead they work with co-operatives which have been formed by several smallholders. It is usually the co-operative that decides how the fair trade premium is used (that is, to buy a van for all members or to build joint storage facilities).

10.2 STRATEGIC INNOVATION AND SOCIAL CHANGE IN THE CAFÉDIRECT MODEL

Fair trade has evolved over the past three to four decades from a form of charity into a viable business model. The following account will retrace the story of one particularly successful ATO, London-based CaféDirect Ltd. However, the account starts long before the foundation of CaféDirect and includes its roots which go back to its four founders: Oxfam Trading, Traidcraft Plc, Equal Exchange, and Twin Trading.

One of the early players to enter charity trade in the UK was the Oxford Committee for Famine Relief (Oxfam). Oxfam was founded in 1942 to raise funds for the International Red Cross to help fight famine in Nazi-occupied Greece. After World War II Oxfam grew into one of Britain's foremost famine and disaster relief organisations. Oxfam generated revenues by asking for cash and in-kind donations such as old clothes. The latter were sold through an extensive network of shops (Coe, 2002, interview). In 1964 Oxfam also began to import and market handicrafts from the South through its extensive network of shops (Oxfam, 2002). This 'Bridge programme' later became the Oxfam Fair-Trade Company.

The story goes that Leslie Kirkley, the then director of Oxfam, was visiting Hong Kong where Oxfam was funding some projects [...] He found that Chinese refugees from the mainland were surviving by making pincushions and other things. Kirkley took everything out of his suitcase, filled it up with pincushions and brought them back to England where Oxfam had opened many shops by that time (Wills, 2002, interview).

Although the majority of the early charity trade was focused on handicraft, there had also been trade in coffee as early as the 1970s. With the invention of freeze-dried granulated coffee the older version of powdered coffee gradually fell out favour. In response to this a UK aid scheme decided to donate the old machinery for making powdered coffee to a group of coffee-producing smallholders in Tanzania. The resulting product, called Africafé, was probably the first fair-trade coffee in the world, which even today can still be found in some World shops (Wills, 2002, interview).

As fair-trade matured in the 1970s, it began to expand beyond the charity movement and to become a force of its own. An important new appeal was solidarity between consumers and producers rather than charity. International politics also entered the field as, for example, in the case of coffee sourced from Nicaragua or the Frontline African States. Trade with these countries was more a political statement than development aid. In this phase, which is usually referred to as solidarity trade (Tallontire, 2001b) or alternative trade (Wills, 2002, interview), two important developments happened.

Firstly, so called alternative trade organisations (ATO) emerged that were dedicated only to fair-trade. For the charities fair-trade had always been just one minority activity among many. The ATOs on the other hand were solely dedicated to promoting fair-trade, and could thus devote more attention towards the development of this new approach. While still selling through the traditional distribution channels (such as charities and church groups), ATOs started to build their own distribution network through specialised World Shops (also called 'Third World Shops' or 'One World Shops').

A second change was what might be called the 'discovery of the producer' as a partner and not just the recipient of donations. This changed the focus of fair trade from charitable towards developmental work. As a consequence ATOs had to build up new capabilities. For example, to engage with producers in long-term relationships, they had to better understand their needs and the different contextual situations of producers in various regions. Furthermore, they started to look at benefits beyond the immediate income from the traded goods, such as training and other support programmes, which would help producers to trade on the world market.

Over time ATOs grew in stature and size as they imposed themselves as the missing link between producers and consumers. Three British ATOs have to be mentioned because they later became instrumental in the foundation of CaféDirect (Hockerts, 2003). These are Traidcraft, Equal Exchange, and Twin:

- Traidcraft was founded in 1979 as a fair-trade mail-order service (Traidcraft, 2002). Traidcraft relied heavily on sales from voluntary reps and church groups, who also helped to raise awareness about the need for fair trade;
- the roots of Equal Exchange go back to 1979 as well (Equal Exchange, 2002). In this year three voluntary workers returned to Edinburgh after working on aid projects in various parts of Africa. Along with a sister organisation in London, Campaign Co-op, they started buying instant coffee from Bukoba on Lake Victoria in Tanzania, launching Campaign Coffee Scotland (CCS);
- the third organisation, Twin, was founded in 1985 when the Greater London Council decided to set up a dedicated developing agency (White, 2002, interview). Very soon Twin realised that the most important knowledge they could transfer concerned the capability to trade efficiently in the world markets. Thus, towards the end of the 1980s, Twin Trading Ltd started to trade jam, honey and nuts with producer groups in Africa and Latin America.

The term fair trade emerged in the mid-1980s when the traditional ATOs reached the limits of their long-established model. Around this time signs became apparent that all was not well with alternative trade. ATOs found it difficult to attract new customers, while old clients were switching back to traditional products. As a result sales remained flat or even began to decrease. At Traidcraft poor mail-order sales and increased market competition led to a trading loss, which in 1991 eventually triggered a major business review and 20 redundancies (Traidcraft, 2002). Other ATOs and World shops also ran into financial difficulty.

The producer focus of earlier periods was associated with the neglect of the consumer. As profits dropped and some ATOs faced bankruptcy, many began to look towards consumer needs and to balance these with the needs of producers. Consumer marketing, product development and product quality all became important concerns of ATOs, marking increased commercial awareness (Tallontire, 2001b: 3).

Most interestingly the initial pressure to change did not come from the ATOs themselves but rather from the producers in the developing countries. 'What we need to understand, is that it was the producers' idea,' explains Penny Newman (2002, interview), CaféDirect's current managing director. Coffee producers suffered huge price drops when in 1989 the international coffee agreement collapsed. The idea of establishing coffee export quotas on a worldwide basis had been adopted in 1962, when the first International Coffee Agreement (ICA) was negotiated by the United Nations (Shoppingplace, 2002). The agreement was renegotiated in 1968, 1976, and in 1983. However, world coffee prices plunged when participating nations failed to sign a new pact in 1989.

The collapse of the international coffee agreement [...] sent the whole market into a freefall. The producers wanted two things. They said: 'First we want a minimum or fair trade price and secondly we want people to understand what happened and what low prices mean for us [...].' It was they who said: 'Why can't we put a mainstream brand in the marketplace?' [...] So with this idea from the producers the four ATOs sat together and came up with CaféDirect. Each of the four founding organisations had to be convinced that this was the way to go. The investment to put the brand into the marketplace was quite something for these organisations (Newman, 2002, interview).

Prompted by producers, the four leading ATOs in the UK, Oxfam, Traidcraft, Equal Exchange, and Twin Trading, came together in late 1989 to discuss options for how to increase growth in the fair-trade market and thus to help producers. The solidarity appeal of alternative trade had reached a small group of committed customers, but it had failed to build a sustainable mass market. The ATOs realised that they had to achieve two goals:

- rather than having each ATO peddle its own coffee, they needed to develop a branded fair-trade coffee that would be available across the four organisations;
- furthermore, they hoped that such a move would allow them to target the mainstream distribution channels such as supermarkets, catering, and coffee bars.

The birth of CaféDirect happened gradually. After having suggested this course of action, three fair-trade co-operatives in Mexico, Peru and Costa Rica each lent CaféDirect a container of coffee and agreed to take payment once the finished product was sold in the UK. The first packets of CaféDirect Medium Roast & Ground Coffee emerged in World shops in the summer of 1991 (White, 2002, interview). After a campaign by fair-trade activists, CaféDirect reached its first trial distribution in some UK supermarkets in 1992 (CaféDirect, 2002). However, it took until 1992 before the company was officially founded, with each of the four ATOs contributing £25 000. By being offered in Oxfam's over 600 shops and Traidcraft's mail-order catalogue, CaféDirect was able to reach out to a large part of potential customers. Thus rather than having to build up a new infrastructure, CaféDirect could draw on the experience of its four founders thus leapfrogging years of painful build-up (Barr, 2002, interview).

In 1993, CaféDirect gained national distribution in the Co-op and other supermarkets, a first for a fair-trade product (Hudghton, 2002, interview). Extending its product range, CaféDirect introduced in 1994 Medium Roast, Freeze Dried Instant coffee, the first fair-trade instant coffee. Given that in the UK about 80 percent of the coffee drunk is instant, this move opened up access to the mainstream market.

At the same time as CaféDirect was founded, another important development began to change the fair-trade world, which impacted the growth of the fair-trade market in general. This was the introduction of fair-trade labels.

The increasing importance of consumers (epitomised through the foundation of CaféDirect) required other changes. In the early days of fair-trade the very reputation of the ATOs had been guarantee enough for their customers. However, as both products and distribution channels multiplied, consumers were increasingly sceptical: Did fair-trade premiums actually reach the producers? Furthermore, consumers faced an increasing range of fair-trade products that each applied its own mix of fair-trade criteria, ranging from very strict standards to products that could at best be qualified as 'fair-trade lite'.

> There are hundreds if not thousands of very small fair-trade initiatives, just based on people wanting to do something to help producers in developing countries. I think one of the main challenges we're facing is to develop a more coherent philosophy as to how these things fit together (Bretman, 2002, interview).

One step in that direction was the introduction of an independent verification and labelling system to guarantee that only products that met certified standards were sold as fair trade. In 1988, the Dutch ATOs were the first to found an organisation dedicated to fair-trade labelling. They named it Max Havelaar after a 19th century book about a Dutch plantation owner who adopted a responsible approach towards his Javanese workers (Roozen and Van Der Hoff, 2002; Wills, 2002, interview). The newly founded organisation was not involved in trading itself. Instead it maintained a fair-trade register of producers that were accredited fair-trade suppliers. Importers and retailers could obtain a label – the fair-trade mark – if they bought from these producers while observing conditions that were audited by Max Havelaar.

The concept was so convincing that soon other countries followed suit. TransFair, the German labelling organisation, was launched by gepa in 1992. In the same year the UK ATOs founded the Fairtrade Foundation, which was to become the British guardian of the fair-trade mark. The same four partners that had founded CaféDirect also launched the Fairtrade Foundation, intending both organisations to be complementary. However, CaféDirect felt that it did not need the fair-trade mark, which comes with a 2 percent license fee on all sales with the mark.

> By the time the mark was launched, CaféDirect products were already on sale. So there had to be serious negotiations with them. They didn't feel they needed the mark. They had the backing of four national organisations that had a fair-trade reputation. They had a distinct brand identity. They said: The fair-trade mark isn't for us. Yet we felt we needed their support. We wanted a clear message to consumers and not have to say that some products carry the mark and some don't. Then CaféDirect said: You want us to put the mark on for solidarity, to help you, rather than us. That sort of rooted the problems. It

illustrates the lack of coherence in the trade movement. The same people who were setting us up were setting up CaféDirect. However there was no coherent strategy for doing that (Bretman, 2002, interview).

In the end the dispute was settled when the Fairtrade Foundation agreed to offer CaféDirect a discount based on its trade volume and the fact that CaféDirect's campaigning often reinforced the Fairtrade Foundation's own work (Bretman, 2002, interview).

CaféDirect's expansion was by no means easy. Its most important growth (increasing turnover by more than a factor of 10) happened between 1994 and 1997. By 1998, CaféDirect had reached a size at which it made sense to move out of Twin Trading's offices into their own space. Furthermore, Ian Lepper, CaféDirect's first managing director, decided to leave CaféDirect. Unsurprisingly this led to a lot of organisational stress.

> By this time, CaféDirect was going through some interesting stages. The partnership was being stretched. Sales-wise it was doing well but its underlying direction – how did its partners and founders work together – that was being stretched. There was a clouding of different roles. I was asked to give it some stability and more importantly direction. [...] I could see potential and a vision for CaféDirect. It was good that I could see that from the outside. My role was taking it out of an NGO vision to making it a commercial and ethical business (Newman, 2002, interview).

It was an important decision of the CaféDirect board to hire an outside managing director with extensive business experience in the area of fast-moving consumer goods (FMCG) rather than a pure fair-trade specialist. Penny Newman had worked at Schwarzkopf, Faberge, a Capital Venture Group and most recently the Body Shop. With growth rates finally levelling off, she faced the challenge to lead CaféDirect into a new management phase. When starting in August 1998, Newman realised that although CaféDirect was more market-savvy than other ATOs, it remained at its heart development-centred.

> Our mission statement is to be the leading brand which strengthens the influence, income, and security of producer partners in the south and links them to consumers. When I joined, its focus was on the developmental aspect. We have added the element of becoming a leading brand, which now gives us

more commercial purpose. We also recognise that we can't do it without the consumer (Newman, 2002, interview).

Since her arrival at CaféDirect Newman has overseen CaféDirect's re-branding and the introduction of several new products (CaféDirect, 2002). In 1998, Teadirect, the first non-coffee product, was introduced, this time using another shareholder, Traidcraft, as the supply chain partner for producer support and quality control. In 1999, realising that its roast and ground sales had been declining recently, CaféDirect launched four new roast and ground coffees, three of which were organic: the Organic Machu Picchu Mountain Special, Fresh Ground, the Kilimanjaro Mountain Special, Fresh Ground, the Organic Full Roast, Fresh Ground, and the Organic Decaffeinated Freeze Dried Instant. The success of the single-origin gourmet coffees was a sign that CaféDirect's quality was finally getting up to par with other gourmet coffees. In order to guarantee high quality, CaféDirect not only controls the produce delivered, it also trains producers on the ground. Thus Amen Mtui, for example, coffee taster for the Kilimanjaro Native Co-operative Union (KNCU), spent two months training with Twin and CaféDirect in London (CaféDirect, 2000). This enabled him to be in charge of quality control at the co-operative.

Several key achievements in 2000 demonstrate CaféDirect's success in attaining high quality (CaféDirect, 2002). Firstly, CaféDirect Medium Roast, Fresh Ground was voted 'best coffee' by Best magazine, awarded 5 stars by Prima magazine and voted 'favourite coffee' by the UK's leading consumer magazine. Secondly, in December 2000, AC Nielsen reported that CaféDirect was the fastest growing brand in the UK roast and ground coffee market, while Teadirect had become the fastest growing brand in the UK tea market. And finally, Costa Coffee Shops decided to sell Fairtrade espresso while at the same time switching the majority of its teas to Teadirect.

The increasing quality of CaféDirect's product made possible the entrance of fair-trade coffee to the mainstream market. However, at the same time it also initiated an important trend that would move it eventually away from its fair-trade roots and transform it into something that might best be described as direct trade. The grudging recognition that customers are also important for the success of fair-trade notwithstanding, most ATOs in the late 1990s saw themselves still primarily as development organisations. Their strategy was to make buying fair trade products less difficult and less unattractive for customers (that is, by offering more choice and using traditional distribution and communication channels). However, their consumer appeal largely remained the same: 'When people buy fair-trade products, there's a very heavy element of altruism. There has to be, with the message that we've got. This isn't about what this product does for you, it's about what somebody else gets out of it' (Bretman, 2002, interview). CaféDirect's most important contribution was to turn this appeal on its head.

> For CaféDirect, the thing they absolutely got right from the beginning was the name. There's an implied consumer benefit out of fair-trade. What we've normally said about direct trade is that it helps producers. It puts them in closer touch with the market. It empowers them in their operations. What CaféDirect said was, this is a better coffee because it comes direct from the producers (Bretman, 2002, interview).

Although it took nearly a decade to fully play out, CaféDirect had laid the groundwork for an inversion of the rationale underlying fair trade. Rather than focusing only on the poor producer's benefit, CaféDirect realised that direct trade was also benefiting the customer. By providing long-term contracts and producer education, direct trade allows importers to obtain high quality coffee – year-in and year-out. While most large coffee importers buy coffee beans on the spot market, direct trade has a built-in supply chain for reliable high-quality gourmet coffee.

With a 6 percent market share CaféDirect roast and ground coffee has become the sixth-largest brand and thus has started to register on the radar screen of the commercial players (Wills, 2002, interview). The Co-op UK, for example, lobbied its traditional coffee supplier, Fine Foods International, to buy from registered fair-trade producers, enabling the Co-op to launch its own-brand fair-trade coffee (Hudghton, 2002, interview). Sainsbury's followed suit with its own fair-trade brand soon after (Marketing Week, 2001).

> If you look at Co-op sales in the UK, [...] fair-trade coffee (that is, CaféDirect and other fair-trade coffee brands) used to account for 10 – 11 percent of our total roast and ground coffee sales. But that plateaued and we were finding it

difficult to grow that any further [...] We then introduced an own-brand fair-trade coffee at a lower price but at the same time gave additional promotion to CaféDirect. And in the next year we managed to double our sales. All fair-trade coffees together now account for 20 percent of our roast and ground coffee sales. Furthermore, we will be launching a standard granule fair-trade instant coffee in September 2002. CaféDirect only operate in the top tier, the freeze-dried sector. So fair-trade sales have been limited by the fact that it's only been operating in one segment of the instant coffee market (Hudghton, 2002, interview).

10.3 COLLECTING, MANAGING AND BALANCING RESOURCES

'Fair-trade activists are passionate about "fair" but very ambivalent about "trade"', muses Lawrence Watson (2002, interview). This fuels a constant tension between the aspiration for commercial success and unease with the trade-offs that commercialisation and growth bring along. How did CaféDirect deal with this issue? When Penny Newman came to CaféDirect, she consciously continued and even accelerated the organisation's shift from charity spin-off to ethical business venture, by pushing for more customer focus.

I've led a culture that's much more business focussed. [...] People were shocked I was using [...] words such as 'sales'. The word 'customer' was another term people thought was too commercial. They asked if we were forgetting the producer in this. [...] I sat in my first meeting on fair trade and talked about customers and there was a deadly hush. I couldn't believe it. [...] I was talking about supply chains, about consumers, and you could see people thinking this is too commercial. This isn't the language of fair trade (Newman, 2002, interview).

Ian Bretman, deputy director of the Fairtrade Foundation and responsible for business development, has had similar experiences.

The key to managing an organisation like the Fairtrade Foundation is to manage the tensions...For us, the key objective is [...] to get fair-trade products into supermarkets. And that means approaching companies like Starbucks. But many activists say you can't work with Starbucks. We're even accused of undermining what campaigners are doing. They claim a sort of greenwash, saying we give outfits the label of fair-trade for a little bit of activity. [...] We have to manage that tension. It's not satisfactory to say we won't work with Starbucks nor to say the whole campaign issue has nothing to do with that. We have to manage that and push the big companies to do even more (Bretman, 2002, interview).

Interestingly, concern about a sell-out of fair-trade ideals comes primarily from activists in the developed world. The smallholder producers seem much less perturbed by CaféDirect's commercialisation strategy.

When I travelled to meet our producers, the first thing they wanted to know was about our customers. They made the link straight away. They wanted to know what consumers like, about taste changes concerning freeze-dried. Producers could more than understand the fact that we need to engage the customer. Underlying the fair-trade movement is the sense of anti-globalisation and anti-commercialisation to some degree. Then add the word profit, and a few people would have heart attacks. But at the basis of a trading relationship with producers is profit. Trading is about buying and selling and making money (Newman, 2002, interview).

Yet many fair-trade supporters remain unconvinced. They are concerned that fair-trade standards might be temporarily relaxed when demand outstrips supply from registered producers, thus undermining the reputation of the whole system.

Imagine a marketing manager would say: I need these products in my range to pay for my budget to cover my operating costs. That's where the commercial side of fair-trade has caused problems. Some people see the need for marketing as a bad thing after what's happened to organizations like Oxfam in the early 1990s. It effectively relaxed its own fair-trade standards, arguing that by trading with these people we can improve their systems. There were some very grey areas (Bretman, 2002, interview).

Bringing in new staff into fair-trade groups to manage commercialisation can augment tensions within the organisation. This problem can be overcome through good induction, believes Wills (2002, interview). She identifies two elements: the induction of existing staff and activists as well as the induction of new employees. Concerning the first point, Wills stresses the need to explain to existing staff why change is necessary and what its goals are.

However charitable the existing staff is, they have the fears of anyone, anywhere when it comes to change. So organisations have to do all they can to upgrade skills or find a way for staff to move on in a dignified way, with proper thanks (Wills, 2002, interview).

The re-branding of CaféDirect's freeze-dried coffee as 5065 is a good example of the problems that can arise if activists are not involved in radical change. Focus groups with customers show that the re-branding is a success with the customers. However, the grassroots supporters felt let down. In their eyes the quality message was becoming more important than the fair-trade message.

For the activists, their problem was not understanding what we do. [...] After research in March this year, people said 5065 was associated with quality and modernity. It was fashionable. For activists, loyal consumers, or people who've been with us for years and years, any change is going to be a hard thing to take. We didn't share with them why we made the change right at the beginning. The press got it before we got to them. So our learning is that we need to talk to them from the beginning (Newman, 2002, interview).

Change management in fair rade also needs to focus on the incoming professionals who are supposed to drive commercialisation and lead change.

Don't count on the people you recruit to absorb the culture just like that. You have to be sure that they have the personal qualities as well as the professional skills. The changing organisations need to teach them about the culture they don't want to lose with the change to professional management. [...] In any induction process there needs to be time for the people recruited to spend time with the people who have been there a long time. Learning what it's about, and why the organisation was set up in the first place; [...] what is sacred and what is less so; and to hear the stories (Wills, 2002, interview).

Again CaféDirect is a good illustration for this point, as shown by Penny Newman's recall of her first months at CaféDirect.

I felt the best way to come to CaféDirect was as an outside consultant to share with them more openly, recalls Newman. It was good that I could see it from the outside rather than as the new Managing Director. With me first sitting in three months as a consultant helped me to act as a catalyst for change (Newman, 2002, interview).

One way to manage tension between developmental mission and commercial venture lies in organisational differentiation, bringing in people with different backgrounds and letting them work together on important strategic issues.

I think the board of the Fairtrade Foundation particularly wanted a director who came from an NGO campaigning background, and a deputy director that was a commercially oriented person. We don't work in opposition to each other, it's much more complex than that. But to the outside world, people look at it simplistically and feel you've got both fields represented at the top of the organization. [...] It is [...] allowing the debate to happen within the organization (Bretman, 2002, interview).

Terry Hudghton (2002, interview) had similar experiences at the Co-op. The Co-op's buyers are usually charged with buying at the best price. Obviously this is not a viable strategy for fair-trade products. On the other hand, letting the price spiral out of proportion would make it impossible to attract a large number of consumers to buy it.

I think there is a role for someone like me to play in those negotiations. I don't have a direct commercial role. So I can act as an intermediary behind the ethical position and the commercial position (Hudghton, 2002, interview).

Recruiting different people for different tasks also allows making a point by deliberately inverting roles having the developmental person talk to businesses and the commercial representative talk to activists.

There are times for me to go and talk to activists – which I'm doing on Saturday, going to a campaigners' conference. The fact that I, who's seen as the commercial person, am talking about the value of campaigning creates a different sort of impact than if it were our normal communications people. Similarly, when our director goes and talks to companies about how fair trade can work for them, and the benefits for them, that message also has more impact (Bretman, 2002, interview).

CaféDirect has also experienced tensions with its owners, who do other things for it apart from owning it. They work on the ground for CaféDirect, with Twin managing the coffee supply chain and Traidcraft managing tea. Oxfam helps out on specific projects (Coe, 2002). On the other hand Traidcraft, Oxfam, and Equal Exchange are customers as well. 'So you have some interesting relationships. A clouding of different roles,' says Newman (2002, interview). One way she decided to address these issues was by assigning different people to look after different tasks. Thus in their roles as founders the four ATOs were managed by the financial controller and the managing director; another person was to negotiate their role in CaféDirect's producer support; and yet another person would deal with sales. This allowed each to focus on her or his primary interests without mixing different motivations and expectations. Lawrence Watson judges that the model of separating organisational marketing in CaféDirect and producer support in Twin is 'perhaps the most interesting and holds out the greatest degree of hope for solving the dilemma' (Watson, 2002, interview).

> What turns people on is different in a business than in a socially oriented organisation. It is difficult to imagine co-existence in the same building of professional business-driven, number-smart budget-attentive individuals on the one hand with people who are concerned with social development on the other hand. This can be solved, if we can get a balance where the business entity is owned by a socially driven organisation and can ensure that the operating values are clearly described, then get good professionals and let them do the job. Let them be paid well. Why should it be a sacrifice to work for fair-trade? However, realistically, this probably needs physical organisational distance between the 'charity' and the 'business'. It would be difficult to get someone who was paid $75 000 a year working alongside someone getting paid $25 000 a year for a job as big or bigger in the social sector (Watson, 2002, interview).

10.4 STRENGTHS AND WEAKNESSES OF DIFFERENT FAIR TRADE VENTURES

Several decades lie between the invention of fair trade and its successful application as a commercial venture. In analysing why CaféDirect has succeeded in creating competitive space in the mainstream markets, two entrepreneurial innovations stand out:

- firstly, CaféDirect has seized upon an opportunity that the traditional fair-trade charities had ignored: Direct trade benefits not only the producer, but also the customer, through better quality;
- secondly, by adopting a branding rather than a mere labelling strategy CaféDirect introduced a new business model for fair trade. Rather than leveraging the reputation of a charitable organisation, CaféDirect has built its own brand, which in the UK has become a synonym for directly traded coffee.

CaféDirect's approach has been copied successfully by other fair-trade ventures such as the Day Chocolate Company in the UK, and AgroFair in the Netherlands, and has recently even motivated mainstream retailers such as the Co-op or Sainsbury's as well as food giants such as Kraft and Nestlé to enter the fair-trade market with their own brands. So why had it to be four ATOs that saw the opportunity for CaféDirect rather than the established coffee producers or retailers?

One explanation lies in time dependency. In order to reap the benefits of quality increases CaféDirect had to go through a phase of low quality, in which it had to rely on the traditional fair-trade messages. Thus the association with the four non-profit ATOs helped to build its fair-trade credentials and reputation in the early years.

On the other hand the question arises why the traditional ATOs were unable to achieve on their own what CaféDirect has achieved. While CaféDirect has been profitable since the late 1990s many of the traditional ATOs are still loss-making. Traidcraft turned a small profit only very recently. At Oxfam, sustained losses even led to the decision to stop trading operations and to focus instead on retail, campaigning, and producer support (Fowler, 2002, interview). Similarly gepa, Germany's oldest ATO, has been facing financial distress for some time. These facts seem to indicate that for-profit ventures with a clear commercial vision are better suited for direct trade than charitable organisations.

> When fair-trade organisations get into difficulties, as a number of them have, it is because their systems haven't kept up with change quickly enough. It's partly to do with the skills in the team. Many fair-trade organisations [...] were set up by individuals (sometimes charismatic individuals), who did not have a business background. They got so busy they didn't have the time to learn things and they perhaps didn't always bring in people who had the financial management skills. The organisations often run into cash flow problems as they grow. [...] Many were set up using voluntary labour, which may not be qualified. Also many fair-trade organisations do not pay very well so they find it hard to attract people with the right skills. Some take the decision to upgrade their salaries. But there is that ethos that you shouldn't be earning vast amounts of money if the producers are earning so little. [...] Enthusiasm gets you a long way. But I think once you get beyond two or three million euros, you do need to get proper systems in place. Ideally they would be in place from the beginning (Wills, 2002, interview).

It may be appropriate to close this chapter with a question: Will demand for fair-trade coffee grow, or has CaféDirect reached the limits of its market niche? Experiences with both the roast and ground sales in 1998 and the instant coffee in 2000 seem to suggest that fair-trade products undergo their own life cycles. The launch of roast & ground 'organic' coffee and the 5056 re-branding have given CaféDirect a new push. However, the question remains how large fair trade can grow. Experiences from the Co-op where roast and ground fair-trade coffee accounts for 20 percent seems to suggest that CaféDirect might still have some way to go. Future chapters in the CaféDirect story can thus be expected to remain interesting for academic scholars as well as practitioners.

11. The Sekem initiative: a holistic vision to develop people[1]

Johanna Mair and Christian Seelos

11.1 THE SEKEM INITIATIVE AT A GLANCE

Sekem – the transcript of a hieroglyphic word that means: 'vitality from the sun' – is the name of an initiative that dates to 1977 when Dr Ibrahim Abouleish, after living more than 20 years in Austria, brought his family to his native Egypt to show them the beauty of his home country. What he found was a country in miserable economic conditions and with increasing social problems. Inspired by the anthropomorphic and holistic approach of Rudolf Steiner, he developed the idea to 'heal the land and the people' (Abouleish, 2004). He envisioned an organization that would not only comprise an economic sphere but also a social and cultural one. This was the beginning of an initiative that earned Dr Ibrahim Abouleish the Right Livelihood Award (better known as the 'Alternative Nobel Prize') in 2003. From the press release (Right Livelihood Award, 2003):

> SEKEM (Egypt) shows how a modern business can combine profitability and engagement in world markets with a humane and spiritual approach to people and respect for the natural environment. The Jury sees in SEKEM a business model for the 21st century in which commercial success is integrated with and promotes the social and cultural development of society through the 'economics of love'.

Starting out with the biodynamic cultivation of herbs and spices, as well as medicinal and aromatic plants, Sekem has become a renowned enterprise and market leader of organic food and phytopharmaceuticals in Egypt. Furthermore it is responsible for the nation-wide application of biodynamic methods to control pests and improve crop yields in the production of cotton (Merckens, 2000).

Today, some 2000 people work for Sekem. In 2003 the Sekem group showed revenues of 76 million Egyptian pounds (1€~7EP). Under the umbrella of a holding organization, the group comprises six business companies. Their activities span from packing and distributing herbs and fresh fruits to the manufacture of phytopharmaceuticals and organic textiles. Besides the businesses Sekem has also established and now facilitates the Egyptian Society for Cultural Development (SCD). Through this non-profit organization Sekem supports a kindergarten, the Institute for Adult Training, a Medical Center, various other social and cultural activities, and is in the process of setting up a university. Finally Sekem's path has been marked by the extraordinary support of individuals and the powerful network of partner institutions it was able to develop over time.

11.1.1 Egypt

When Dr Abouleish returned to Egypt in the mid seventies, he found a devastated country. Suffering from a socialist economic system initiated by the former president Gamal Abdel Nasser and the aftermath of the Yom-Kippur War against Israel in 1973, Egypt was struggling to improve living conditions for its population. Reforms to liberalize markets by the succeeding president, Anwar Sadat, put additional stress on living conditions, and income inequality increased, leading to violent demonstrations and riots in 1977.

Although economic conditions have improved, Egypt still has poor health care and inadequate education systems. In 2002, 16 percent of the population was living under the national poverty line, life expectancy was around 68 years and the adult literacy rate was 67 percent for males but 43 percent for females (United Nations Development Program, 2004). Gender inequality is also high.

The agricultural sector is Egypt's major employer accounting for 40 percent of the workforce. However periodic droughts and unpredictable hot, driving windstorms can have a devastating effect on its output. Today only 3.5 percent of the land is actually arable having been dramatically reduced by the completion of the Aswan High Dam, which altered the time-honoured place of the

Nile River in the agriculture and ecology of Egypt. Increasing soil salination, the growing popularity of monocultures and the lack of former flooding which redistributed fertile Nile soils have led to ever increasing use of pesticides and the pollution of limited natural fresh water resources.

11.2 THE BEGINNINGS OF A HOLISTIC VENTURE

Sekem started to take shape when Abouleish bought some untouched desert land on the fringe of the Nile delta near Belbeis, 60 km north east of Cairo. With this bold move he wanted to prove that fruitful land could be claimed back from the desert to produce natural medicines and foodstuffs that are healthy and environmentally friendly. Time and patience as well as continuous learning were essential to face the numerous challenges: securing property rights from the administration for a piece of desert; coming to an arrangement with the once nomadic Bedouin, who had started to settle nearby; pacifying rural communities who adopted a hostile attitude toward the 'intruder'; fighting against the Egyptian army when it occupied the land; and finally ensuring water supply and protection against desert storms.

Before biodynamic cultivation began on a small scale at the 'mother farm', the first three years were devoted to infrastructure preparation: electricity, roads, houses, irrigation systems, a sewer system and many other elements. One of the most important challenges Abouleish had to master was creating a culture for biodynamic agriculture within Egypt. This included transforming skepticism of farmers into collaboration, gaining the trust and support of public authorities, and finally raising awareness among consumers.

Along this journey the question of how to finance further progress also had to be addressed. In this respect Abouleish was able to create and act on opportunities by combining the few available resources in new and meaningful ways. An American company was looking for a provider for a special plant extract. Although Abouleish did not even know the name of the desired substance, he met with the company and won the deal. His expertise in pharmacology was vital in convincing the Americans and planning the build-up of the extraction facilities and machinery. A loan from a local Islamic bank provided essential funding, although this turned out to be another major challenge as the bank cut the deal unilaterally half-way through the startup phase of the project. A lack of contracts and accountability made it difficult to establish long lasting business relationships. Nevertheless, these first commercial activities laid the foundations for Sekem's further development.

11.2.1 Developing the Business Side

The first shipment was sent to the United States in 1981, followed by successful entry into the local Egyptian market two years later. Sekem's operations expanded steadily thereafter in both the domestic and international markets, focusing on three lines of products: phytopharmaceuticals, foodstuffs from biodynamic cultivation and textile products from organic cotton. In 1985, Isis brand herbal tea was launched, both in the domestic market with the support of a strong advertising campaign, and in the international market through German and Dutch companies with which Sekem had established business relations. Sekem distributed its production among four subsidiaries specializing in particular lines: Atos (established in 1986) was a joint venture producing phytopharmaceutical products; Libra (1988) packaged and exported fresh produce to Europe and coordinated organic production; Conytex (1990) manufactured various organic cotton textile products; and Isis packaged and distributed organic cereals, oils, spices, condiments and a wide variety of herbs and teas.

Sekem has been equally innovative and creative in marketing, establishing a chain of shops called Nature's Best to promote and sell organic and health products in the domestic market and also with ten foreign partners in Europe and the United States. A company named Mercury was created to handle local distribution for the Sekem group, and another, named Perfect, was established to provide consultation and general services.

11.2.2 Broadening Impact

The success of the Sekem initiative in the biodynamic cultivation of herbs, cereals and vegetables prompted the Egyptian Government to task Sekem in 1990 with developing a biodynamic cultivation method for cotton. Sekem established the predecessor of what later was to become the Egyptian Biodynamic Association

(EBDA) as a knowledge and learning institution to support and instruct the slowly growing network of farmers in biodynamic agriculture. EBDA was an important success factor for the cotton project.

Cotton was Egypt's most important cash crop. Unfortunately, it was also a magnet for countless insidious pests and one of the world's most pesticide intensive crops. Worldwide, 18 percent of all chemical plant protection active ingredients were used in cotton fields which accounted for only 0.8 percent of the total area under cultivation. In close cooperation with scientists, farmers, consultants and consumers, Sekem developed a biodynamic concept for organic cotton cultivation based on the use of pheromones to control cotton insects. The results were so convincing that the Egyptian authorities officially promoted the methodology. Over the following years, the total use of pesticides in Egyptian cotton fields was reduced to less than 10 percent of the previous amount on nearly the same cultivation area, thus saving about 30 000 tons of pesticides per year. By 1999, these methods had been applied to nearly 80 percent of the entire Egyptian cotton-growing areas. The average yield of raw cotton increased by nearly 30 percent to 1,220 kg per acre and a number of fiber quality parameters were better than those of cotton from conventional agriculture.

11.3 THE SEKEM INITIATIVE TODAY

By 2001, Sekem was organized as a joint stock holding company. All economic activities were under the umbrella of Sekem Holding, which managed the capital and offered centralized services to its subsidiary companies. The holding company was also responsible for positioning the various brands. While all the group companies made their own strategic plans, the holding company ensured that the chosen strategies fitted with Sekem's overall mission. The Managing Director of the holding company was Helmy Abouleish, the son of Ibrahim Abouleish. Sekem had a strong set of guiding principles including: the development of biodynamic methods for all crops suitable for Egypt; the production of high quality products based on a responsibility to the environment; the human oriented marketing of these products; access to development, education and training for all employees; a social framework of cooperation between employees and organizations to promote cultural development in Egypt; and spreading the Sekem idea throughout the country thus providing a base for future generations. These guiding principles were translated into mission statements for all the Sekem Group companies and organizations.

In 2003, Sekem consisted of three main parts (numbers of employees in brackets):

- the Sekem Group: Atos (450); Conytex (260); Hator (51); Isis (100); Libra (240); Sekem Co. (63); Sekem Holding (56);
- the Egyptian Society for Cultural Development (420);
- the Cooperative of Sekem Employees (50).

11.3.1 The Sekem Group

All Sekem firms were autonomous business units, with full P&L responsibility. They were managed by factory or enterprise managers, who coordinated their activities in a weekly strategic meeting as required under ISO 9001. Each company had a monthly management meeting that also was attended by central functional managers at the holding company level.

Demand for Sekem's products grew strongly between 2000 and 2003 and the focus had shifted from export to the local market which, in 2003, was generating more than 50 percent of the revenues. Some of the products were sold under the fair trade label of the Fair Trade Labelling Organization (FLO). FLO was a worldwide standard-setting and certification organization that aimed at strengthening the position of disadvantaged producers and workers in developing countries. Standards stipulated that traders had to pay a price to producers that covered the costs of sustainable production and living; pay a premium that producers could invest in development; partially pay in advance when producers had special needs; and sign contracts that allowed for long-term planning and sustainable production practices.

11.3.2 The Egyptian Society for Cultural Development (SCD)

Established in 1984, the SCD was Sekem's way of reaching out beyond its commercial activity in pursuit of the goal to contribute to 'the comprehensive development of Egyptian society' and to realise 'Egypt's unique contribution to global development'. It was a private nonprofit organization registered as an NGO with the Ministry of Social Affairs. At the core of SCD was an emphasis on people's moral and cultural awareness as a basis for improving living standards. It considered raising individual integrity and consciousness an important part of achieving sustainable development. The SCD initially started with educational programs but had expanded to include the arts and sciences as well. It focused on three fields of activity: education and training, medical care, and the arts.

Through the SDC Sekem set up a private kindergarten, primary and secondary school, and a special needs education program for the children of all employees and the neighbouring community. It also set up a vocational training center to enhance Egyptian workers' skills so that local businesses could meet world market standards in the quality of their products. Opened in 1996 to provide health care for the Sekem community, the medical center turned out to be in high demand; it was soon providing comprehensive basic health care services to around 30 000 people each year from the surrounding villages as well as Sekem. Finally, the Academy was established in 2000 to promote scientific research that served the needs of Egyptian society and to strengthen the links between development-oriented researchers and development practitioners. It was active in the areas of medicine, pharmacy, biodynamic agriculture, sustainable economics and the arts.

11.3.3 The Cooperative of Sekem Employees

Setting up a Cooperative of Sekem Employees (CSE) had two major goals: first, to ensure that the democratic rights and values of co-workers were adequately implemented, and second to educate all members of the Sekem community towards taking responsibility for society.

Sekem's recognition and reward system was designed to ensure that everybody felt part of and understood how she contributed to the overall success of Sekem. Simple initiatives were introduced to underline this message: the employees – assembly line workers, farmers and executives – of every Sekem company met at the beginning of the workday in a circle to report on their current projects and activities. Standing side by side, hand in hand, they prepared mentally for the day ahead and recited a brief text that reminded everyone of the shared values of Sekem. This symbolic ritual not only fostered team spirit, it was also highly effective in encouraging punctuality and work discipline.

11.4 BUILDING A NETWORK OF PARTNERS

From the very beginning Sekem adopted an opportunistic and yet strategic approach, cooperating closely with a number of individuals and partner organizations. Sekem was also innovative in the case where no potential partner institutions existed: it established them itself. Among them were the Egyptian Biodynamic Association (EBDA), the International Association of Partnership (IAP), and the Centre of Organic Agriculture in Egypt (COAE). This collaborative approach allowed Sekem to gather necessary scarce resources it did not have itself and at the same time ensure sustainable impact. Partnering was crucial in building processes, facilities, and trust.

11.4.1 The Egyptian Biodynamic Association (EBDA)

This association was established to promote the organic agriculture movement in Egypt. In 1996 it was registered with the Ministry of Social Affairs as a non-governmental, non-profit organization providing training, research, and advisory services in the field of organic farming. EBDA consultants worked with the farmers, particularly during the transition periods, to ensure efficient implementation of biodynamic methods as well as farm management and documentation to enable their farms to be inspected by national and international auditors. EBDA regularly organized training seminars and workshops for farmers and agricultural engineers and supplied them with seeds and planting materials from plants grown organically in EBDA's experimental farms.

EBDA also performed applied biodynamic research in cooperation with Egyptian and international research scientists to solve any problems the farmers might have with plant nutrition, plant protection and post-harvest conditions and quality. A 'Scientific Committee' coordinated all research activities, and representatives of universities and national and international research centers sat on the board.

EBDA also set up a committee to draw up the 'Egyptian Biodynamic Guidelines'. These guidelines were based mainly on the EU and IFOAM regulations but were focused on the private labelling scheme 'Demeter', an international ecological association that represented about 3000 producers in 40 countries. EBDA's marketing committee developed strategies to introduce organic labels in the local market and support its farmer network with marketing expertise.

11.4.2 The Centre of Organic Agriculture in Egypt (COAE)

The COAE was jointly established by Demeter, the Swiss-based Institut für Marktökologie (IMO), and Sekem in 1990 as an independent inspection and certification body to ensure quality control in line with international standards for organic production. In 1992, COAE was appointed by the Ministry of Agriculture as a private inspection body, responsible for inspecting and issuing organic products to the EU.

11.4.3 The International Association of Partnership (IAP)

The IAP was founded in 1997 by Sekem and eight business partners, most of them European, to foster dynamic interaction between farmers, producers and traders. All the partners worked in different fields of natural and organic products:

- Dr Schaette AG (successor company of Gebrueder Schaette), biological veterinary products, Germany;
- Lebensbaum, organic and biodynamic herbs and spices, Germany;
- Aarstiderne.com, organic fruits and vegetables, Denmark;
- Cotton People, organic clothing, Egypt;
- Piramide, organic and biodynamic herbs and spices, Holland;
- Eosta, organic fruits and vegetables, Holland;
- Euroherb, organic and biodynamic herbs, Europe;
- Organic Farm Foods, organic and biodynamic fresh produce, UK.

The IAP partners agreed to an approach that would combine economic, social and cultural aspects and to develop modern forms of cooperation in three areas:

- economic cooperation, which included the exchange of market information, joint strategic planning, marketing, and joint financing concepts to develop organic movements worldwide;
- social cooperation, referring to the development of a code of ethics as a basis for a modern fair trade concept and to the development of a contractual basis and an arbitration concept to improve cooperation;
- scientific and cultural cooperation to develop new association concepts that clarified the roles of traders, producers, farmers, and consumers including property and asset management and ownership issues, as well as to develop new ways to enhance labour motivation, for example through effective salary schemes or profit sharing.

11.5 ECONOMIC AS WELL AS ENVIRONMENTAL SUSTAINABILITY

Financial viability was key for Sekem to reach its mission of holistic development. The path Sekem chose exemplifies a high level of creativity and resourcefulness. From an early stage Sekem complemented the earned income generating activities of the Sekem group with a professional approach towards applying for external funding and donations for its non-profit activities.

11.5.1 Internal Financing

Efficient management of the Sekem Group companies was essential to ensure financial viability. In 2003, the Sekem Group had revenues of 76.2 million Egyptian pounds (EP), up from 59.7 million EP on the previous year, and earned a profit of 3.7 million EP, up from 2.6 million EP. 5 percent of the consolidated revenues provided financial support for SCD and other non-economic activities. There were plans to increase revenues to 200 million EP by 2005.

SCD schools received 45 percent of their funding from tuition fees and the rest from Sekem and external funds. For the medical center, its status as a recognized partner of health insurance companies was essential in securing funds. About five per cent of patients paid privately for health services, while 80 percent were covered by health insurance. The vocational training center was set up with help from EU grants and aimed to let students produce products that could be sold in the local market.

EBDA was independent from public funding: the members themselves raised the association's financial resources. Farmers and processing companies paid a yearly fee for the services they received. All products sold with the 'Demeter' trademark were charged a percentage administrative fee. EBDA was also using foreign donations to promote organic farming methods in Tunisia, Morocco, Palestine, and Lebanon. The Sekem Academy, a part of the SCD, was almost 75 percent self-financed by acting as an outsourced product development center for Atos.

11.5.2 External Financing and Support

Due to Sekem's explicit commitment to developing social and cultural values, it had access to various sources of financial, social, and human capital. Sekem projects received funding from several development funds: the International Finance Corporation (IFC), Deutsche Investitions-und Entwicklungsgesellschaft (DEG), The Acumen Fund, and the North African Enterprise Development Fund (NAEDF) for example. It also received donations from individuals who often spontaneously decided to contribute and support the initiative. A good example of this was a program in Germany that allowed young men to perform social assistance in foreign countries as an alternative to mandatory military service: it was successfully used by Sekem to set up infrastructure, including the entire internal fiber network for Sekem's intranet. Artists who spent time at Sekem left their mark by contributing wall-paintings, and a German architect helped design the stunning architecture of many of the Sekem buildings. In 1981, a German medical doctor, Hans Werner and his wife Elfriede, met Abouleish during a cultural trip to Egypt. They became very excited about the Sekem vision and spontaneously founded the German Society for Cultural Development in Egypt, a German based institution which became a vital source of financial, in-kind and moral support for Sekem.

11.6 LEARNING POINTS

The purpose of this chapter is to illustrate Sekem's entrepreneurial journey to realise the complex vision of integrated social, economic and cultural development in Egypt. The Sekem initiative exemplifies entrepreneurial value creation along multiple dimensions in a developing country. It developed from a mere vision to a fully fledged multibusiness company with a complex organizational structure comprising both for-profit and non-profit organizations. Remaining true to its vision, Sekem was able to sustain its entrepreneurial character and to grow and develop organically.

The case offers new insights for studying social entrepreneurship understood as activities that aim at creating multiple dimensions of value. It illustrates the nature, role and challenges of social entrepreneurship in a developing country. Some of the most valuable insights include:

- value creation. Sekem explicitly created value in economic (jobs, income, taxes), social (health services, education, social inclusion and self-esteem), and cultural (expression of creativity) terms. An important aspect in this discussion is the role that fair and trusted institutions play in enabling a healthy society. Sekem effectively institutionalized new norms in a number of areas (human rights, labour rights, reduced pesticide use, a system of fair trade) and established various institutions (a medical center, an academy, schools, COAE, CSE) over time. Moreover, the case illustrates how these various dimensions of value creation are interwoven and are necessary to enable broad-scale development and growth. This suggests that merely focusing on one aspect might not have been a sustainable approach in this context. Karl Weick's notion of small wins (Weick, 1984) provides an excellent conceptual framework to analyze how Sekem was able to create value over time. Guided by the vision of Dr Abouleish Sekem isolated and focused on small tangible problems. With the vision as a source of energy Sekem engaged in a series of small steps: it solved problems, felt successful and empowered, and meanwhile built skills and capabilities to address the next problem. Some of these small wins include: finding the land and water; building roads and providing electricity; planting 120 000 trees; building houses; enhancing soil fertility; founding the first small businesses; opening a kindergarten and school; creating an academy and a medical center; and setting up various institutions (the academy, SCD, EBDA, IAP). Finally Sekem provides a wonderful example for a discussion of 'success' in the case of a social entrepreneurial initiative. Traditional financial metrics clearly do not suffice to capture the impact of Sekem;

- the meaning of 'entrepreneurial. Sekem represents a fascinating case to rethink the defining characteristics of entrepreneurship such as resourcefulness, opportunity recognition, innovation, and creativity. For example the case provides interesting insights on the notion of resourcefulness. Across the different phases, Sekem was able to configure its limited resources in ways that allowed it to develop unique capabilities. Also interesting in this context is Sekem's value network, which enabled it to secure valuable resources. Another striking characteristic of Sekem was its ability to recognize and pursue emerging opportunities in the absence of a detailed plan of action. Dr Abouleish was indeed starting with almost no resources except a solid knowledge base, which he used in a systematic way. He had limited capital, could not rely on physical structures, could not count on support from local partners (except for his family) and had no patents or products. However he possessed specific knowledge (pharmacology) and the capability of scientific inquiry and systematic problem solving. Furthermore he could draw from his knowledge of the local context (he grew up in Egypt);

- replicating and scaling activities without losing the social entrepreneurial character. How easy is it to replicate Sekem outside of Egypt? Indeed, it would be very difficult to replicate an initiative like Sekem without the holistic vision underlying it. While replicating Sekem in other developing countries might fail because of a lack of this holistic approach and/or the exceptional leadership of Dr Abouleish another interesting question is whether Sekem could be replicated in the developed world. An important aspect that needs to be taken into consideration here is the fact that SEKEM was able to experiment, explore opportunities, and develop capabilities in the absence of direct competition.

Companies that operate in developed countries however, seldom have a 20-year timeframe in which to form and grow organically. The time dimension is clearly an important aspect to understanding the success of Sekem. Interesting points for the future also revolve around the issue of whether Sekem should scale and how it might do so. Sekem could scale deep by extending its service and product offering to the community it is serving currently; it could scale up its organization by increasing current capacity; or it could scale out by targeting new countries or regions. It is important to note that scaling is not the same as replicating. While scaling might require Sekem to change its business model and alter existing formulas, replicating involves the use of the same model with minor adaptations. Both represent important challenges for the future of Sekem as well as for many social entrepreneurial initiatives worldwide. In 2005, there was no sign of a slow-down in Sekem's growth – either in scale or in scope – as was reflected by two of Sekem's latest projects: the Sekem University and the Sekem Chamber Orchestra. Sekem felt that a number of its social initiatives in the arts and other fields had contributed to Egyptians' development, raising their self-esteem and promoting mutual respect, and that a University inspired by Sekem's philosophy would finally make its vision complete. The idea behind hiring the retired Director of the Cairo Opera to form an orchestra was to spread music from the big cities into the rural areas of the country and to build relationships with European orchestras that were willing to participate in the pursuit of this mission.

NOTE

1. This chapter builds on a manuscript presented at the Business Solutions for Alleviating Poverty Conference at Harvard Business School, December 2005. It has been prepared with the support of the European Academy of Business in Society (EABIS) as part of its Research, Education and Training Partnership Programme on Corporate Responsibility. This Programme has been made possible due to the financial support of EABIS' founding corporate partners, IBM, Johnson & Johnson, Microsoft, Shell and Unilever.

12. Teleserenità®: home-assistance services for non-autonomous elderly people in Italy

Alessandro Marino

12.1 INTRODUCTION: DEMOGRAPHIC DEVELOPMENTS AND EMERGING SOCIAL NEEDS

According to projections by the Ministry of Labor and Social Affairs, Italy is second only to Japan in the international ranking of countries that in the next 50 years will be most affected by population aging (Ministero del Lavoro e delle Politiche Sociali, 2003). The chief causes of this are to be found in the sharp fall in the fertility rate between 1975 and 1985. In other European countries such as Sweden and France, efforts to resolve the problem have followed a strategy of providing incentives for new births to mitigate the demographic impact of the growing number of elderly. If Italy were to align itself with the average European birth rate, the annual number of newborns would remain at its current level (520 000) for the next 30 years, rather than declining to just over 400 000 by 2030. The ratio of over-65s to under-15s would rise from 127 percent today to 140 percent by 2010, rather than to 146 percent if the current trend persists; and rise to only 208 percent rather than 242 percent by 2030 (Ministero del Lavoro e delle Politiche Sociali, 2003).

Regardless of which economic and demographic policies are adopted to achieve a more balanced population, the inescapable fact is that in the near future the elderly population is set to grow considerably. This will be accompanied by correspondingly strong growth in aggregate demand for services for the elderly such as daytime and night-time care in the home and hospital, welfare and health services, nursing assistance and emergency medical aid

(Censis, 2002). The elderly and invalids will increasingly expect to receive assistance in their own homes, and avoid unnecessary hospitalization or accommodation in assisted care facilities.

Italy does not appear to be adequately prepared for the impact of this demographic shift. The national health plan for 2002–2004 draws attention to the delays in creating an efficient network of home-based assistance for the elderly and invalids. Specifically, Italy lacks post-acute rehabilitation and lie-in centers and day-care support centers for the elderly. The country also lacks a system of global care tailored to the health and social needs of the elderly, guiding them through a disorienting maze of services.

Other European nations have already taken steps to create insurance funds to cover the risk of a loss of autonomy. The funds are intended to provide older people who are no longer self-sufficient with sufficient resources to allow them and their families to continue to lead a dignified existence.

The priority functional goal is to develop a form of in-home 'hospitalization'. In other words, all parties benefit if some of the services now provided in hospitals are brought into the home, including palliative care, infusion therapies, dialysis and so on.

Partly as a result of efforts to contain public expenditure, these needs have driven an exponential rise in the supply of private-sector healthcare services. The growth has been further boosted by the fact that the incremental increase in demand for healthcare services is backed by the adequate surplus savings and financial resources of the beneficiaries (Censis, 2002).

This survey of the current state of healthcare in Italy looks at the size and variety of the opportunities available for social enterprises that intend to operate in this sector. Later, we look at how innovative operational models can be used to deliver healthcare services, whether by the public or by the private sector. As regards the private sector, we look in detail at the experience of the social enterprise Teleserenità.

12.2 HOME ASSISTANCE FOR NON-AUTONOMOUS ELDERLY PEOPLE IN ITALY: AN ANALYSIS OF CURRENT DEMAND

We have noted the unquestionable rise in average life expectancy and in elderly people's quality of life. Demographic figures clearly reveal a substantial gap between the duration of biological life and the duration of an active and autonomous existence. Consider, for example, that although average life expectancy for 2020 will rise to 78.3 years for men and 84.6 years for women, the incidence of chronic degenerative diseases and, in general, diseases commonly associated with old age are constantly increasing (Terenziani, 2001). The demand for home assistance is thus increasing in size and scope. Yet the estimated penetration of home care services in Italy is less than 1 percent, compared with a European average of around 9 percent (CNR, 1998). Meanwhile, it is estimated that roughly 10 million Italians channel around €2000 million into supplementary healthcare insurance (ISVAP, 2000). The insurance industry is producing made-to-measure products for the elderly, such as long-term care policies. Insurance companies therefore look forward to the arrival of a larger number of professional and efficient organizations to provide home care assistance. In parallel to this, company funds, funds run by associations of workers and professionals as well as health insurance providers are progressively expanding the range of services they offer customers. Even so, the provision of home-based nursing assistance forms only a marginal part of the services covered by policies, mainly owing to the absence of adequate providers in Italy. Furthermore, budget constraints are prompting clinics, retirement homes, municipal assisted care facilities, local health authorities (for integrated home care assistance) to turn to outsourcing as the best means of obtaining less expensive and more flexible nursing and/or welfare-healthcare services.

Pharmaceutical companies are also in favor of home-based assistance, which offers them a way of selling their products and defending or even widening their profit margins. For them, home care constitutes an emerging retail channel.

To get an idea of the size of potential demand, let us examine some of the relevant statistics (Censis, 2002; ISTAT, 2002; Teleserenità Report, 2002). As of 1 January 2001, there were 14037876 over-60s in Italy. Of these, 8.1 percent received assistance from professionals, so-called 'home helps', who receive their pay directly from the elderly person himself or herself. A further 2.1 percent were assisted by helps paid by members of the family; and 6 percent needed assistance but did not receive it. Consequently, more than 1 400 000 elderly people in Italy were receiving assistance from home helps, and 840 000 require assistance but receive none. Assuming that a person who declares that he or she receives assistance from a help is looked after for at least two hours a day, a quick calculation shows that this person spends around €5400 a year. The resulting global turnover of home-care alone, excluding care in hospitals and clinics, therefore comes to just under €8 billion.

12.2.1 The Structure of the Supply of Services: an Overview

Various different types of operators are currently active in Italy catering to the demand for services that we have examined. We previously observed that the process of service privatization is a central factor. For the time being, the prevailing model seems to be based on the contracting-out of services, in which the state is the source of funding but not the provider of the services themselves. The prevalent model can therefore be described as a form of 'quasi free market' (Terenziani, 2001) still regulated by formal statutory requirements. Only a few isolated cases of innovative private-sector services have been accepted. It is estimated that in Italy today more than 2000 agencies and/or cooperatives deliver services to the elderly. Most of them work with public sector entities either through competitive tenders or private negotiations. Neither the quantity nor the quality of supply, however, is sufficient. The new welfare mix, the system of vouchers for assistance services and the coming de-hospitalization mean that there will soon be little room for improvisation in either the public or the private sector.

The following box offers a brief account of the public sector experience with the Progetto Anziani (Project for the Elderly) organized the Fondazione Monte di Bologna e di Ravenna (see Box 12.1). We then consider the case of Teleserenità®, a private sector company. Both cases are examples of concrete efforts at social innovation in the welfare-healthcare sector.

BOX 12.1 'PROGETTO ANZIANI' BY THE FONDAZIONE DEL MONTE DI BOLOGNA E DI RAVENNA

In line with the new 'welfare mix' principle, the chief aim of which is to augment resources by leveraging every possible synergy with civil society (IRESS, 2000), *Progetto Anziani* was an attempt to systemize all social stakeholders that, in one way or another, provide in-home care for non-autonomous elderly people. The project had a dual objective: on the one hand, to enable households with a dependent non-self-sufficient elderly member to access inexpensive services, and, on the other, to stimulate competition to deliver those services.

The Del Monte Foundation therefore had to operate on two fronts. First, it had to select eligible families in accordance with their needs and issue them vouchers to spend on healthcare services. The innovative element in this scheme was that the benefits were assigned to the caregivers. The underlying principle was that family members (the care-givers) who were willing to dedicate a greater number of hours to looking after their elderly charges would receive vouchers for a value in excess of the price of the services. So, the more committed a family was to providing care, the more it saved on the cost of complementary services. Secondly, the foundation developed a mechanism for selecting and affiliating the providers that would enjoy exclusive rights to deliver services in exchange for the vouchers. Effectively, this meant that private companies wishing to serve customers with vouchers had to undergo a selection process based on the assessment of the quality of their personnel and organization. Following an assessment, a company might receive the right to deliver some, or all, of the services through the assignment of specific 'counter vouchers'. To maintain price competitiveness, reverse tenders were held to assign credits. Every company was free to quote its own price for a service. Based on the prices quoted, shortlists could be made of suppliers from which the customer could then choose.

Both the underlying concept of *Progetto Anziani* and the method it uses for assessing services for non-autonomous elderly people are highly innovative. Faced with the inability of the public sector to cater on its own to the growing and increasingly diversified demand in this area, the foundation developed a system that supplies healthcare from the private sector while minimizing costs and maximizing the resources of the community (Terenziani, 2001, p. 103).

12.3 PRIVATE ORGANIZATIONS FOR THE DELIVERY OF HOME-CARE: THE TELESERENITÀ® EXAMPLE

12.3.1 History

Teleserenità® is a private-sector social network. It provides remote emergency medical response and assistance and care to the elderly and the sick. The company was formed in 1993 on the initiative of Dr Orgero and Dr Facibeni, who realized that qualified home-based social and healthcare services for old people and the sick were lacking. The first Teleserenità service centre was set up in Alessandria and quickly became an established figure in local and provincial social and healthcare services. In 1995, a nationwide project, Teleserenità® Franchising, was launched with a view to attracting aspiring social entrepreneurs. Under this system, social entrepreneurs acquire and apply know-how and operating methods that have been tested by Teleserenità's pilot centre. The entrepreneurs then set up their own local service centers and receive vital operational support from national headquarters. The franchising circuit came into existence at the end of 1996 with the first affiliations. Between 1997 and 2002, 17 main service centers and one satellite centre were established, in addition to the pilot centre located in Alessandria. By 2002, the growth projections for the circuit envisaged a network of 100 affiliates within 10 years.

Teleserenità's management, led by Pierluigi Morelli, therefore encompassed skills focusing on the operation of affiliates, training and management skills for the franchising network, as well as marketing and personnel management skills.

Recently, however, the company produced a development plan that effectively offers a growth model based on the opening of proprietary facilities throughout the country, thus moving away from the franchising model that characterized its expansion in the late 1990s. Below we describe both strategic models and the different business development visions they imply.

12.3.2 The Franchising Model

Teleserenità management believed that the best way of building an extensive healthcare delivery system throughout the country was to develop a network of locally-based affiliates that offered an efficient service based on as standardized a model as possible. The first solution developed by management was to spread the company brand and best practices to third-party social entrepreneurs throughout the country under franchising arrangements. Under the franchising agreement, the parent company would offer potential franchisees:

- a renewable five-year contract;
- exclusive operating rights in areas with 40 000 to 100 000 inhabitants;
- the payment of a one-off franchise fee;
- the monthly royalty payment to the parent company both of a minimum fixed fee and a variable component based on turnover generated from the provision of healthcare services;
- the payment of a fee amounting to 1 percent of turnover (with a minimum amount being set annually) to contribute to the costs of advertising carried out by the parent company;
- initial training and tutoring;
- periodic consulting/refresher courses/support;
- the right to use the brand name;
- the right to exploit all opportunities generated by the parent company;
- the obligation to participate in group agreements and calls for tenders;
- the obligation to comply with the guidelines and quality standards set by the parent company;
- the obligation to refrain from the marketing of services/products other than those envisaged in the franchise agreement, unless authorized.

The company used a number of geomarketing surveys to map out an expansion plan for affiliates throughout the country. Under this plan, national coverage would entail the creation of between 200 and 300 centers. Specifically, it was estimated that the average peripheral centre would service a customer base of around 40 000 inhabitants, and at least one hospital.

12.3.3 The Activities of a Teleserenità Affiliate

The core business of every Teleserenità affiliate was the delivery of hospital and home-based healthcare assistance. It is common practice within hospital structures to offer assistance as a commercial option. For example, the hospitalization of a family member may often require night-time assistance. The most common solution is to engage the services of home helps, who, however, often lack the proper preparation, are not authorized, and are not organized to provide long-term service. The affiliate centers were intended to fill this gap by providing a high quality, organized service by selecting and managing adequately trained healthcare personnel. The same applied for home care. Following hospitalization, or whenever an elderly person begins to become less self-sufficient, the alternative to a nursing home is the provision of care in the home. The affiliate directly supplied and managed the delivery of such care, which must not be confused with the presence of a home help (who usually lives in the elderly person's home and works full-time for a single family).

Another reason for opting for the franchising formula was the belief that it was the best method for establishing the company in a given area and negotiating partnership agreements with pharmaceutical companies, insurance companies, mutual health insurance funds and public and private healthcare providers. For example, in a manner similar to other operators, affiliates sought to forge agreements with municipal water and gas companies for the joint development of remote medical assistance and emergency response systems for private households. The Alessandria branch of the Italian Federation of General Practitioners endorsed the protocol for the management of these services. The potential competitive advantage of Teleserenità's remote assistance system was that whenever necessary the affiliate centre could actively interact with general practitioners, and not limit itself to forwarding written communications, which risked having no follow-up.

Another line of business expansion for the affiliates consisted in becoming authorized providers of services for public and private entities (municipalities, local health authorities, assisted care facilities, complementary home care providers, hospitals, clinics, etc). The competition here consisted of social cooperatives. The idea was to leverage the organizational strength of the company and its ability to guarantee quality both in the services themselves and in related aspects such as punctuality, speed of delivery, and so forth. The business activities needed to accomplish this goal were as follows:

- general management of relations with customers and healthcare operators;
- coordination of the services provided in the local district;
- monitoring of service quality;
- promotion of brand (by means of public relations and advertising) at a local level through local marketing and advertising campaigns planned by the parent company;
- organization of local training courses for healthcare personnel in accordance with the guidelines set by the parent company;
- public relations activities in hospitals, nursing homes and retirement homes.

Generally, the services that Teleserenità affiliates provided to the public, whether on the basis of private agreements or public tenders, were as shown below in Table 12.1.

12.3.4 The Selection of Affiliates

As we have seen, finding, selecting and training potential affiliates were a key task in the Teleserenità business model. To facilitate its accomplishment, the company prepared a list of requirements delineating the ideal profile of the potential social entrepreneur. The ideal candidate had to:

- be a motivated, participatory entrepreneur;
- demonstrate strong motivation and have a high propensity for operating in the social sector;
- believe firmly in the philosophy of franchising;
- know how to work as part of a network and display strong interpersonal skills;
- have excellent organizational, management and coordinating skills;
- be, preferably, between 25 and 50 years old;
- carry out the activities full-time and be willing to commit totally to the job (looking after the local affiliate and remaining on call);
- possess unquestionable moral qualities of integrity and reliability;
- be strongly determined to achieve goals;
- be prepared to commit to continuous training.

Table 12.1 The services of a typical Teleserenità affiliate centre

Assistance Services	Health Services
Personnel hygiene assistance	Nursing care
Meal assistance	Medical care
Motor exercise	Therapeutic support for chronic and acute illness
Daytime and nighttime attendance	Therapeutic support for terminal illnesses
Monitoring and support	Therapeutic training
Remote emergency response and medical assistance	Monitoring and diagnostics
Auxiliary domestic services	Rehabilitation therapies
Home catering	Telemedicine
Tidying up of living space	Delivery of pharmaceutical products

The potential entrepreneur would also preferably have some experience in the assistance sector, although this requirement could be met by training by the parent.

Proposed locations for affiliates had to meet a number of general guidelines. As mentioned above, the user base had to consist of at least 40 000 inhabitants in an area containing at least one hospital. Central districts or frequently used travel routes were preferred and, in any event, the centers were to be situated near hospital and healthcare facilities. Ideally, an affiliate would be housed in a premises with a glass display window fronting the street and an internal floor space of around 30–50 square meters. Furnishings were supplied centrally in accordance with the standards set for the project. The number of staff needed was an estimated 20–30 healthcare practitioners, one internal manager and one manager in charge of dealing with external relations, commercial arrangements and partnerships.

12.3.5 Teleserenità's New Development Plan

In July 2002, the Teleserenità® brand was acquired by Lineassistenza Srl, a company owned by operators in the social assistance and healthcare sector. The new owners, who already had healthcare structures, steered the company towards a new course of development, which is still unfolding, based on a different business rationale from that used in the late 1990s. The development plan has a number of innovative aspects which both derive and depart from past experience. They can be summarized as follows:

- governance: The project for expansion through franchising has effectively been shelved. The accumulated experience of years of operation has persuaded management to internalize the expansion of sales outlets by means of centralized proprietary operations. The main reason for this choice is that franchising poses difficulties relating to the guarantee of adequate standards of quality, corporate identity and branding;
- redefinition of services delivered: the previous range of services has been complemented with other activities such as the transportation of patients and the sale of insurance and parapharmaceutical products;
- new marketing concept: the new mission of Teleserenità is to provide a one-stop shop supplying home services for the elderly. The underlying marketing strategy seeks to increase customers' cost of switching providers through the creation of a dedicated technological channel, namely remote emergency medical assistance. Management decided to supply the remote emergency call devices free of charge because they establish a relationship with customers with a view to securing their loyalty;
- new technologies: under the new development strategy particular attention has been given to internal marketing tools based on new technologies. Specifically, the company has designed a project management platform that uses mobile telephones to manage healthcare personnel: worker shifts and systems for allocating working hours can be managed automatically by means of integrated instant messaging systems;
- new partnerships for development: Teleserenità management

has decided to pursue new strategic and financial partnerships. The new corporate goals require additional skills and external resources in the form of equity capital.

With reference to this last point, the company has focused its search on two categories of potential allies. The first consists of a corporate partner that would use the network to place its own products and services. This might be an insurance company or a small bank that could offer innovative products to the same target segment. Another possibility could be a pharmaceuticals/medical or industrial enterprise that wishes to place its products using Teleserenità as a means of direct access to customer homes. The second category consists of financial partners. The aim here is to find a player capable of financially backing the development of the project. It is essential, however, that the partner provides all-round high-quality management support and a network of useful contacts. Accordingly, the preference has therefore been for institutional risk capital investors.

12.4 CONCLUSIONS

Although the general trend in the Italian public sector is moving towards the decentralization of responsibility for the delivery of healthcare services, it is still too early to claim that a fully fledged private sector of social entrepreneurs exists to provide home-based healthcare to non-autonomous elderly people. Genuinely innovative and sustainable business models are still rare, and the pioneers who introduce them will have a solid and defendable competitive advantage.

A number of observations regarding emerging operational best practices are in order. Operating in this sector effectively means acting as intermediaries in communities whose fundamental characteristics differ considerably. On the one hand, it is necessary to secure the loyalty of the final customer by offering a full package of services that is both competitive and, above all, socially responsible. This implies that final prices must be controlled by modulating margins rather than costs, in accordance with the segmentation of the market. In other words, a successful operator must assume the responsibility of offering services that are differentiated by the spending capacity of customers, yet also meet common standards of quality and ensure the services always remain adequate to the needs they are intended to satisfy. This differentiation may take the form of, for example, the inclusion of optional extras (such as healthcare practitioners with additional qualifications) or the extension of the range of services (such as, in the case of Teleserenità, the inclusion of packages of complementary products).

Second, it is essential to design highly effective systems for staff recruitment, training and management. This is a sensitive issue in view of the developments directly related to it: given that demand outstrips the supply offered by institutionalized services, many households have turned to the 'black market', which is mainly made up of immigrant women. These are people without training, without insurance and without pension cover, with little scope for shift-work and very low wages. The presence of an efficient market for home-based healthcare services would therefore help put the work done by these people on a legal footing, as long as the organizations operating in the sector do not underestimate the difficulties associated with personnel management.

It is worth stressing the importance of partnerships with both public and private institutions. They are only secondarily a constraint, as they are primarily a source of opportunity because they provide the means for the indirect financing of the company's activities without overly weighing on the budget of the customer.

13. Technology social venture and innovation: process at Benetech

Geoffrey Desa and Suresh Kotha

13.1 INTRODUCTION

Technology has great transformative potential but, on its own, is not a panacea for social ills. Despite this recognition, some of the largest active philanthropic organizations in the United States are committed to technology-based solutions to social problems. Similarly, like-minded entrepreneurs are beginning to address social problems through information and communications technology. The World Summit on the Information Society, attended by representatives from 177 countries, portrayed information and communication technology based ventures as:

> Making it possible for a vastly larger population than at any time in the past to join in sharing and expanding the base of human knowledge, and contributing to its further growth in all spheres of human endeavor as well as its application to education, health and science (WSIS, 2005).

This chapter attempts to understand innovation in technology social ventures (TSVs): ventures situated at the nexus of social entrepreneurship and technology innovation. It is based on the following premises (a) social enterprises increasingly develop and use technology to solve critical social problems, and (b) traditional technological-innovation frameworks may not be readily applicable to the social entrepreneurship context. This is because social entrepreneurs operate in a resource-limited context. Although social needs are often clearly defined, the absence of supranormal financial returns precludes financial investment from traditional sources such as venture capitalist and corporate venture funds. Also, technology commercialization usually pursue investment capital backed, for-profit, high growth technology ventures (e.g. Shane 2000; Mowery et al. 2001) and often refrains from social need-driven markets where the motives are balancing financial sustainability (not superior returns) and social impact.

By merging the social and technology entrepreneurship domains, we explicate how a technology social venture (TSV) innovates in a resource-limited context. Specifically, we address the following research question: What role does knowledge-bridging play in this process? Knowledge bridging is a type of boundary-spanning search in which firms apply knowledge from one technical domain to innovate in another (Hsu & Lim 2005). In this process, ideas are used from one technical domain to create innovation in another area. The applicability of the knowledge-bridging concept and its importance has yet to be examined in the context of social entrepreneurship, specifically technology social ventures (TSVs). We show that knowledge bridging is a critical underlying mechanism that enables the formation and the subsequent technological innovation addressed in TSVs.

We study Benetech, a pioneering TSV, which has a demonstrable track record of innovation across multiple technological and social domains. Although this TSV has limited financial resources relative to a typical for-profit technology venture, it draws from a broad community of social workers and technical experts in different knowledge domains to create innovative social products and services. Across eight technology projects (Table 13.1) at Benetech, the company applies knowledge from diverse technological domains to create innovative social products.

We first show how Jim Fruchterman, a technology entrepreneur, employed knowledge bridging to conceive and start Benetech. We then highlight and discuss three knowledge-bridging approaches that Benetech employed to recombine knowledge from diverse, highly technical areas to pursue different social causes. The technical fields spanned include optical pattern recognition, learning disabilities research, data encryption, and statistical analysis, among others.

Through such knowledge bridging approaches, the firm has, in rapid succession, created innovative, low-cost technological products and services specifically designed to target social needs in multiple domains.

Table 13.1 Technology projects at Benetech

PROJECT	DESCRIPTION
Bookshare.org	An Internet library where members of the blind, visually impaired and reading disabled community can legally store and share scanned publications.
Martus	Provides for the creation, ancryption and secure storage of reports of human rights abuses. The system improves the accessibilityof human rights information to help assure that violations will be recorded and those responsible held accountable.
Human Rights Data Analysis Group	Applies information technology solutions and statistical techniques to help human rights advocates build evidence-based arguments.
Route 66-Literacy (ALL-Link)	Internet service providing best-practice reading and writing instruction to student with significant disabilities.
Bookaccess	An initiative delivering digital books to improve access to information for poor and illiterate populations in the developing world.
Landmine Detector Project	Adapts cutting-edge technologies to the needs of humanitarian landmine removal.
Libre	Seeks to bring truly affordable and usable open source software to users in the developing world and schools, nonprofits and government agencies in the industrialized world.
ReadingCam	Developing a prototype device for people with visual disabilities tha can locate, recognize, and speack text found in the general environment.

Source: www.benetech.org, 2005

13.2 BACKGROUND LITERATURE

Entrepreneurship has been defined as the formation of a new venture to create a product or a service of value (Gartner 1988). Entrepreneurship research goes further to examine how, by whom, and with what effects future goods and services are created (Venkataraman 1997). A review of the literature suggests that three factors are important to understanding new venture formation – the entrepreneur, the opportunity, and the mode the entrepreneur uses to exploit the opportunity (Shane and Venkataraman 2000).

Although these three factors have been studied extensively in the 'for-profit' entrepreneurship domain (Kirzner 1997, Shane 2000), it is only recently that they have attracted scholarly interest in the social or 'non-profit' entrepreneurship domain (cf., Dees, 1998; Brinckerhoff, 2000).

13.2.1 Distinguishing Social Ventures and For-Profit Ventures

Social entrepreneurship involves the innovative use of resources to explore and exploit opportunities that meet a social need in a sustainable manner (Mair and Marti, 2004), and two important factors distinguish social ventures from 'for-profit' entrepreneurship ventures. First, mission statements of such new ventures address a social need (or problem) that is either ignored by 'for-profit' sector or not adequately addressed by the government sector. In contrast, 'for-profit' ventures typically highlight the market segment addressed or expected financial returns to the providers of capital, who are often, but not always, venture capitalists. Thus, it is addressing the social need first that forms the defining characteristic of a social venture.

Second, social ventures invariably straddle the boundaries between the 'for-profit' business world and the social-mission driven world of the 'non-profit' organization. These social ventures take on a complex array of forms that include for-profit, non-profit, and intermediate hybrids (Mair & Marti, 2004). Figure 13.1 illustrates, irrespective of the form these ventures eventually take, that social ventures serve three masters by operating at the nexus of public, economic, and social authorities.[1]

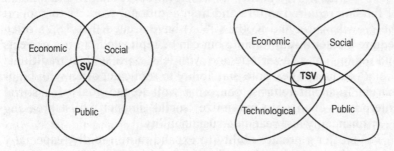

Figure 13.1 Social ventures and technology social ventures

13.2.2 The Emergence of Technology Social Ventures

The TSVs represent a unique aspect of social ventures in that they represent a venture that attempts to meet a social need through a technological innovation. They have, as their core mission, the development and use of scalable technology to serve social needs. As Figure 13.1 illustrates, they represent a boundary-spanning entity situated at the nexus of public, economic, social, and technological domains. TSVs, similar to other social ventures, address the twin cornerstones of social entrepreneurship – ownership (financial return) and mission (social impact); but they do so using advanced technology.

For example, Voxiva represents one such venture. By leveraging the web, phone, fax, email, and text-messaging, Voxiva has deployed a technology solution to track diseases, monitor patients, manage programs, report crime, and respond to disasters in many regions of the developing world (Casas, Lajoie and Prahalad 2003). Voxiva's solution is a real-time data collection, analysis, and alert system that combines established telecommunications networks with decision support and structured communication and information sharing systems. The founders of Voxiva have backgrounds in information technology, public health, non-profit development, and humanitarian law. They drew on their multiple knowledge domains to envision, start, and grow this specific venture.

TSVs differ from traditional social ventures in some unique ways. Traditional social ventures are driven by human-power and principally scale with the number of volunteering and employed social workers. This ability to scale is proportional to the amount of funding required to hire and train additional workers to support the growth. Desa and Kotha (2005) have argued that TSVs often require greater initial funding but can be replicated (across projects and regions) at a faster rate and with less expense than traditional social ventures. They note that ability to replicate, often with high-margin financial returns, conforms well to the goal of a social enterprise, which is to maximize 'social' impact whilst breaking even financially and reaching sustainability.

TSVs offer a greater ability to expand more rapidly, especially those built on opportunities that involve high fixed costs and low marginal costs (e.g., IT-based solutions or vaccines for disease prevention in developing nations). Creating the original unit incurs the majority of the cost of a technology-based product: every additional unit has relatively low replication costs (Shapiro and Varian, 1999). However, such ventures face significant financial challenges in developing technology solutions to meet social needs.

The high fixed costs required to develop the technology to initiate the venture have important implications. They necessitate financial resources that are typically larger than those needed to start a traditional social venture. Although the needs for the service or product are relatively straightforward to demonstrate, gaining venture capital backing for a social venture is extremely difficult because venture capitalists tend to focus on financial and not social returns. And as Bhide (2000, p.145) argues, 'every venture VCs invest in must hold the promise to provide returns in the tens of millions of dollars, rather than in the tens or even hundreds of thousands of dollars'. In other words, the market need and target segment addressed by the technology social entrepreneur do not attract funding from VC sources.

Additionally, advanced technologies developed in university or private research labs are often proprietary and protected by an array of copyrights or patents. Licenses to use such technologies are difficult to obtain because universities or private labs require that the entrepreneur demonstrate a large and viable market (with good future revenue streams) before a license can be awarded. Further, since many of these technologies represent advances in basic sciences, they need more nurturing and development before they can be deployed in a market setting. Translating such embryonic ideas to marketable products requires access to specialized technical expertise that most technology social ventures do not possess. Hence, it is not surprising that most technology commercialization processes pursue the well-established 'for-profit' track and seek VC funding to get started (e.g. Shane 2002; Mowery et al. 2001). This raises an interesting question about how technology social ventures originate and grow.

How does a resource-limited technology social venture develop and deploy advanced technology to address a known market need? While the technology related costs can be partially mitigated by building ventures on top of existing technology infrastructure (Fruchterman 2004, Peizer 2001), we contend that knowledge bridging is the process that enables technological innovation in the social venture domain.

13.2.3 Knowledge Bridging and Innovation

Knowledge bridging is a type of boundary-spanning search in which firms apply knowledge from one technical domain to innovate in another (Hsu and Lim 2005). In this process, ideas are used from one technical domain to create innovation in another area.

The creative application of knowledge across technical domains has been researched not only across disciplinary lines, but also across levels of analysis, including the idea or invention level (Fleming 2001, Hsu and Lim 2005), the product level (Katila and Ahuja 2002), and the firm level (Kogut and Zander, 1992).

At the risk of oversimplification, we note that much of this research pertains to the 'search' literature (March and Simon, 1958), where the primary focus is on new knowledge creation. In the search literature, firms build their knowledge base by recombining knowledge gathered either through local or distance search (March 1991). Whereas local search produces re-combinations of familiar knowledge and is often the mode used by firms (Cyert and March, 1963), distant search helps generate combinations of unfamiliar knowledge with knowledge residing within a firm. Research has shown that distant search is critical in reconfiguring a firm's existing knowledge and capabilities (Nagarajan and Mitchell, 1998). In other words, the type of search a firm uses can impact its ability to innovate (Katila and Ahuja, 2002). But the applicability of the knowledge-bridging concept and its importance is yet to be examined in the context of social entrepreneurship, specifically technology social ventures (TSVs).

In the following sections, we illustrate how knowledge-bridging is used by our focal technology social venture, Benetech, to create innovative technological products in a resource-constrained environment. The technical fields spanned by Benetech include optical pattern recognition, learning disabilities research, data encryption, and statistical analysis, among others. The TSV created innovative, low-cost technological products and services designed to target multiple social needs in rapid succession by drawing from mature technical fields.

13.3 METHODS

To understand innovation within a technology social venture, we deliberately chose Benetech, a pioneering technology social venture based in Silicon Valley. The firm has been the recipient of numerous social venture industry awards including the Skoll Award for Social Entrepreneurship and the Schwab Foundation Award for 2003. In the same year, the firm was awarded one of 20 Social Capitalist awards from Fast Company, Inc, and was the only technology organization to receive an award. The awardees were selected from a list of 117 top social entrepreneurs, and were evaluated on entrepreneurship, innovation, social impact, aspiration, and sustainability (Dahle, 2004). For these reasons, Benetech may be considered to be an exemplar entrepreneurial organization developing technology for social purposes and can thereby serve as the role model for new firms aspiring for similar outcomes. In other words, it represents a revelatory case (Yin, 1994).

The projects undertaken by the firm appear in diverse fields of social entrepreneurship, for example, human rights, education, literacy, disability access, civic participation, and the environment (Table 13.1). We started with a broad research question, asking how a single technology social venture was able to develop useful products across multiple social domains. Following guidelines for inductive research, we were as descriptive as possible until major themes emerged from the data (Kotha 1998, Tsoukas 1989). As 'knowledge-bridging', a promising technology innovation theme, emerged, we used multiple sources of data and within-case analysis to understand the role knowledge-bridging played in Benetech projects.

Types of archival data (from Benetech's inception in year 1999 to 2005) analyzed include newspaper articles, an independent non-profit study, project summaries, business plans, press releases, non-retrospective quarterly data from the president, blog summaries of meetings (captured by independent participants), and archived public speeches and presentations. We supplemented this data with interviews with project leaders at Benetech, including the company founder. We periodically returned to the literature on innovation to develop the categories of knowledge bridging, which were grounded in our observations of the technology social venture.

13.4 INNOVATION AT BENETECH

Jim Fruchterman founded Benetech in 1999 on the recognition that most big companies do not address small markets. Benetech as conceived by Jim is a non-profit venture that combines the impact of technological solutions with the social entrepreneurship business model to help disadvantaged communities. Jim has modeled Benetech as a technology incubator where a company team and the board decide to fund the initial technology and business development plans for different ideas in the social entrepreneurship domain. Depending on the venture, the finances are either obtained from an internal unrestricted operating budget or from external corporate, public, or private funding sources.

The genesis of Benetech relates back to Arkenstone, Jim's first social venture.[2] Jim, drawing from his optical character recognition technical expertise, founded Arkenstone in 1989 to develop reading tools for people with disabilities. Over a decade, the venture had grown to provide reading tools in 12 languages to 40,000 people in 60 countries. With the money in his pocket from the sale, and with time to spare, Jim founded Benetech in 1999 with a goal of spreading the original Arkenstone model to other fields, all with the common thread of technology in the service of humanity. While actively looking for opportunities worthy of pursuit at Benetech he chanced upon an idea that blossomed into the Bookshare.org initiative.

13.4.1 Case Illustration 1: Bookshare

Early in January 2001, Jim came home after a long day at Benetech. Stopping by to say hello to his teenage son, he noticed a program called Napster[3] running on his son's computer. A quick demonstration later, he was completely intrigued by the music and file sharing program which allowed users to access and share thousands of files. The acting CEO of Napster happened to live two doors down and so Jim got the opportunity to talk to her about Napster. Recalls Jim: 'That's pretty cool, I thought. What if you can do something similar for digital books? Perhaps an online digital book distribution service for the blind?' Out of this chance encounter came one of the first product ideas for Benetech – the Bookshare initiative.

13.4.1.1 Recognizing the opportunity

Jim conceived Bookshare as a subscription service providing an extensive online library of accessible digital books to United States residents with print disabilities. Print disabilities represents a condition where people affected by the condition are unable to read print materials due to vision, physical or cognitive disabilities. Jim was vaguely aware that less than 5% of published books were available in accessible formats to people of print disabilities, mostly in Braille or four-track audiotape. In an effort to increase the number of published books available in accessible format thousands of schools and tens of thousands of individuals in the blind, visually impaired and reading disabled community used computers to scan books into digital formats. The process was slow and time consuming with each book requiring the investment of several hours of scanning.

Jim was also familiar with the National Library Service for the Blind and Physically Handicapped of the Library of Congress (NLS) and Recording for the Blind and Dyslexic (RFB&D) that offered high-quality digital book services. However, since contract narrators at NLS and volunteers at RFB&D recorded the audio books, the cost per book was quite high because of quality control requirements. This approach severely limited the availability of books in the desired format.

Two governmental agencies were involved in providing this sort of service, but no 'for-profit' entrepreneur perceived this domain as an opportunity worthy of pursuit because the potential financial returns were limited, given the size of the market. In contrast, Jim wondered, what if he provided a vast library of low-cost scanned books instead of a small library of high-quality digital books? With Jim's solution acting as an accessible 'Napster meets Amazon.com', he hoped to revolutionize book access for people with disabilities by acting as a pioneer in delivering accessible digital books.

13.4.1.2 The Benetech solution

Following this epiphany, Jim modeled Bookshare as a cross between Napster and Amazon. He conceived of Bookshare as a subscription-based online file-sharing community that enables the upload and download of digital books exclusively for use by people with print disabilities. By providing a central repository, the same materials need not be scanned over and over again but can be accessed by any Bookshare member.[4] The member-scanned book collection was stored on a centralized server at Benetech and was appropriately named Bookshare.org. A nationwide group of volunteers contributed scanned books, using an online interface to process them and decide which to recommend for approval by staff. Each digital book was processed to ensure that minimal character recognition quality guidelines were met before being added to the collection.[5] An extensive digital rights management plan including encryption, digital watermarks and digital fingerprinting protected against copyright infringement.

To create such a low-cost system that provided more accessible books than existing governmental agencies, Jim had to not only draw extensively from his deep experience in optical character recognition technology, but also from other technical domains such as digital rights management, website and database expertise, and print-disabled software and hardware expertise. Yet, the combination of these different domains only occurred when Jim, with his prior experience in optical pattern recognition and print disabled software, came across the Napster service by a chance encounter. Once Bookshare began gaining traction, Jim and his team at Benetech began looking for other social ventures to add to their portfolio.

13.4.2 Case Illustration 2: The Martus Venture

One area of keen interest to Jim and others at Benetech was the human rights domain. While looking in to this field, the team became aware that grassroots NGOs needed a tool to collect, organize, and securely store narratives that describe human-rights violations. The most effective weapon against human-rights abuses was the timely and accurate distribution of information about such violations.

13.4.2.1 A systematic search for product specifications

In early 2001, Marc Levine, a project manager at Benetech, visited human rights activists in Sri Lanka, Cambodia and Guatemala. His objective was to gain insight into the need for technology in the human-rights domain, and for specific input for a potential Benetech solution. He and the team he led discovered that testimonies taken by human rights groups often got lost, files were destroyed when people got arrested, computers got seized, or termites ate paper files. What workers needed most was a secure, simple way to manage and store information on abuses. Jim, Marc and a few others at Benetech, drawing from their past pattern-recognition experience, initially thought of documenting human-rights violations via sophisticated technological solutions such as satellite imagery and spy drones. However, after talking with human-rights workers in the field, the need for a more practical approach emerged.[6] The team learned that information collected by NGOs on the field was the core product of the social-justice sector, and often this information was lost to outside forces such as confiscation and destruction or through neglect due to resource limitations. In response, the Benetech team developed Martus, their first TSV product for the human-rights sector.

After systematic understanding of the issue, the Martus prototype was aimed at the grassroots activist with the skills to use e-mail and the World Wide Web. The Benetech team led by Marc built an information and documentation management system based on client software and Internet-based infrastructure. The prototype consisted of a simple and secure application with an e-mail type of interface for gathering, organizing and backing up the documentation of human rights abuse around the world. Additionally, any information earmarked as public was published to a human rights information search engine on the Internet. The Martus prototype provided human-rights grassroots teams with power over their own information, allowing them to decide what to make public and what to keep securely private.

13.4.2.2 The Benetech Solution

Martus reached a need in a particularly difficult social domain that was apparently known to many who worked in the field of human rights. Although there existed numerous organizations (for example, Amnesty International and Human Rights Watch) dedicated to the dissemination of human-rights information, there was no simple, secure documentation system available to field workers gathering information on human-rights abuses. The local human rights groups did not have the resources to buy off-the-shelf commercial software that could be then modified to fit their need nor did they have the expertise to develop the requisite tools themselves. Also, since the market for a tailored solution was rather limited, no commercial entity came forward to produce a software product to meet this rather apparent need – an easy-to-use, and inexpensive software solution with secure encryption capabilities suited for fieldwork.

Martus existed through a unique combination of sophisticated technology and social venture business savvy. Software development costs for Martus were borne by philanthropic groups including Benetech, and third-party organizations interested in the dissemination of human-rights information such as the media, members of the academic community, concerned citizens, activists, and international human rights NGOs. With the Martus project underway, the Benetech team turned their attention to another project that drew on their growing competences and skill base in information technology and the Internet-based delivery of services – Route 66 Literacy project.

13.4.3 Case Illustration 3: Route 66 Literacy (ALL-Link)

The genesis of this project was a strategic alliance formed in 2003 between Benetech and the Center for Literacy and Disability Studies at the University of North Carolina (UNC).

The idea was simple: To provide best practices reading and writing instructions to students with significant disabilities.

13.4.3.1 Recognizing the opportunity

Although students with significant disabilities could learn to read and write, 70–90% lagged behind their peers in literacy learning. Students with autism or Down syndrome, for example, learned in a number of different instructional settings – from special classes in special schools (for example, resource room settings) to regular classrooms in regular schools.

The need to address this concern was especially critical because special education teacher preparation programs did not provide any training to teach children with significant disabilities to read, and existing commercial learning tools and materials were often inadequate.

High-interest, low-level reading materials were often not available below the second grade level and this shortage frustrated efforts by teachers to engage beginning readers.7 Market research at Benetech showed that over 800,000 public school students in the U.S. were identified with prevalent developmental disabilities. Once again the need was clear, but no commercial ventures supplied products or services to address this need.

Literacy researchers and educators realized that low-cost universally accessible instructional materials were required to address the need for disability access to literacy. The solution required knowledge from at least two distinct domains, instructional materials on literacy for the disabled, and a web-based platform to deliver the instructional materials to a wide audience at a low cost. The resulting Route 66 Literacy project was designed as an Internet service providing best practices reading and writing instruction to students with significant disabilities. Moreover, the alliance between Benetech and UNC leveraged the expertise of these two organizations to find a low-cost solution and unlock this important market segment that commercial enterprises were reluctant to enter.

13.4.3.2 The Route 66 Literacy Solution

The alliance between Benetech and UNC enabled the development of a commercial prototype for Route 66's first product, ALL-Link. The alliance helped move it from a research prototype toward an innovative product that could potentially reach large underserved markets. ALL-Link drew from initial research and prototype development by UNC researchers Dr. Erickson and Dr. Koppenhaver, and was specifically designed to address the needs of adolescents and young adults with developmental disabilities.[8] Additionally, Benetech obtained a $50,000 grant from a California-based community foundation to further the prototype and develop a business plan for literacy technology. Benetech executives identified the market as public school students with developmental disabilities in need of better literacy education. As part of the agreement with UNC, Benetech transferred the ALL-link prototype built with the active assistance of researchers and students at UNC and 'web-enabled' it.

The ALL-Link interface for the Internet addressed the literacy learning needs of individual students and supported the instruction given to them by their teachers, even if these individuals had no teacher training or experience. In early testing ALL-Link generated impressive results and received positive feedback from both teachers and students with severe speech and physical disabilities in 28 schools across the country.

13.5 DISCUSSION

The purpose of this chapter was to understand how a technology social venture (TSV) innovates in a resource-limited context and what role knowledge bridging plays in this process. We defined knowledge bridging as boundary-spanning search in which firms applied knowledge from one technical domain to innovate in another. We focused on Benetech and its ventures to understand how entrepreneurs bridged technical knowledge from different domains to create ventures that focused on social (as well as financial) aspects. In the process, Jim and his team at Benetech opened up markets that were not pursued by 'for-profit' enterprises.

Earlier we noted that numerous scholars have implicitly or explicitly used the concept of knowledge bridging in the innovation and search literature (March & Simon, 1958). The search literature has primarily focused on the types of searches undertaken by firms and has examined the impact of search type on a firm's ability to innovate. Research from this literature has shown that 'distant' search is critical to reconfiguring a firm's existing knowledge and capabilities (Nagarajan & Mitchell, 1998; Katila & Ahuja, 2002).

Using this understanding as our point of departure, we examined knowledge bridging in the social entrepreneurship domain to describe how mature technologies in different domains were combined to create innovative solutions to well recognized problems. Using Benetech as our revelatory case, we show how this manifestation of knowledge bridging translates into opening markets that traditional 'for-profits' have ignored or are unable to enter. Each of the three TSVs – Bookshare, Martus, and Route66 Literacy – required extensive knowledge bridging from multiple technology domains to satisfy customer needs in their particular markets (see Table 13.2).

In each case the social needs were clear but the market was neither large enough to support a for-profit venture, nor was the technology solution readily apparent to traditional non-profit organizations. Each case presented an opportunity for a socially oriented technology entrepreneur to find a low-cost solution that enabled the firm to provide a viable solution to the needs identified. Our analysis shows that the technologies that are employed are well-developed (and are often mature), and require little investment for further development for application in the new context. Each venture also illustrates different approaches to knowledge bridging as discussed below.

13.5.1 Bookshare Venture

In this first case, we observed that in order to create a web-based system that supplied books in digital format to people with print disabilities, knowledge-bridging had to occur from at least four distinct technological domains:

- optical scanning and character recognition to convert hardcover books to digital format;
- digital rights management software to prevent copyright infringement;
- an e-commerce website and database expertise to manage a centrally located content server;
- print-disabled software and hardware to allow users to access the digital books.

Table 13.2 Comparing models

Project	Bookshare	Martus	Route-66/Literacy
Project Description	Web-based system that supplies books in digital format to people with print disabilities	Software, secure server and search engine to preserve records of human rights violations	Web-based service providing reading and writing instruction to students with significant disabilities (Autism/Down Syndrome)
Technology Domain 1	Optical scanning and character recognition	E-mail client / server	Literacy and adaptive technology educational research
Technology Domain 2	Print disabled software formats, screen reading software and hardware	Data encryption	Mass-customized digital reading and writing instructional material
Technology Domain 3	Digital rights management	Secure data storage and backup	Interface with print disabled software formats, screen reading software and hardware
Technology Domain 4	E-commerce website and database expertise	Database search and data analysis expertise	E-commerce website to deliver services and database expertise

Interestingly, the combination of the above domains occurred only when Jim came across the Napster software by a chance encounter. Through this chance encounter, he was able to conceptualize a social venture that represented a cross between Amazon.com and Napster. Bookshare was conceived through the fortuitous combination of different technological domains within the social context where the need was readily apparent. Jim's background technical experience in optical character recognition reading machines, and experience with the Arkenstone non-profit organization helped him recognize this social opportunity.

This 'unintentional' knowledge bridging is akin to Kirzner's (1997) notion of 'entrepreneurial alertness'. He described alertness as an 'earlier sheer ignorance, a receptive attitude to available (but so-far overlooked) opportunities and an ability to correct for the earlier ignorance' (Kirzner 1997:72). The entrepreneur becomes aware of the significance of potential new combinations that are critical to the process of discovery (Table 13.3). This example also represents the 'discovery view' of entrepreneurial opportunity (Dew et al., 2003) where opportunities tend to be discovered through an inductive process. One of the important characteristics of the discovery view of entrepreneurship is that only one side of the 'supply-demand' equation exists a priori. In this case, the need for accessible books for the disabled was apparent, but the 'supply' had to be discovered before the product and service to address that need could be created.

13.5.2 The Martus Project

Similar to Bookshare, the Martus project required knowledge-bridging from at least four distinct technical domains:

- e-mail client/server expertise to build a reporting tool;
- data encryption to keep transmitted information secure;
- secure data storage and backup to prevent loss or unauthorized access to sensitive human rights information;
- database search and data analysis expertise to rigorously analyze systematic occurrences of violations to provide legal evidence.

Table 13.3 Comparing discovery views

Benetech projects: combining technological solutions from other domains	*Bookshare.org*: Combines online file-sharing with optical text recognition to create a digital book library	*Martus*: Combines email client/server with secure encryption and database search to create a secure searchable archive of human-rights violations	*Route 66/Literacy*: Combines literacy research for disabled students with print-disability based software formats, and mass-customized digital instructional materials
Knowledge-bridging incident	Bookshare.org founder comes across online file-sharing by chance	Martus product managers conduct field research among human-rights workers while the prototype is developed	Benetech and the Center for Disability Services at UNC enter into a strategic alliance to develop an online literacy product
Knowledge-bridging mechanism	Unintentional	Systematic search	Strategic alliance
Description	An earlier sheer ignorance, a receptive attitude to available (but so-far overlooked) opportunities and an ablity to correct for the earlier ignorance	Through target-market research and expert opinion, knowledge corridors are explored with the intent of finding feasible product solutions	Different but complementary technological resources owned by one organization that are beneficial in the operations of the partner through an alliance
Example literature	Kirzner, 1997	Fleming, 2001; Hayek, 1945	Mowery, Oxley, Sillverman, 1998

In contrast to Bookshare, the knowledge bridging combinations that resulted in the Martus prototype were a result of 'systematic' search by members of Benetech. The Benetech team decided which technology domains to draw from after systematically searching for a viable product that met the needs of human rights groups. While some software development expertise was available in-house, Benetech enlisted the help of encryption experts and a human rights data analysis expert to develop the product.

Systematic search for a solution to known problems is a learning process through which firms respond to changes in their environment (Baum, Li & Usher, 2000, Fleming 2001). Using systematic knowledge bridging, firms can develop new competencies and improve current skills and technologies in order to adapt to the changes. As in the case of the Martus project, knowledge creation is a recombinant process that comes about when different streams of knowledge are purposefully brought together in search of a solution to a known problem. Such recombination involves combining known components of a firm's knowledge base, or combining known components with new, external knowledge (Katila & Ahuja 2002). Both such types are likely to result in an accretion to the firm's knowledge base. In the case of the Martus project, the Benetech team used directed search to draw from multiple technology domains and develop software and encryption capabilities to address the needs of human rights groups.

13.5.3 Route 66 Literacy

Product development for the Route 66 Literacy prototype required a combination of knowledge from multiple domains of expertise:

- literacy and adaptive technology educational research;
- mass-customized digital reading and writing instructional material;
- the ability to interface with print-disabled software formats, screen reading software and hardware;
- website delivery and database expertise.

Neither the UNC nor Benetech on their own had such expertise to provide innovative online literacy product, but by joining forces they were able bridge knowledge from multiple domains to provide a solution.

This observation is consistent with what others have found in the literature on strategic alliances. First, strategic alliances are an important tool to promote inter-firm knowledge bridging (Mowery, Oxley and Silverman 1997). Second, the organization's capacity for learning from its alliance partner depends upon its endowment of relevant technology based capabilities when entering the alliance (Cohen and Levinthal 1990). Third, knowledge-transfer may not merely be dependent on the alliance, but also on the level of pre-alliance overlap between the two organizations, technological capabilities (Mowery, Oxley and Silverman 1997). The Route 66 Literacy case shows that each alliance partner had relevant technology-based capabilities; Benetech had useful software programming capabilities, while UNC had experience with literacy research for disabled students. The development and transfer of the ALL-link prototype helped create the overlap between the two organizations' capabilities.

13.6 CONCLUSION

The challenges for technology social enterprises are numerous. A social venture must be able to communicate its mission effectively, establish its legitimacy in multiple domains, maintain low costs and financial sustainability, monitor the evolution of social needs, and innovate in service delivery (Desa and Kotha 2005, Borzaga and Solari 2001). Under these resource constraints, that knowledge bridging is a particularly important mechanism for meeting needs is readily apparent, yet the solutions for meeting all those needs are not quite so apparent.

- technology social ventures (TSVs) are a unique form of social enterprise. The requirement to create technologically innovative replicable products at a low cost presents unique challenges;
- TSVs can employ 'knowledge bridging', a type of boundary spanning search, to innovate in resource limited environments;
- knowledge-bridging mechanisms can include unintentional discovery, systematic search and strategic alliances;

- unintentional knowledge-bridging draws on the advantage of spontaneous discovery at a particular time and place, but it can be hard to predict a priori;
- systematic search enables TSVs to explore solutions that specifically target a social need but comprehensive search can be resource intensive and is rarely undertaken;
- strategic alliances allow complementary technological assets to be efficiently leveraged to build unique innovative combinations but execution can depend on the prior level of technological overlap between the two organizations.

NOTES

1. Social authority represents the communities, voluntary organizations and corporations which operate in the same field as the focal venture. Public authority refers to regulatory government organizations that represent and aim to protect and promote public welfare, while financial markets represent the economic authority (Shaw and Carter, 2004; Leadbeater 1997; Mair and Noboa, 2003).
2. Prior to his foray into the social entrepreneurship domain, Jim was involved with some 'for-profit' venture. Jim had co-founded Calera Recognition Systems, a manufacturer that developed and marketed a line of optical character recognition machines, in 1982. Following this venture, he co-founded RAF Technology in 1989, which created mail address-recognition systems eventually used by the U.S. Postal Service.
3. Napster, originally created by Shawn Fanning in mid-1999, was an online-file sharing program that allowed users to share music files and search for music from a large centralized database.
4. This service offers blind, dyslexic and other disabled individuals instant access to a large and growing library of digital books. The resource is built by directly involving members and hundreds of volunteers in growing and improving the collection, and by involving publishers and authors who donate original digital versions of their books to help increase access to literacy.
5. To gain access to the Bookshare collection of copyrighted books, users must register at the website, buy a subscription and submit proof of a qualifying disability. Once this information is processed, they can log onto Bookshare.org and begin searching for books or browsing the collection. After choosing a book, they can download it in the format of their choice and then decrypt and read it using free software provided as part of their subscription.

6. Based on feedback from NGOs on the field, the Benetech team found that such workers did not want fancy sophisticated technology. The needs were rather more mundane; they had a difficult time managing and preserving text documents cataloguing abuses, and transmitting this information to the appropriate destination was a slow and expensive process.

7. Commercial electronic learning products did not effectively combine reading comprehension, word study and writing instruction. Moreover, it required the user to already know how to read and write, thus providing information but not building basic literacy. The need was especially acute in public schools, where software costs were a key barrier to adoption of the commercial available software despite its limitations.

8. ALL-Link provided a comprehensive, universally accessible, age-appropriate instructional program that supported and motivated literacy learning. ALL-Link's balanced set of exercises in reading, word study and writing were built around high interest subjects which allowed each student to personally address his or her strengths and weaknesses by engaging in sustained, self-selected and varied repetition.

14. The NYC Watershed agreement: sustainable development and social entrepreneurship

Joan Hoffman

14.1 INTRODUCTION

Watershed collaborations provide experience in the practical problems of achieving sustainable development because they entail simultaneous consideration of economic and environmental goals, albeit through the lens of water quality concerns. In contrast to broad macroeconomic problems such as unemployment (Cook et al., 2003), the challenges of watershed collaborations are natural milieus for social entrepreneurs. The term social entrepreneurs here refers to innovators who tackle social problems not addressed by existing organizations, creating social value in the process and producing new multi-sectoral organizations (Davis, 2002; Johnson, 2000).

The economic concept of externalities, or impacts of market transactions on third parties, can be extended to describe the need for social entrepreneurs. Transactions undertaken not only by market but also by government, community and existing non-profit participants can create external costs or fail to account for available benefits resulting from their actions. The new organizations fostered by social entrepreneurs are designed to internalize consideration of these externalities. Social entrepreneurship can emerge from any sector. Watershed collaborations can be said to arise not only because decisions on water use in each sector have external impacts on water quality in other sectors, but also because government decisions about how to protect water quality have external impacts on businesses and community costs. Collaborations require the creation of new social organizations to address the hybrid goal of enhancing the health of both the water supply and the local economy.

The drive to collaboration can be spearheaded by persons from any of the involved sectors, but success is likely to require innovative and entrepreneurial leadership from all participating sectors. Collaborations are geographic organizations whose borders do not correspond to historical political boundaries. Social entrepreneurs creating collaborations must forge a system of cooperation among diverse stakeholders that is essentially a system of networks. The study of networks has demonstrated that they have general properties (Amaral and Ottino, 2003). This paper explains the rise of watershed collaborations, analyzes the network properties of social entrepreneurship in watershed collaborations and describes their operation in a case study of the Watershed Collaboration of New York City.

The paper draws on the author's extensive research on the New York City Watershed Collaboration (Hoffman 2005). Section 14.2 discusses the rise of watershed collaborations. Section 14.3 describes the general properties of networks and their interactions with social entrepreneurship in collaborations. Section 14.4 provides a case study of New York City's Watershed Collaboration. The last section presents some of the lessons that the experience provides.

14.2 COLLABORATIONS

Watershed collaboration as a means of water quality control has increased in the US over recent decades (NRC, 1999; Heathcote, 1998)[1]. Two factors help explain the rise of collaborations. One is that direct regulation, while successful in reducing point pollution from sources such as factories, has been characterized by lack of cooperation and expensive conflicts. The second is that water quality problems now often derive from diffuse non-point pollution sources such as septic tanks and farms, and these are less amenable to direct regulatory control (Lubell et al., 2002; Heathcote, 1998; NRC, 1999). Collaborations are well suited to non-point pollution problems.

The building of collaborations requires the skills of social entrepreneurship not only because the new organizations require participation by multiple sectors, but also because the conflicts of collaboration require ongoing innovation (Davis, 2002; Johnson, 2000; Wondollock and Yaffee, 2000). The collaborative process has been described as a reframing of conflicts to a productive process which includes identification of problems, consideration of options, and experimentation with solutions. Use of the process increases the efficacy and reduces the costs of water quality protection (Richter et al., 2003; Heathcote, 1998; Lubell, 1999). The skills and commitments of social entrepreneurship enhance the possibility of positive outcomes of collaborations. Water problems increasingly cross international political and cultural boundaries. The concomitant increase in complexity of the water use conflicts and communication process in international collaborations creates a heightened need for the skills of social entrepreneurship.

14.3 NETWORKS

Watershed collaborations themselves are networks, and social entrepreneurs in collaborations must link to other networks to achieve desired ends. These networks are the social structures in which social entrepreneurs must build social capital (Sobel, 2002) to promote collaboration effectiveness. Network properties can be divided into four categories: structure, characteristics, purpose and effectiveness. These general properties of networks can be used to examine social entrepreneurship in watershed collaborations.

Structural elements of networks include nodes (both local and border), links and link properties, density, extent, efficiency and Nadel's Paradox. A static description of network structure would include its nodes and connecting links (Amaral and Ottino, 2003). Networks have been described as a system of relationships (Jönsson et al., 1998) and the relationships between nodes can be positive or negative and balanced or unbalanced (Cartwright and Harary, 1956). In watershed collaboration networks the stakeholders are nodes, and the social entrepreneurs are likely to be well-connected and therefore especially powerful nodes. The links among sectors might be thought of as negative since they entail negotiations to serve their separate interests, but they can also be viewed as checks and balances within the system. If one sector becomes too strong, the goals of the collaboration may be undermined.

Network structure, its pattern of nodes and links, can change overtime; networks are dynamic (Berry et al., 2004). Because collaborations involve so many diverse interests, collaborative networks are especially likely to change their structure over time. Networks vary in their degree of formality (Jönsson et al., 1998). It is the informal components of collaboration networks that would provide the most fluidity in the face of need for change.

Networks can be described by the density and extent of their nodes, and denser networks tend to be more efficient. In practice most networks are clustered or dense, meaning that the nodes are richly connected with one another, but their reach may also be extensive through border nodes providing connection to other networks (Amaral and Ottino, 2003). While watershed collaborations, like most networks, are likely to be dense, the breadth of collaboration issues, ranging from market profits to water quality, means that social entrepreneurs in collaborations will have to extend their reach through border node connections to be effective. Links with universities which can supply scientific expertise are examples of border nodes relevant to collaborations.

A network's purpose serves as a criterion for judging its effectiveness. However, the alleged purpose may differ from the ends actually served due to Nadel's paradox (Berry et al., 2004). While networks have the general properties described above, Nadel's paradox refers to the fact that each node in the network is local and is acted upon by local expectations, which may be contrary to the purpose for which the network has been organized. Nadel's paradox is present in watershed collaborations by design, because stakeholders participate in order to represent their local interests.

Several general characteristics affect network effectiveness. Two factors known to enhance effectiveness are density and, in the case of human networks, access to proper skills (Berry et al., 2004). Impediments to effectiveness include aging, which is the withdrawal of well connected or powerful nodes from the network, and high transactions costs that can prevent important nodes from connecting to the network or the purchase of necessary communication tools (Amaral and Ottino, 2003). Collaborations face the challenge of the aging problem because the collaborations are relationships built on understanding, experience and trust. If social entrepreneurs or other well connected long term participants depart from the collaboration, they take with them some of the valuable social capital of the collaboration process. The importance of transaction costs is reflected in watershed collaboration research that has shown that funding is important to success (Lubell et al., 2002; Leach and Pelkey, 2001). From a network perspective, sufficient funding allows social entrepreneurs to finance both network transaction costs, and thereby network density, and access to skills.

14.4 NEW YORK CITY'S WATERSHED COLLABORATION

New York City's watershed collaboration, hereafter to be called the Collaboration, offers the opportunity to examine social entrepreneurship in a complex series of networks. The Collaboration evolved from a system of direct regulation. The system began with the 19th century search for water sources outside of the City. Eventually the City constructed a vast system of 19 upstate reservoirs spread over a 1972 square mile area on both sides of the Hudson River, which passes through the City. Construction of these reservoirs lasted from 1835 to 1967 and involved the aggressive use of eminent domain, which stirred up considerable community resentment (NRC, 2000; Galusha 1999; CCCD, 1997).

The current era of water protection in the City began in 1986 when the US Environmental Protection Agency (EPA) promulgated a rule that all surface water suppliers serving more than 100 000 consumers had to filter their drinking water. In 1989 it allowed effective alternatives to filtration. Because water from the Catskill/ Delaware (C/D) Watershed, 120 miles to the north of the City, was considered relatively clean by the EPA and constitutes 90 percent of the City's water supply, the City had the opportunity to avoid the $6 billion estimated cost of filtration by instituting alternative programs to assure the quality of the water.

The City first sought a filtration avoidance determination (FAD) from the EPA by taking steps to directly regulate the water supply. However, upstate community residents whose families' or neighbors' lives had been disturbed by the City's creation of the reservoir system and local business interests organized to prevent the City from using eminent domain and to affect the conditions under which the water supply would be protected (NRC, 2000;

Galusha, 1999; CCCD, 1997; IATP, 1997). Three fourths of the C/D Watershed was privately owned (NRC, 2000, p. 260). The City needed local cooperation both because the size of the watershed precludes effective protection through inspection and police action alone and the EPA had to consider City programs to be effective to be willing grant the FAD.

The City negotiated with local communities in order to obtain FADs in 1992, 1997, and 2002.

14.5 COLLABORATION SHAPING: DYNAMIC NETWORKS AND SHIFTING ROLES FOR SOCIAL ENTREPRENEURS

While collaborations are increasingly common, they do not occur automatically: strong entrepreneurial leadership is required. Social entrepreneurship in the creation of the City's collaboration came from at least three networks: the local communities, the non-profit organizations, and the City's Department of Environmental Protection (DEP). These entrepreneurial leaders worked to bridge communication gaps among participating networks in an effort to create a system of collaboration that would create more social and economic value than would have occurred from direct regulation alone.

The shaping of the City's Collaboration provides an example of social entrepreneurship operating in networks undergoing dynamic change. There were three stages: informal protest, formal negotiation and collaboration shaping and formal collaboration.

During the first stage environmentalists from both the upstate area and the City and local politicians and business people created informal networks to affect the system of water protection. The environmentalists were more concerned about water protection and the political and business leaders about local economic interests, but some leaders shared both concerns and kept communication open between the groups (Dewan, 2005; Galusha, 1999). They served in essence as border nodes to one another's networks, enlarging the effective size of the protest network working for accommodation with the City. The politicians who were members of State government used that network to increase the power of local residents in their bargaining with the City. For instance, Senate committee on State government held public hearings on the Watershed. The City at this stage was conducting its relationships with local communities primarily through its upstate operations and regulatory offices (Galusha, 1999; Graf, 2005).

During the second stage, the networks evolved and the shape of the collaboration was negotiated. Three networks formalized their structure while one, the non-profit organizations (primarily environmental), met regularly but remained informal. The communities created a formal network of the Coalition of Watershed Towns (CWT). The CWT had funds for skilled help such as lawyers (Galusha, 1999). The City and Watershed farmers regularized their relationship in two stages. First the City DEP under the leadership of the Commissioner participated with leaders from the agricultural community in a citizen based task force to address the conflict. Then as a result of task force discussions and negotiations, the City provided financial support for the creation in 1992 of the non-profit Watershed Agricultural Council (WAC) whose task included enlisting farmers in a voluntary water protection program in lieu of direct regulation (NRC, 2000; IATP, 1997). The Chair and some members of the WAC board of directors had served as leaders in the initial protest movement. A second evolution of the City network occurred under the leadership of a new female commissioner in 1994. She altered the communication link with the local communities. She not only visited the Watershed to listen to local community concerns, she also brought City decision makers to the Watershed (Galusha, 1999). In addition she initiated the creation of a community relations office, Watershed Lands and Community Planning (WLCP), to handle the communications with the local communities. The head of that office helped shape the Collaboration (Graf, 2005; Galusha, 1999).

The third stage of the formal collaboration agreement was achieved with the help of pressure from the State's Governor (Galusha, 1999). The official document of the Collaboration, the Memorandum of Agreement (MOA) was signed in 1997 (MOA website). The MOA established two more formal watershed wide organizations. The Watershed Protection and Partnership Council (WPPC) of all signers of the MOA[2] was created to meet annually, hear conflicts and issue reports. The non-profit WAC continued to exist[3] and the City funded another non-profit organization, the Catskill Watershed Corporation (CWC), to implement water protection programs and pursue appropriate local economic development. Similarly to the case of the WAC, the CWC's Executive Director, Chair and some board members were drawn from leaders of the protest and negotiating stages of the Collaboration. The participating environmental organizations, although they have membership on the Partnership Council and a seat on the CWC board of directors, remained and remain informally networked (Alworth, 2005; Dewan, 2005; Budrock, 2005; Galusha, 1999). As the formal collaboration began, social entrepreneurs found their roles shifting from creators of a collaboration structure to leaders in collaboration organizations which were themselves designed to change their societies through the connected tasks of educating a far flung public, protecting water quality and promoting economic development compatible with good water quality.

14.6 SOCIAL ENTREPRENEURSHIP, NETWORKS, AND COLLABORATION PROCESS

New York City had committed over a billion dollars to its well funded collaboration by 2002, and the funds supported not only direct water quality protection but also social entrepreneurship. The City financed the upgrading and construction of local waste water treatment plants and subsidies for the repair and replacement of septic tanks and storm water prevention. The City funded non-profit organizations, the CWC and the WAC. They obtain the bulk of their funds from the City, but also obtains outside grants and each has one minor revenue earning activity. CWC manages a loan fund to stimulate local business, and the WAC now sells tote bags to obtain seed money for a program to promote regional farm products (Rauter, 2005; NRC, 2000; CCCD, 1997).

The entrepreneurial tasks of the WAC include the creation of a network of farmers who would voluntarily participate in a system of water quality protection called the 'Whole Farm' program. The WAC successfully met the City's requirement that 85 percent of farms in the most agricultural section of the Watershed join the program, and it is now estimated that over 90 percent of all Watershed farms participate. Farms are signed up through a system of 'kitchen table diplomacy' in which farms are recruited individually and offered benefits such as financial aid for water quality protective infrastructure and advice from Cornell University agricultural specialists (Rauter, 2005; NRC, 2000). In essence, the City funded the transaction costs of creating the network and providing access to essential skills. The WAC also engages in the entrepreneurial tasks of promoting markets for local agriculture and forestry products to create incentives to keep land in farms and forests, which are a preferred land use in the Watersheds. Promoting links to the network of New York City markets and promoting businesses which add value to local natural resources products both achieve this end. Education to improve water quality consciousness is another WAC task (NRC, 2000).

The CWC also undertakes a range of social entrepreneurial tasks. In addition to implementing City water protection programs, the CWC awards education grants to New York City and local schools, sometimes involving student exchanges. Local economic development is promoted in diverse ways. Grants are made to local community and cultural groups. It also administers the loan fund, the Catskill Fund for the Future (CFF). While the City provided the initial $60 million funding for the CFF, it is a revolving fund which is expected to be maintained as a continued resource to stimulate appropriate local businesses. The CWC joins the WPPC and NYS Department of State in holding annual conferences to foster the success of the agreement by promoting interaction among stakeholders and providing workshops on Collaboration issues from regulation to innovation in the local economy. One conference was specifically designed to engage the local Watershed community in identifying their needs and in visioning an alternative future. The staff of the CWC also attend conferences about local, rural and sustainable development (NRC, 2000; CWC website).

The Collaboration contains several examples of Nadel's Paradox. In the case of CWC, the board of directors is dominated by elected officials whose very job is to meet local expectations. The design was purposeful in order to foster responsibility to the electorate (Triolo, 2005). Also, representatives from the county, with the largest land mass in the Watershed, Delaware, constitute a majority on the board of directors and can dominate the voting. Environmental and watershed wide goals can potentially be undermined by local interests and the power of Delaware county and resolving tensions between the competing interests is part of the task of the collaboration. There are two factors that lessen the problem inherent in the paradox. One is that the goals of the Collaboration include fostering local development, so it is appropriate for directors to consider local concerns. A second is that the creators of the Collaboration had the foresight to establish a check list of requirements, including protection of water quality, to be met in order for a loan to be granted. The check list has been used in an effective manner according to the CWC board's environmentalist (Dewan, 2005). In the case of the WAC, whose board is dominated by local farm and agro business interests, potential conflict between local and watershed wide concerns is addressed by the establishment of review committees to oversee the awarding of grants and the fact that Federal grants overseen by the WAC come with guidelines attached (interview Rauter, 2005).

The network aging problem is a fact of Collaboration life in part because New York City mayors appoint their own Commissioner of DEP. Staff consistency helps to reduce each Commissioner's learning curve, but the changes guarantee the need to periodically restructure trust relationships in the networks. Aging challenges caused by leadership shifts at the CWC and the WAC have been helped by several factors: promotion from within the organization (WAC), informal links among political leaders (CWC), and the informal network of people from the local area working throughout the Collaboration organizations. Those with local experience help to educate newcomers. Among the local employees are young people who have obtained higher education in natural resource protection and have returned to work in the Collaboration (Rauter, 2005).

Factors external to the Collaboration affect its goals. For instance, while Collaboration subsidies for infrastructure and economic development were designed to aid low income Watershed residents, these residents are also vulnerable to the national problems of the high costs of housing, health care and child care (Hoffman, 2005). Such problems are not easily solved at the local level. To address such issues, Collaboration entrepreneurs have to seek help at the State and National level through lobbying for appropriate government policy and linking to more broadly based social organizations.

14.7 LESSONS TO BE LEARNED: POSITIVE AND NEGATIVE

Consideration of the New York City collaboration experience provides a variety of lessons for social entrepreneurship and collaborations. The first is that the necessity of linking networks from varied sectors in the economy during both the creation and operation of the collaboration creates a need for social entrepreneurship.

A second set of lessons are related to structure. One is that collaboration networks change structure. Social entrepreneurs involved in collaborations can expect the focus of their activities to change over time from the creation of collaborations to the creativity required of collaborations. A second is that social entrepreneurs need to develop relationships with persons who serve as border nodes to other networks which can provide skills or resources vital to their tasks. The New York City Collaboration has relied on a wide variety of border nodes throughout its life. A third is that informal networks are critical to collaboration life. In the New York example, the environmental networks remain informal, and the network of home-grown employees helps educate new arrivals to Collaboration work. A fourth is the importance of identifying potential conflicts from the tension between global and local concerns and to establish procedures to protect organizational goals. The check list of requirements for awarding of grants and loans in the New York Collaboration provides an example of a protective procedure. A fifth is that methods to protect against the loss of skill, connection and information from aging, should be considered. New York's Collaboration has been protected by promotion from within, staff consistency and informal local networks, but more explicit attention to the problem would be wise. A sixth is that the scale of social entrepreneurship determines the problems it can solve. Problems with broad roots call for relationships with border nodes that link to larger scale networks that can have effect on the problem.

A third set of lessons relates to funding of collaborations. First, the funding of social entrepreneurship is important to support the transaction and communication costs of creating and maintaining collaboration networks, such as the Whole Farm program. Second, funding creates incentives for local communities to cooperate.

Third, the funding of social entrepreneurial organizations like the CWC and WAC can have multiplier effects, such as their success in obtaining outside grants.

A fourth lesson is that sticks as well as carrots can be important to social entrepreneurs working in watershed collaborations. The necessity of obtaining the EPA's signature on the FADs creates pressure for the City to work effectively with local communities. The desire of local people to avoid more direct regulation is another incentive for cooperation. Also, local communities share an interest in local water quality protection with the City.

Watershed collaborations provide practical experience in the effort to attain sustainable development. Viewing them as social entrepreneurship in a milieu of networks reveals some of the necessary processes and challenges. Analysis of the New York City Collaboration teaches us that although the struggles to balance the interests and needs of diverse stakeholders are real, there are a variety of means for social entrepreneurs to work through the challenges and effect positive change.

NOTES

1. The Conservation Technology Information Center (CTIC) listed 962 watershed collaborations for 2000, but as the inventory is based on returned surveys, this total underestimates their actual number (CTIC 2005). They are seeking funding to update the survey.
2. The MOA was signed by New York City and State, the US EPA, a coalition of 34 Watershed towns (CWT), 9 villages and 5 Watershed Catskill/Delaware counties, other Watershed communities, and locally active non-profit organizations (CCCD, 1997).
3. The Agricultural components of the WAC negotiate with the City directly but its easement and forestry programs are part of the larger MOA (interview Rauter, 2005).

15. Investing in social innovation: harnessing the potential for partnership between corporations and social entrepreneurs

Jane Nelson and Beth Jenkins

One of the key leadership challenges of our time is to find new ways to harness the innovation, technology, networks and problem-solving skills of the private sector, in partnership with others, to support international development goals. And to do so in a manner that makes sound business sense, and does not replace or undermine the role of government. Business leaders have a growing interest, both in terms of risk management and harnessing new opportunities, to get engaged.

(The World Economic Forum, the International Business Leaders Forum, and the CSR Initiative, Nelson, Prescott and Held, 2005)

15.1 INTRODUCTION

The growth in corporate responsibility and social entrepreneurship represents one of the most exciting social trends of the past decade. Around the world there is increased awareness of the potential to harness the core competencies, assets and resources of corporations in helping to find new solutions to complex social and environmental problems. At the same time, there has been a dramatic growth in awareness of, and support for the crucial leadership role played by social entrepreneurs – individuals who apply innovative, entrepreneurial, performance-driven, and scalable approaches to solving societal problems, and who often act as bridge-builders between different sectors, communities, institutions and/or cultures.

Yet, with a few notable exceptions, relatively little analysis has been done on the linkages between these two trends and between the corporate leaders and social entrepreneurs that drive them. This is especially the case in developing countries where there are both enormous development needs and great opportunities for increasing engagement between corporations and social entrepreneurs.

This chapter looks at some of the innovative alliances that already exist in both developed and developing countries. It suggests a conceptual framework for thinking about the different ways through which companies can support social entrepreneurship focusing on: a company's core business operations in the workplace, marketplace and along the value chain; its social investment and strategic philanthropy activities; and its engagement in public policy dialogue, advocacy and institution building. The chapter outlines the 'business case' for how such alliances can help companies meet their business goals and support their corporate values. And it offers a set of recommendations for business leaders, social entrepreneurs, foundations and governments on how they can work together to increase the scale and effectiveness of these alliances for mutual benefit.

15.2 CORPORATE INNOVATORS SERVING THE PUBLIC GOOD

The ability to turn good ideas into deliverable solutions – the distinguishing feature of an entrepreneur – has never been more important to the success of business and society (Jackson and Nelson, 2004). Innovation is the lifeblood of corporate competitiveness, value creation and sustainable growth. It is also vital to solving many of the major environmental and social challenges that our world faces – from global warming to poverty and the lack of access to livelihood opportunities, education, health, nutrition, water, energy, housing, technology, credit, property rights and other essential goods, services and resources that underpin such poverty.

Some of the world's leading companies are recognizing that by harnessing innovation for the public good they can manage risks, gain competitive advantage and/or enhance their reputation and stakeholder relationships while helping to solve complex social and environmental problems. Such companies are focusing on ways to integrate social and environmental considerations into their R&D activities and into the sourcing, manufacturing, marketing, use and disposal of their products.

At a minimum, these companies are aiming to ensure that their business activities do not create or exacerbate social and environmental problems, but many companies are going further. They are exploring ways to *create new value* by developing products, services, and business models that meet social and environmental needs and generate a profit at the same time. For instance, they are exploring opportunities to reach low-income customers underserved by traditional markets, as our examples of Cemex and Amanco illustrate. And they are looking at feasible and mutually beneficial ways to source from small-scale and micro-enterprises, as our example of SC Johnson illustrates.

These companies are also looking to their philanthropic, community investment and employee volunteering programs as sources of innovation for the company, its partners and the communities and countries in which it operates, as illustrated by our examples of Nokia, Bank of America, Cisco Systems, and the Abdul Latif Jameel Group. And they are supporting institutional innovation to improve the effectiveness and efficiency of public policy and market frameworks in order to better address important economic, social and environmental challenges.

Some examples of these innovative new approaches are outlined in Box 15.1. As our examples in this chapter illustrate, innovative and world-class approaches to corporate responsibility are not only the preserve of multinational corporations, but also driven by leading companies headquartered in developing countries.

BOX 15.1 Innovative new business approaches to serve the poor

Some of these examples are hybrids – philanthropic models that harness core commercial competencies, skills and products; others are profit-making ventures and business activities. All are focused on improving the access of low-income households, entrepreneurs and communities to essential products, services, resources and opportunities.

Spreading access to economic opportunity

In Ghana and Tanzania, Unilever is working with small-scale producers to source raw materials from indigenous plants, and enabling small-scale distributors to sell affordable products to low-income households in countries such as Brazil, India and Indonesia. In Colombia, Starbucks is working with Conservation International and local farmers to support sustainable coffee production and more reliable incomes. SC Johnson is undertaking similar efforts with KickStart and small-scale growers of pyrethrum in Kenya. Cemex is cooperating with Ashoka in Mexico to deliver low-income housing. In Kazakhstan, Chevron and Citigroup are working with the UN and local partners to deliver small business services, as is BP in Azerbaijan. In the Middle East, where over 60% of the population are under the age of 25, companies such as Abdul Latif Jameel, Nokia and Shell are supporting youth enterprise and micro-finance initiatives.

Providing access to pro-poor financial services

Citigroup, Deutsche Bank, Credit Suisse, Barclays, ABN Amro, Calvert, ANZ, Standard Bank, and Merrill Lynch are among leading financial institutions that have started to develop financial services for the poor, ranging from micro-credit to insurance, saving and investment products.

Improving access to information technology

Efforts to harness information and communications technology to support education, enterprise development and humanitarian relief are being undertaken by Cisco Systems, Microsoft, Vodafone, Nokia, IBM, HP, Ericsson, Dell, Ayala, and Infosys, among others.

Ensuring access to clean and affordable water and energy

Shell is working with the UN and others in Uganda to catalyze the pro-poor market for solar home systems, aimed at both increasing access to energy and tackling indoor pollution and health problems. BP is doing likewise in the Philippines, EDF is supporting off-grid energy access in Madagascar, and ABB is working with WWF on sustainable energy access in Tanzania. Companies such as Thames Water/RWE, Suez, General Electric and Coca-Cola are exploring new business models and technologies to improve access to clean water and sanitation.

Increasing access to health and safety

Most major pharmaceutical companies are now engaged in efforts to improve access to essential medicines through a variety of R&D initiatives, preferential pricing and product donation programmes. Companies with large developing country workforces, such as Coca-Cola, Anglo-American, Chevron, Rio Tinto, Unilever and ExxonMobil, are also developing new approaches to support employees and local communities in the fight against infectious diseases. Major food companies are engaging in food fortification efforts and companies such as 3M, GM, InBev and SABMiller are working with local communities and social entrepreneurs to improve road safety and responsible vehicle use.

(Source: Nelson, 2005)

15.3 SOCIAL INNOVATORS HARNESSING THE POWER OF ENTERPRISE

In approaching many of these opportunities to innovate for the public good, large companies are finding a new type of partner: the social entrepreneur.

The Schwab Foundation for Social Entrepreneurship defines social entrepreneurs as people who:

> Identify practical solutions to social problems by combining innovation, resourcefulness and opportunity. Deeply committed to generating social value,

these entrepreneurs identify new processes, services, products or unique ways of combining proven practice with innovation, driving through pattern-breaking approaches to seemingly intractable social issues. Most importantly, they act as social alchemists, converting under-utilized resources into productive assets by working with, and motivating, groups of people and communities (Schwab Foundation for Social Entrepreneurs, 2005).

Social entrepreneurship pioneer Ashoka describes a social entrepreneur as:

An extraordinary individual with unprecedented ideas for change in his or her community. The job of the social entrepreneur is to recognize when a part of society is stuck and to provide new ways to get it unstuck. He or she finds what is not working and solves the problem by changing the system, spreading the solution and persuading entire societies to take new leaps (www.ashoka.org).

Social entrepreneurs whose visions and approaches are profiled in this chapter and who believe in harnessing the power of markets and the private sector for social goals include:

- Dr. Muhammad Yunus, who founded Grameen Bank in 1976 as a young economics professor in Bangladesh, investing his own limited resources to make small loans to poor women whom he passionately believed would pay him back, support each other, and use their loans to improve the health and prospects of their families and communities. In doing so, he not only established a bank which today serves some 5 million clients and has diversified into other services for low-income markets, but also pioneered the concept and practice of microfinance and launched a global movement that generates reasonable financial returns, is attracting the interest of commercial banks, insurers and investors, and improves the lives of millions. Grameen Bank and its strategic partner, the Grameen Foundation USA (GFUSA), have both started to partner with large companies to scale-up the impact of their activities. Our example of the evolving partnership between GFUSA and the Abdul Latif Jameel Group in the Middle East illustrates one such case;
- Bill Drayton, the founder of Ashoka, has pioneered the application of a venture capital model for investing in

exceptional individuals with new ideas for public service using a combination of financial stipends, professional support services and opportunities to leverage connections and networks. A social entrepreneur even in his schooldays, Bill founded Ashoka in 1980, after working with the management consulting firm McKinsey and then serving as an Assistant Administrator of the US Environmental Protection Agency designing innovative tradeable 'pollution rights' as a market-based alternative to environmental regulation. Since then, he has applied his business skills, networks and passion to investing in social entrepreneurs and promoting awareness of their critical role in society. Ashoka invests in people who meet the following criteria: creativity in goal-setting and problem-solving; entrepreneurial spirit and temperament; an idea with potential for large-scale social or environmental impact; and strong ethical fiber. Since 1982, Ashoka's investments have enabled over 1500 people in 53 countries to make change in areas such as education, the environment, health, human rights and economic development. Bill and his colleagues are now pioneering the concept of the Hybrid Value Chain™, a framework that enables companies to design, test and implement commercial business models to serve low-income citizens in profitable ways, through partnership with social entrepreneurs. Our examples of Cemex and GrupoNueva working with social entrepreneurs in Mexico illustrate the Hybrid Value Chain™ approach in practice;

- Rick Little has launched several initiatives that have transformed the lives, self-esteem and prospects of millions of youth around the world. In his 20s, he launched Quest to equip students with valuable life skills. After enduring over 150 rejections, Rick finally met Russ Mawby, President of the Kellogg Foundation, who took the necessary risk to fund his vision. Today, Quest reaches students in thousands of schools in over 40 countries, and Rick has gone on to found the International Youth Foundation (IYF), a global network of in-country partners that improves the prospects of young people in over 70 countries, and more recently the ImagineNations™ Group, which is helping to build bridges among youth of different cultures and religions and expanding the practice of youth enterprise. Our example of

Finnish mobile communications company Nokia illustrates how one company has aligned its corporate vision of connecting people to IYF's vision of connecting youth, with benefits for both;

- Jacqueline Novogratz began her career in international banking before consulting for UNICEF and the World Bank in Africa, founding a micro-enterprise organization in Rwanda, and managing special projects at the Rockefeller Foundation, including creation of 'The Philanthropy Workshop,' an international philanthropic education program. Now she is drawing on her diverse skills and experiences as well as her passion for social progress as Founder and CEO of Acumen Fund. This is an innovative non-profit venture fund that focuses on entrepreneurial solutions for access to affordable health, housing and water. Our example of the venture philanthropy approach Cisco Systems took to help create Acumen Fund in 2001 illustrates another way that large companies can invest in social entrepreneurs: by supporting innovative financing mechanisms that harness market disciplines to tackle social problems;

- Alan Khazei and Michael Brown were roommates at Harvard Law School when they had the vision for creating City Year, a youth service corps that harnesses the power of young people from all walks of life working together to address pressing social issues. Ira Jackson, former Executive Vice President of BankBoston (now Bank of America) was one business leader who saw the potential of this vision and put his companies' financial and in-kind resources behind it. Established in 1988, City Year today enlists over a thousand young adults in communities across the United States and has a growing alumni of young leaders who are making a difference. It has helped to inspire the creation of AmeriCorps, a federal program that supports national youth service in the USA, and has now been adopted in South Africa, while Bank of America continues to reap concrete business benefits from being a strategic partner;

- Martin Fisher and Nick Moon were working with subsistence farmers in Africa for a British charity, ActionAid, when they decided to set up a social enterprise called ApproTEC. Their goal was to demonstrate that low-tech agricultural equipment could be designed and marketed to poor farmers in a manner that was both appropriate to their needs and affordable, and that such technology could help bring these farmers into the market economy, returning the initial investment in three to six months. Family-owned SC Johnson was one of the first major companies to recognize that a partnership with ApproTEC could help the company manage the quality and reliability of small-scale producers along its global supply chain. As our example illustrates, their partnership is now improving the livelihoods of thousands of Kenyan farmers, while also helping SC Johnson to meet its supply needs for pyrethrum.

These eight people are among the world's most respected social entrepreneurs and their partnerships with large companies are helping them not only to achieve their own missions, but also to inspire an increasingly professional approach to combining market-driven approaches with social purposes.

It is important, however, not to 'pigeon-hole' the concept of social entrepreneurship or to give the impression that social entrepreneurs only operate in the 'social sector' or 'citizen sector'. As the above personal stories illustrate, many social entrepreneurs start out their careers and gain their early leadership experience in the commercial, private sector, often working for large companies. Others decide to stay there, using their business skills, their companies, and the wealth they create to drive social change through supporting other social entrepreneurs either through corporate partnerships or philanthropy.

Our examples in this chapter of Ira Jackson, former EVP at BankBoston, and Tae Yoo, VP at Cisco Systems, illustrate such cases – corporate executives who shared the social vision, clearly understood the entrepreneurial potential, and toof the financial and reputation risk to be early investors in individual social entrepreneurs.

In summary, the mindset and practice of social entrepreneurship are not confined to a particular sector, nor to a particular set of issues or approaches. At the individual level, social entrepreneurs can be found in nonprofits and companies; at the organizational level, both nonprofits and companies can be social enterprises. As a result, combining these forces can be a logical and powerful way to effect large scale, economically sustainable social change.

What are some of the mutual benefits that can be gained by large companies and social entrepreneurs working together?

15.4 THE MUTUAL BENEFITS OF PARTNERSHIPS BETWEEN COMPANIES AND SOCIAL ENTREPRENEURS

In periods of economic and political change and uncertainty, where business budgets tend to be tight and community needs high, there is greater incentive than ever for companies, communities and public officials to work together to leverage social and commercial investments as effectively and efficiently as possible.

As Elizabeth Riker, Portfolio Manager at New Profit Inc. comments:

> For corporations, working with social entrepreneurs can be one of the most effective ways to make a difference in the communities in which they work. They can prove to be very valuable not only in terms of strengthening the company's reputation, but also in providing an opportunity for corporate leaders to learn from their counterparts in the social sector, and in some cases to develop new markets and competitive advantages or to manage unfamiliar risks. As corporations are increasingly tasked with managing and influencing a broader set of stakeholders, they have a great deal to learn from social entrepreneurs who possess remarkable skills and experience in building support and driving action from a diverse set of constituents. At the same time, social entrepreneurs have much to gain from working more closely with corporate leaders. Non-profits that have developed strong alliances with corporations have benefited from their strategic advice, access to networks, marketing/branding networks, and of course funding (Interview with Elizabeth Riker, 20 October 2005).

Ashoka also argues the case for mutual benefit. Looking at companies interested in serving low-income markets in profitable ways, it makes the case that

> businesses can enter these markets more efficiently, and they can provide a more integrated solution to low-income clients, by partnering with citizen sector organizations "along the value chain" of product and service development, production, distribution and logistics, sales and marketing, and

financing. On the other hand, social entrepreneurs and their organizations can develop and test new ways to significantly increase their social impact by leveraging the core competencies of businesses, while creating a sustainable source of revenue for their organizations (www.ashoka.org).

In their report Partnership Alchemy, Jane Nelson and Simon Zadek outline the following seven areas of potential mutual benefit (Table 15.1) that can result from new types of partnership between

Table 15.1 Potential participant benefits from new social partnership

1. Development of 'human capital'	Creating new opportunities for training, mentoring, exchanges, incentive programs, awareness raising, volunteering and leadership development.
2. Improved operational efficiency	Achieving reduced costs, increased process efficiency and better service delivery.
3. Organizational innovation	Helping the organization to develop new, creative ways of operating to meet complex challenges and opportunities.
4. Better access to information	Learning about the people or communities in which an institution (business, government or NGO) is operating and delivering products and services. This can help the institution in question to improve service delivery, but also to improve risk management and conflict prevention measures.
5. Product and service innovation	Partnerships can create openings for the more effective and responsive design and delivery of goods and services.
6. Enhanced reputation and credibility	Building better relationships with key stakeholder groups which are benefiting directly or indirectly from the partnerships.
7. Creation of a stable society	This is in the critical long-term interest of business and a direct objective of government and many NGOs.

Sorce: Nelson and Zadek, 2001

commercially driven companies and social entrepreneurs and their organizations (Nelson and Zadek, 2001).

15.5 A FRAMEWORK FOR BUSINESS ENGAGEMENT WITH SOCIAL ENTREPRENEURS

Companies can support or invest in social entrepreneurship in three main ways, all of which can also create benefits for the company.

First, through investing directly in social entrepreneurs and their organizations. Such investment can be carried out in two main ways. First, as a fundamental part of *core, commercial business operations*, where social entrepreneurs work with companies along various parts of the value chain – to offer affordable goods and services to low-income communities, for example, or to source from micro-enterprises or small-scale producers. This approach lies at the heart of Ashoka's Hybrid Value Chain™ approach, which is illustrated below in Figure 15.1:

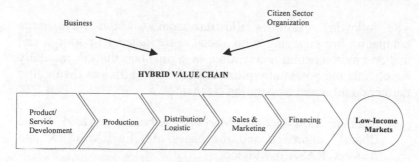

Source: http://www.ashoka.org/global/fec_hvc.cfm

Figure 15.1 Ashoka's Hybrid Value Chain™ approach

Another direct approach is through companies' philanthropic and community investment activities, where social entrepreneurs can partner in ways that mobilize not only corporate money, but also people, products and premises to help support and strengthen local communities and non-profit organizations. The growing practice of venture philanthropy or social venture capital, in which venture capital principles are applied to support social enterprises, provides a good model for such investment. Companies and individual business leaders share their management skills, provide seed financing, and engage in active, performance-driven partnerships. Some of the differences between venture philanthropy and traditional philanthropy are summarized in Table 15.2.

Second, companies can encourage social entrepreneurship through engaging in public policy dialogue, advocacy and institution building in order to create an enabling environment for social enterprise.

Third, companies can create internal climates for social entrepreneurship. For example, by encouraging employees to be innovative in developing new business models, products, services and processes that combine profitable business opportunities with social or environmental solutions.

Leadership within the company is essential in all three cases.

15.6 PARTNERSHIPS IN ACTION

The following examples illustrate some of the ways large companies are engaging with social entrepreneurs to spur social and/or environmental innovation in a manner that is mutually beneficial, and potentially more effective and efficient than either partner could achieve operating on their own:

- reaching Low-Income Markets: Ashoka's Hybrid Value Chain^{TM} approach and the cases of CEMEX/SISEX and Amanco/RASA in Mexico;
- improving global supply chain management and livelihood opportunities: The case of SC Johnson and KickStart in Kenya;
- investing in Innovative Financing Mechanisms: Social Venture Capital and the case of Acumen Fund and Cisco Systems;
- investing in Innovative Financing Mechanisms: Microfinance and the case of Grameen Foundation USA and the Abdul Latif Jameel Group in the Middle East;
- harnessing Technology for Social Progress: The International Youth Foundation and Nokia;

- mobilizing Corporate Competencies to Develop the 'Next Generation': City Year and Bank of America, formerly BankBoston.

Table 15.2 From 'check book' philanthropy to social venture partnership

	Old Paradigm Giving: One-way	New Paradigm Partnerships: Strategic
Philosophy	• Discretionary giving • Corporate obligation	• New business discipline • Societal opportunity
Methods	• Formulaic • Responsive • Conventional • Incremental • Risk averse	• Opportunistic • Anticipatory • 'Out of the box' • Transformative • Risk-taking
Decision-makers	• CEO and spouses • Board members • Department of 'good deeds'	• Line business managers • Stakeholders • Core strategic competence
Purpose	• Conformity • Good will	• Differentiation • Results and reputation
Recipients	• The 'usual suspects'	• New social entrepreneurs and innovators
Reach	• Local	• Local and global
Impact	• Minimal and not measured	• Potentially high, leveraged and measured
Employee involvement	• Minimal	• Direct and intense
Relationship management	• One way • Arms-length • Bureaucratic • Paternalistic	• Strategic partnership • Entrepreneurial • Mutual learning
Nexus with core competencies	• Peripheral	• Linked to core business purpose and competence

Source: Jackson and Nelson, 2004.

15.6.1 Reaching Low-Income Markets: Ashoka's Hybrid Value Chain™ approach and the cases of CEMEX/SISEX and Amanco/RASA in Mexico

Social entrepreneurship pioneer Ashoka recommends that companies interested in expanding into 'Bottom of the Pyramid' markets – markets of low-income consumers and producers at the bottom of the world's economic pyramid – partner with social entrepreneurs and their organizations to do so.

From the company's point of view, the partnership approach has the advantages of accelerating learning and eliminating the need to develop new competencies internally, by leveraging the existing experience, relationships, infrastructure, skills, and/or distribution systems of partners. From the social entrepreneur's point of view, the approach allows poor people's needs to be served more sustainably and at greater scale, and generates earned income to support his or her non-profit activities.

Two examples in Mexico that illustrate Ashoka's evolving approach to Hybrid Value Chains™ are illustrated below:

15.6.1.1 CEMEX and SISEX

CEMEX, headquartered in Mexico and a global leader in the cement industry, launched its Patrimonio Hoy initiative in 1998 in an effort to target the low-income, do-it-yourself homebuilders who constitute a growing percentage of new home construction in Mexico. These homebuilders typically start off with a small core structure and then add on, one room at a time, as cash flows and saving habits permit. However, short-term needs and cultural norms often mitigate against saving for the future, with the result that it can take an average of four years to build a single, modest-sized room of 100 square feet.

CEMEX has succeeded in tapping this difficult market through a savings-and-credit program that leverages and improves upon its low-income customers' existing, incremental building habits. Its product offer is no different – CEMEX standard cement – but its business model is highly tailored to these customers' specific needs.

First, Patrimonio Hoy accommodates low incomes by allowing customers to pay in small but regular weekly instalments. After a certain number of payments are made on time, the company will disburse the construction materials – in effect, providing credit 'in-kind'.

Second, Patrimonio Hoy provides auxiliary services such as design and technical assistance (useful in increasing quality and reducing waste, both common problems for do-it-yourselves) as well as home delivery of materials (useful for those without trucks or time off work to do the transportation).

Third, Patrimonio Hoy helps build cultural acceptance for saving by marketing housing as 'patrimony,' or an asset to pass down to one's children. CEMEX uses well-respected local women, working on commission, to market the program, and throws a small fiesta whenever a room is completed to celebrate and reward that family's success.

To date, CEMEX's Patrimonio Hoy program has enabled more than 120 000 families to improve their homes in 1/3 the time and at 4/5 the cost, on average, of methods previously available to them. Patrimonio Hoy has also generated a stable source of demand for CEMEX – because its PH families are generally not employed in the formal sector, they are less affected by the ups and downs of formal business cycles, in contrast with the company's large corporate and government customers. The program has contributed to the bottom line, albeit in a small way, and earned CEMEX widespread international recognition for the leadership and innovation it embodies.

As part of the challenge involved in scaling Patrimonio Hoy, CEMEX sought to widen its marketing outreach and make it more efficient. At the same time, the company realized the advantages its network of local promotors brought – including local relationships, trust, on-the-ground presence, and access to information. They saw the potential for partnering with effective social entrepreneurs.

One such entrepreneur is Patricia Nava, an Ashoka fellow who runs the National System of Promotion and Sexual Health (SISEX), an association of civil society organizations offering sex education and reproductive health information to people of both genders, all ages and socio-economic backgrounds in 16 Mexican states. SISEX's mission is to fill a critical gap in awareness about sex and reproductive health – a gap that lies at the root of many challenging social issues, including gender inequality and domestic abuse, diseases such as HIV/AIDS, and unplanned pregnancy. To execute on its mission, SISEX has built an extensive information distribution network based on grassroots marketing techniques. As many as 75 000 people per year receive training from SISEX member organizations.

CEMEX and SISEX may seem unlikely bedfellows, but as David Wheeler of the York University Schulich School of Business has noted, businesses and social entrepreneurs/their organizations do not have to have the same ultimate objective for partnerships between them to work (Wheeler et al., 2005). In this case, SISEX's large social network is the asset that makes it an attractive partner for CEMEX. From Patricia's point of view, 'improving housing conditions is a strategic issue that she views as a way to address her core topics of domestic violence and a balanced life' (www.ashoka.org). SISEX has now trained a number of promoters to liaise with the organizations in its network to cultivate future Patrimonio Hoy customers. In return, these promoters generate commission-based income for SISEX.

15.6.1.2 Amanco & RASA

Amanco, a subsidiary of Grupo Nueva, is a leader in the production and marketing of piping and lightweight construction solutions in Latin America. 25 percent of the Mexican population, approximately 25 million people, lives in rural areas. 2 million of these are small-scale farmers with less than 4 hectares of land (FIRCO, 2004). These small-scale farmers fell outside the networks of Amanco's existing independent distributors, and indeed outside of their capacity to serve. Individual transaction costs were high, and potential customers could not afford the systems without financing.

Social entrepreneur and Ashoka fellow Arturo García founded Red de Agricultores Sustentables Autogestivos (RASA), a network of farming cooperatives in the state of Guerrero, in 1993. His mission is to ensure sustainable livelihoods for small-scale farmers. These cooperatives allow the farmers to own and manage the production, marketing, and distribution of local crops – primarily coffee, wood, and coconuts – as an alternative to the repressive tactics of the privileged class, and the ineffective ones of the government. In a farming society traumatized by inequality and conflict, Arturo has been able to build the relationships required for a successful cooperative structure by remaining strictly apolitical, focusing solely on the economic advantages of his work. RASA now encompasses 12 000 farmers.

Amanco and RASA have partnered to develop a new distribution system to enable the company to sell its irrigation systems, and small-scale farmers to buy them, in poor, rural areas. The partnership is advantageous for the company as a means of expanding its marketing and distribution reach cost-effectively; it is advantageous for RASA because it contributes directly to the organization's mission. The systems increase productivity and incomes among farmers.

With an initial loan from Ashoka, RASA hired a staff of promoters who aggregate demand for Amanco systems among the farmers in its cooperative network. In addition to marketing, these promoters perform distribution, installation, and maintenance of the Amanco systems. RASA also channels financing in the form of subsidies and loans to help farmers afford the systems. Amanco, for its part, provides irrigation technology, promotional materials, and training for the promoters. The company also pays promoters on commission, which contributes to diversification and stability in RASA's funding base.

The partnership is especially strategic for Amanco in the sense that RASA, as an organization dedicated to ensuring sustainable livelihoods for farmers, already provides a set of services that enable those farmers to become good Amanco customers – ranging from facilitating financing to make the initial purchase possible, to providing agricultural extension services and market development support to increase productivity and incomes, thus enabling them to repay their loans and become repeat customers.

15.6.2 Improving Global Supply Chain Management and Livelihood Opportunities: The Case of SC Johnson and KickStart

SC Johnson is a US-based, family-owned company that has a longstanding reputation for its commitment to sustainable development and corporate social responsibility. As Chairman and CEO Dr. H. Fisk Johnson describes it, 'Environmental and social responsibility is so much a part of our legacy – what we have done for well over 100 years at SC Johnson and what we continue to do today. In fact, it remains a top priority for the company as it is one of our seven key corporate strategic objectives' (Nelson et al., 2005).

This commitment is reflected in the company's ongoing efforts to monitor and manage the environmental impacts of its large portfolio of household products and to use naturally sourced inputs and recyclable materials as much as possible in their production and distribution. One example is its use of the pyrethrum plant as an active ingredient in its production of insecticides such as Raid® and Baygon®.

Kenya produces two-thirds of the world's supply of pyrethrum, which represents the country's fifth-largest export crop, and SC Johnson is the largest buyer of the crop. The crop itself is grown by some 200 000 subsistence farmers, who in turn support more than a million people. SC Johnson has sourced from these farmers since 1970, working closely with the Pyrethrum Board of Kenya (PKB) a national governmental or parastatal agency that manages the country's supply and export of the crop, working through farmer cooperatives representing the individual growers.

In the 1990s SC Johnson made a decision to continue the use of natural pyrethrins in their insecticides despite facing the advent of lower-cost synthetic ingredients and some challenges with the reliability of their sources due to weather and other challenges facing the Kenyan growers. In addition to continuing to work closely with the PKB to improve reliability, quality and efficiency of pyrethrum production, the company looked at other alternatives for securing and enhancing their supply, while helping to improve livelihood opportunities for farmers.

ApproTEC (Appropriate Technologies for Enterprise Creation) emerged as a partner. Founded in 1991 by social entrepreneurs Nick Moon and Martin Fisher, ApproTEC's mission is to promote sustainable economic growth and employment by developing and promoting simple money-making tools that can be used to run profitable small-scale enterprises and farming operations. Examples include micro-irrigation, cooking oil, building, sanitation, hay baling and transport technologies. They use the following market-driven approach in achieving their goals: researching the markets to identify high potential small-scale business opportunities; designing new technologies and business models to respond to these opportunities; training local manufacturers to produce the new technology; using innovative marketing and communications approaches to promote them to small-scale entrepreneurs; and undertaking a rigorous approach to monitoring both the cost-effectiveness and development impact of the technologies once adopted.

Recently renamed KickStart, the social enterprise has to date developed and marketed affordable and appropriate technologies that have helped over 39 000 families start profitable new businesses, averaging some 750 new businesses per month. These generate an estimated $37 million a year in new profits and wages, and produce new revenues equivalent to more than 0.5 percent of Kenya's GDP and 0.2 percent of Tanzania's GDP, delivering measurable benefits in terms of family incomes, local and national economic growth and in some cases export revenues. KickStart's vision is now to expand from Kenya, Mali and Tanzania, to 6 new countries in Africa over the next 3 years and reach more than 400 000 people (www.kickstart.org).

The two organizations saw the mutual value that could be gained by providing pyrethrum farmers in Kenya with better access to appropriate and affordable irrigation technologies, in this case small, manually operated pumps. They established a joint program aimed at marketing such pumps to farmers to enable them to irrigate their crops, with the ultimate goal of raising household income levels while ensuring the long-term availability, quality and lower cost of natural pyrethrum for SC Johnson products.

A pilot was formally kicked off in July 2004. In the first year, more than 10 000 farmers have had an opportunity to learn about the pumps through a variety of creative marketing and communication efforts, ranging from radio and posters to promotional events and competitions. The number of distributors has been increased and hundreds of pumps have been sold or given away. With every pump sold, farmers are also receiving a pack of pyrethrum seeds from the PKB and a can of Raid® and Baygon® from SC Johnson Kenya, helping to establish the company's brand among potential consumers.

Ongoing efforts are being made by the partners to measure the impact that micro-irrigation and clonal seeds have on improving the quality and quantity of pyrethrum being grown. KickStart's staff will measure and record the true economic and social impacts of the pump, looking at measures such as net household and diversity of income, pump sales and usage patterns, household food security, health and nutrition, and market awareness of the pump. The government's PBK will also monitor crop production of some of the farmers who have purchased a pump, focusing on both quantity and quality.

15.6.3 Investing in Innovative Financing Mechanisms: Social Venture Capital and the Case of Acumen Fund and Cisco Systems

Founded just over 20 years ago by a small group of computer scientists from Stanford University, Cisco Systems has become a global leader in developing hardware, software and service offerings to create Internet solutions that improve the connectivity and productivity of individuals, companies, and countries. The company's stated vision is 'to change the way people work, live, play and learn.' Since its creation, the company has focused on developing innovative new approaches to customers' challenges and has emphasized the power and potential of networking.

While Internet ecosystems are the company's value proposition for achieving one of its two core values – customer focus – the Cisco Corporate Citizenship Ecosystem enables it to apply a similarly entrepreneurial, networked approach to its corporate citizenship activities. The company's work in this area is directed by Tae Yoo, Cisco's Vice President of Corporate Affairs, who brings strong experience in new business development and alliance building to this role, having led various business units in the company focused on new markets and sales channels.

The company's corporate citizenship activities aim to drive sustainable change by fostering mutually beneficial partnerships between local and global nonprofits, corporations and government bodies, which leverage the partners' varying skills, networks and resources to solve problems in the areas of education, access to basic needs, capacity building and economic development.

The company looks for social investment opportunities with partners who take a similar approach to developing innovative new models and mechanisms that address public problems. One such example is the role Cisco Systems Inc. and the Cisco Systems Foundation played, together with the Rockefeller Foundation and several individual investors, in providing the seed capital for social entrepreneur Jacqueline Novogratz to establish Acumen Fund, which operates like a venture capital firm for the poor. Established as a nonprofit organization, Acumen Fund identifies innovations with high potential to solve demanding issues, currently in the areas of health technology, housing and water, which may operate in either the profit or nonprofit sector. It then supports these innovations and the social entrepreneurs who drive them via a combination of financial capital, in the form of loans, equity investments and occasional grants, and intellectual capital and technical assistance, delivered through a network of connections and partners. In each organization in its portfolio, Acumen Fund focuses on the areas of effective design, pricing, marketing and distribution of critical goods and services to the poor.

Current investments range from A to Z Textile Mills in East Africa, which produces long-lasting anti-malarial bednets (now 3 million a year, with a new factory completed and plans to achieve a yearly rate of 7 million on the next year), to the establishment of a mortgage guarantee facility with National Bank of Pakistan, to stimulate a private mortgage market for the poor, many of whom live on less than $4 a day (targeting over 6,000 poor urban families), and IDE in India, which has sold more than 30,000 affordable drip irrigation units to poor farmers, giving them an opportunity to move out of poverty while also managing scarce water resources better.

Experienced portfolio managers monitor the portfolio's performance based on a set of indicators and benchmarks that cover both the social and financial returns of its investments, and provide regular reports to investors. Acumen Fund evaluates its own effectiveness as a social enterprise across five main areas: financial sustainability; portfolio performance; strength of its community; internal operations; and thought leadership, in addition to measuring key outputs and lives changed as a result of its investments.

Acumen Fund's investment approach is based on the following core principles: take a few big bets; focus on sustainability and scale; build effective networks; provide financing and management expertise; demand accountability; and measure the results. The core of its business model is to combine the flexible capital of philanthropy, the skills of business and the rigor of the marketplace to help build enterprises that have the potential to serve the poor on a large scale.

This approach aligns well with Cisco Systems' own philosophy in both its business activities and its approach to corporate citizenship. Both organizations focus on developing and promoting high-impact solutions. As one of Acumen Fund's founding investors and now one of its sustaining partners, Cisco Systems Inc. as well as the Cisco Systems Foundation engages with Jacqueline and her colleagues in a number of ways. Tae Yoo serves on Acumen Fund's Advisory Council and the company has an opportunity to participate in a range of investor briefings and field trips to meet with social enterprises in Acumen Fund's portfolio, offering useful learning opportunities and exposure to innovative new approaches to social problem-solving.

15.6.4 Investing in Innovative Financing Mechanisms: Microfinance and the Case of Grameen Foundation USA and the Abdul Latif Jameel Company

The Abdul Latif Jameel (ALJ) Group is the world's largest independent distributor of Toyota vehicles, operating in the Middle East, Europe, Asia and Africa, with other activities in real estate, electronics and home appliances, advertising and financial services. Over 50 years ago, ALJ's founder instilled a strong commitment to community engagement in the company's overall approach to doing business. His son, Mohammed Abdul Latif Jameel, has built on this legacy of service to develop an increasingly strategic, solutions-driven approach to corporate citizenship that aims to align the company's values and competencies with the capacity building needs and societal challenges of the communities where it operates.

As a leading company based and operating in the Middle East, ALJ identified job creation opportunities for young people and increased economic opportunities for women as two crucial areas warranting a more focused, rigorous and partnership-driven approach. Over 60 percent of the population in the Middle East is under the age of 25 and many young people are leaving school without the necessary skills or motivation to do the jobs most needed in the region to ensure its long-term economic development and stability.

At the same time, an estimated six million Arab families live in extreme poverty, and there is growing awareness by leaders in the region that market-driven microfinance approaches offer a great opportunity for poverty alleviation. This includes the challenge of providing finance, technical assistance and broader support to women entrepreneurs, even more challenging in this predominantly Islamic region than elsewhere.

Drawing on a business relationship of over 50 years with the Toyota Corporation, and a commitment to benchmarking his business operations against world-class practices, Mohammed Abdul Latif Jameel decided to take the same rigorous approach to identifying world-class social enterprises that he and colleagues could learn from in order to address the challenges of job creation and enterprise development most effectively. His research and a long-standing relationship with the Massachusetts Institute of Technology led him to Muhammad Yunus, the founder of Grameen Bank, and from there to Grameen Foundation USA (GFUSA).

Building on the models and lessons of Grameen Bank, GFUSA is a nonprofit organization that combines microfinance, new technologies, and innovative business models to empower the world's poorest people to start their own enterprises and escape poverty. It champions innovation in three areas: information and communications technology as a strategy for poverty reduction; pursuing industry standards for data tracking and reporting; and developing and executing financing models to expand available capital for microfinance programs. Established in 1997, GFUSA has already built a global network of some 50 partners that have reached nearly 1.4 million families in 20 countries.

In 2004, GFUSA and the Abdul Latif Jameel Group joined forces and resources to launch a programme aimed at building the capacity of leading Arab Microfinance Intermediaries (MFIs) and the broader microfinance sector. The initiative is providing badly-needed capital for expansion around the Middle East, helping to jump-start the microfinance sector in some Arab countries, and building a network of social entrepreneurs who can raise awareness and build local capacity in order to increase the scale and impact of such activities throughout the region.

In addition to providing funding, the initiative is also supporting efforts to improve the evaluation, investment portfolio monitoring and technical assistance provided to Arab MFIs. It is offering targeted training and scholarships to these MFIs, including opportunities to spend time in Bangladesh learning first-hand from the Grameen Bank experience, as well as technology support to improve their information management systems and translation of microfinance training materials and research publications into Arabic.

In ALJ's home country Saudi Arabia, the initiative has helped to pioneer a new microfinance program that has already empowered hundreds of poor Saudi women to start small businesses and improve their families' prospects through the provision of micro-loans. Launched in June 2004, this Program for Productive Families had benefited over 550 women without a single loan default by the end of 2004, and has set an ambitious goal of reaching 2000 women by the end of 2005. It is expected to provide about 25 percent of the 6300 new jobs that the ALJ Group has committed to create through its overall Community Services program in 2005. During the implementation phase, over 800 Saudi women applied for six positions as loan officers, resulting in a well-qualified and highly motivated staff team.

This programme is not only helping to alleviate poverty by starting microfinance programs and encouraging greater entrepreneurship, but is also, in the words of GFUSA, 'beginning to break down entrenched barriers and stereotypes by addressing economic hardship through the use of microfinance' (Grameen Foundation, 2005).

From Mohammed Abdul Latif Jameel's perspective, the combination of a strong sense of social responsibility with rigorous evaluation, market-driven disciplines and innovative financing models, offers one of the best hopes of creating the necessary jobs and sense of entrepreneurship that are so crucial to securing a stable and prosperous future in the region.

Partnering with social enterprises such as those operating in the Grameen network helps the ALJ Group to bring world-class microfinance skills and capacities to the Middle East, thereby more effectively leveraging the resources his own company can contribute to tackling poverty, and helping to pursue the long-term interests of both the company and the wider society in which it operates.

15.6.5 Harnessing Technology for Social Progress: The International Youth Foundation and Nokia

Nokia has been one of the business success stories of the global technology revolution. Virtually unknown outside its home country of Finland in the 1980s, today the company is one of the world's leaders in mobile communications. Its clearly stated corporate mission is 'Connecting People.'

A passion for innovation has been a key factor in the company's success, as has a systematic focus on stakeholder relations. This is a key characteristic of the company's collegial culture and leadership style, and also feeds into its innovation processes, its operational capability and its brand equity. The company explicitly defines its stakeholders as 'employees, customers, suppliers, shareholders, governmental and non-governmental organizations, the media, the communities where it does business and other parties that have influence over or are influenced by Nokia' (Ibid).

Given Nokia's leadership in future-oriented communications technologies, young people are an increasingly important stakeholder group. The company is establishing mechanisms to listen to and learn from this group, integrating feedback from young people into its innovation processes and future visioning. Youth and education have also been made the strategic focus of Nokia's corporate citizenship activities. According to Jorma Ollila, 'In the future that Nokia's business is shaping, people will have the technology to communicate anytime, anywhere. Helping young people improve their skills, knowledge and connections to society is a natural outgrowth of Nokia's business, vision and values' (Ollila, 2002).

As a company that revolves around innovation, Nokia is keen to work with social entrepreneurs in delivering its youth and education programmes. After extensive consultation, Nokia decided that the International Youth Foundation (IYF), founded by social entrepreneur Rick Little, would be an effective and creative partner in helping it to implement its global commitment to youth development. IYF's programs seek to build young peoples' character, confidence and competence and to connect them to their families, peers and communities. This purpose fits strategically with Nokia's own vision of connecting people.

In April 2000, Nokia and the IYF launched a multi-year, multi-million dollar partnership called 'Make a Connection.' This global initiative focuses on locally driven programmes that improve educational opportunities for young people and teach them life skills. Nokia's initial financial commitment to 'Make a Connection' was about $10 million over four years, with the aim of leveraging more money, as well as ideas and technology through partnerships and employee volunteer efforts.

It also aims to mobilise in-kind and professional support from Nokia, its employees, business partners and other companies and non-profit organizations. Not surprisingly, an important element is making effective use of information and communications technology. One example is *YouthActionNet*, an Internet site for youth interested in making a change in their communities. It provides information on events, resources, and issues that young people can get involved in and enables them to interact with peers around the world. The site was developed, with support from Nokia experts, by a group of young people from eight different countries.

Today, 'Make a Connection' is operating on five continents in 20 countries and has directly impacted more than 180 000 young people – helping to create the life skills and technological capacity that will enable them to be effective and responsible citizens, employees, customers and leaders of the future.

15.6.6 Mobilising Core Corporate Competencies to Develop the 'Next Generation': City Year and Bank of America (formerly BankBoston)

BankBoston, now part of Bank of America, is America's oldest commercial bank. From the China Trade to the textile mills of the early industrial revolution, from the first movie studios in Hollywood and the birth of McDonald's, to the high tech revolution along Boston's Route 128, the bank has been a vital part of America's economic history. By the late 1980s, it had grown into a formidable regional and international presence and had been steadily paying dividends longer than any corporation in North America. It had also grown complacent, however, as well as inwardly focused, bloated, bureaucratic and even arrogant. In 1991, like so many other storied US companies, BankBoston almost went bust.

Management knew that it had to act decisively – and it did. Layers of management were eliminated, scores of uncompetitive businesses were sold or discarded, demanding new metrics imposed a tight financial discipline, and a comfortable, conventional corporate culture was transformed and reinvented into a leaner, more flexible, market-driven and customer-focused company. The results were impressive. By the late 1990s, the bank was producing record earnings and growth, its stock had soared to $118 a share, and its market value exceeded $15 billion.

As part of its corporate turnaround and reinvention, the bank was determined to transform its traditional corporate giving programme into a more strategic investment initiative. In other words, instead of just giving out small grants to many community organizations as it had for decades, engendering little goodwill or recognition in the community and realizing little quantifiable benefit to society, the company decided to pursue a new approach. One that was driven by a desire to make a difference and to harness not only its philanthropic dollars but its other corporate strengths in advancing a limited number of community needs.

In 1988, Ira Jackson, an Executive Vice President at the bank, was thinking about this new approach to social investing and partnership, when he was approached by two young Harvard Law School graduates, Alan Khazei and Michael Brown, who wanted seed funding to start a youth service program called CityYear. Khazei and Brown thought that young people recently graduated from high school could be tapped to be part of the solution to inner city problems, and that idealism backed by a disciplined and entrepreneurial approach could result in changed lives and vastly improved communities. Jackson decided that the idea was promising, even if untested, and that CityYear had the potential of becoming a transformational initiative for young people and their communities; one where the company's philanthropy, combined with other corporate resources, might really make a difference.

Khazei and Brown had no track record, no infrastructure or support system, and virtually no organizational capacity. The bank gave its 'Good Housekeeping Seal of Approval' by being the first company in the nation to fund a CityYear team, and then helped line up five other corporate sponsors to launch a summer pilot programme. It provided funding to CityYear's founders so that they could methodically evaluate the results of their summer 'test' and thoroughly plan for a full year programme the next fall. The bank provided meeting space, a surplus vault, office furniture and banking privileges. It took out advertisements celebrating CityYear's potential and signed on to fund the first year-round CityYear team. It trained the first year-round corps in financial literacy, provided them with free checking accounts and ATM privileges, and allowed a middle manager to serve 'on loan' as CityYear's first director of corporate development and fundraising.

When CityYear decided to expand into a national programme, the bank funded its first non-Boston-based team, introduced CityYear to bankers and prominent customers in other major communities, and hosted a breakfast with big city mayors from across the country to learn about CityYear's promise. Today, Bank of America remains one of City Year's most important corporate partners and in 2004 committed to become the first national lead partner for City Year's Young Heroes program, which helps middle school students to understand social issues facing their community and how they can be part of the solution.

CityYear, over 15 years later, has grown and expanded into cities around America and has been implemented in South Africa. In 1992, Bill Clinton visited the organization while campaigning for President, and was so impressed with what he experienced that he modelled AmeriCorps on the CityYear precedent. AmeriCorps, in less than a decade has attracted over 250 000 young people to full-time national and community service, more than have served in the forty-year history of the Peace Corps.

City Year's strategic partnership with the bank has enabled it not only to raise the finances, but also to develop the institutional capacity and core internal competencies to grow, expand, control its expenses, secure its funding, ensure for quality programs and deliver on its promise. The bank and other corporate partners have gained a variety of employee development, reputation and brand recognition benefits, while investing in the longer-term stability of the communities in which they operate.

15.7 RECOMMENDATIONS FOR INCREASING PARTNERSHIPS BETWEEN COMPANIES AND SOCIAL ENTREPRENEURS

If partnerships between businesses and social entrepreneurs make so much sense, both in terms of mutual organizational benefit and of social or environmental impact, why are there so few good examples? Business-social collaboration is a new and growing field, to be sure, but there is also more that can be done to expand the number, scope and impact of such partnerships. Following are five recommendations that would contribute to moving this emerging field forward.

1. Increase the exposure of leaders in both sectors, business and civil society, to each other and 'their' issues: they may find some of those issues are actually shared. Ways to do this include experiential learning, project visits, integration of corporate responsibility and social entrepreneurship studies into regular business and public policy curricula at universities, joint international fora, and increased diversity of experience on corporate boards of directors and advisory committees.

2. Linked to this, increase understanding – by companies AND civil society organizations or social entrepreneurs – of the critical social and environmental roles companies play. We find that corporations are urged, sometimes on pain of legal action, to spend more time and money understanding their social and environmental impacts and we agree that this is a valuable endeavour. However, civil society organizations who work with (and even against) companies would also benefit from a fuller understanding of both the negative and positive multiplier effects companies' core business activities have within the larger systems of which they are part, and also the very real operational and competitive constraints that even some of the world's largest companies face.

3. Create systems to harvest employees' own ideas for social innovation. Imagine employees were granted one day per month to volunteer, on the condition that they bring back every quarter two ideas applicable to the organization. A number of staff could be tasked with reviewing all these ideas and bringing the best to the attention of the CEO or president. Such a system for cross-sectoral knowledge and idea transfer could be equally applicable for companies and nonprofits. Some companies are also offering some of their high potential employees the opportunity to take several months leave to work with social enterprises and development agencies, with two notable examples being the Pfizer Health Fellows program and PriceWaterhouse Coopers' Ulysses programme.

4. When business-social partnerships are implemented, be rigorous about planning, monitoring, and measuring results. This may sound obvious, but in our view does not yet happen regularly enough. Those in charge of business-social collaborations should set targets, measure results,

communicate, and hold each other accountable as rigorously as in any other business- or mission-critical endeavour. Evidence that business-social collaborations deliver, as well as promise, will provide incentives for others to undertake them despite the well-recognized transaction costs to working across sectors (and could also yield lessons in cross-sector management that reduce those transaction costs in future).

5. Provide funds and other incentives for such partnerships. Companies could also join forces with foundations, bilateral and multilateral development agencies and other government bodies to invest in sector-focused, national or even regional or global challenge funds, matching grants and fiscal incentives aimed at supporting the growth of social enterprises.

The public challenges we face, both nationally and globally, are too large and too integrated, and the resources and capacities we have for addressing them too scarce and disintegrated between different sectors, that no one sector – government, business or civil society – can find the solutions on their own. There is a growing need for public officials, business leaders, civic leaders and social entrepreneurs to come together to explore new approaches to problem-solving; approaches that combine the best of social vision and public purpose with the best of business acumen and market disciplines. The examples and frameworks in this chapter offer some ideas for the way forward.

Bibliography

Abell, D. (27 March 1998), 'Leading Business beyond the Bottom Line', *Financial Times*.

Abouleish, I. (2004), *Die Sekem: Vision*, Stuttgart: Mayer Verlag.

Ackerman, R.W. (1975), *The social challenge to business*, Cambridge: Harvard University Press.

Ajzen, I. (1991), 'The Theory of Planned Behaviour', *Organizational Behaviour & Human Decision Process*, **50**, 179-211.

Aldrich, H.E. and Fiol, C.M. (1994), 'Fools rush in? The institutional context of industry creation', *Academy of Management Review*, **19**, 645–670.

Alkhafaji, A.F. (1989), *A Stakeholder Approach to Corporate Governance. Managing in a Dynamic Environment*, Westport: Quorum.

Allen, D.N. and McCluskey, R. (1990), 'Structure, Policy, Services, and Performance in the Business Incubator Industry', *Entrepreneurship Theory & Practice* **15**(2), 61-77.

Alter, K., Emerson, J., Shoemaker, P. and Tuan, M. (2001), 'When is it time to say goodbye? Exit strategies and venture philanthropy funds', Virtue Ventures Report, Social Venture Partners and the Roberts Foundation.

Altman, B.W. (1998), 'Corporate community relations in the 1990s: A study in transformation', *Business and Society*, **37**(2), 221-228.

Altman, B.W. and Vidaver-Cohen, D. (2000), 'Corporate citizenship in the New Millennium: Foundation for an architecture of excellence', *Business and Society*, **105**(1), 145-169.

Alvord, S.H., Brown, L.D. and Letts, C.W. (2002), 'Social entrepreneurship and social transformation: An Exploratory Study', WP #15 November, The Hauser Center for Nonprofit Organizations and The Kennedy School of Government, Harvard University

Alworth, Thomas, Executive Director, Catskill Center for Conservation and Development, Arkville, New York, interview with the author (2005).

Amaral, L.A.N. and Ottino, J.M. (March 2003), 'Complex networks: Augmenting the framework for the study of complex systems', *European Physical Journal*, 38(2), 147-163.

Andriof, J. and McIntosh M. (2001), *Perspectives on corporate citizenship*, Sheffield, UK: Greenleaf.

Argyle, M. and Henderson M. (1985), *The Anatomy of Relationships*, London: Penguin.

Ashoka (2005), 'Full Economic Citizenship: A global initiative of Ashoka. What is a Hybrid Value Chain?', November 2005 (available at www.ashoka.org).

Ashoka (2005), 'Hybrid Value Chain', November 2005 (available at www.ashoka.org).

Attenborough, David (1987), *The First Eden: The Mediterranean World and Man*, Boston, US, and Toronto, Canada: Little Brown and Company.

Axelrod, R. (1984), *The Evolution of Cooperation*, New York: Basic Books.

Backman and Dees (1994), 'Social Enterprise: Private Initiatives for the Common Good', *Harvard Business School*, publishing division, 9-395-116.

Bank of England (1998), 'Finance for small firms: A fifth report', London: Bank of England.

Bank of England (2003), 'The financing of social enterprises', London: Bank of England.

Baraldi, C. and Piazzi, G., 'The Community Seen from the Bottom, Children at San Patrignano'.

Barendsen, L. and Gardner, H. (2004), 'Is the social entrepreneur a new type of leader?', *Leader to Leader*, Fall **34**.

Barlett, C.A. and Ghoshal, S. (1994) 'Changing the role of top management: Beyond strategy to purpose', *Harvard Business Review,* **72**(6).

Baron, R.A. (1998), 'Cognitive mechanism in entrepreneurship: why and when entrepreneurs think differently than other people', *Journal of business venturing,* **13**, 275-294.

Barr, S. (2002), Personal interview with the author, 10 April 2002, London: CaféDirect.

Barrett, R. (1998), *Liberating the Corporate Soul*, Butterworth Heinemann.

Baum, J.A.C., Li Stan, X. and Usher, J.M. (2000), 'Making the next move: How experiential and vicarious learning shape the locations of chains' acquisitions', *Administrative Science Quarterly*, pp. 766-801.

Baumol, W.J. (1986), 'Entrepreneurship and a century of growth', *Journal of Business Venturing*, **13**(4), 141-145.

Baumol, W.J. (1990), 'Entrepreneurship: Productive, unproductive, and destructive', *Journal of Political Economy*, **98**(5), 893-921.

Bergquist, W.H. (1992), *The four cultures of the academy: insights and strategies for improving leadership in collegiate organizations*, San Francisco: Jossey-Bass.

Berry, F.S., Brower, S.O. Choi, W.X. Goa, H.S. Jang, M. Kwon and J. Word (2004), 'Three Traditions of Network Research: What the Public Management Research Agenda Can Learn from Other Research Communities', *Public Administration Review*, **64**(5), 539-552.

Bhide, A. (2000), *The Origin and Evolution of New Business*, New York: Oxford University Press.

Bollier, D. (1996), *Aiming Higher*, Amacon

Bornstein, D. (2004), *How to change the world. Social entrepreneurs and the power of new ideas*, Oxford: Oxford University Press.

Borzaga, C. and Defourny, J. (eds), (2004), *The Emergence Of Social Enterprise,* London: Routledge.

Borzaga, C. and Solari L. (2004), 'Management Challenges for Social Enterprises', in Borzaga C. and Defourny J. (eds.), *The Emergence of Social Enterprises*, New York, London: Routledge, 333-349.

Boschee, J. (1998), 'What does it take to be a social entrepreneur?', National Centre for Social Entrepreneurs, June 2005 (available at http://www.socialentrepreneurs.org/whatd oes.html).

Boschee, J. and McClurg, J. (2003), 'Toward a better understanding of social entrepreneurship: Some important distinctions', June 2005 (available at http://www.se-alliance.org/ better_understanding.pdf),

Bowen, H.R. (1953), *Social responsibilities of the businessman*, New York: Harper & Row.

Bowie, N.E. (1988), 'Challenging the Egoistic Paradigm', *Business Ethic Quarterly*, **1**, 1-21.

Bradach, J.L. (1998), *Franchise Organizations*, Boston: Harvard Business School Press.

Bretman, I. (2002), Personal interview with the author, 23 May 2002, London: Deputy Director, Fairtrade Foundation.

Briassoulis, H. and Van Der Straaten, J. (2000), *Tourism and the Environment: an Overview in Tourism and the Environment: Regional, Economic, Cultural and Policy Issues*, Boston, US: Kluwer Academic Publishers.

Brinckerhoff, P.C. (2000), *Social entrepreneurship: The art of mission-based venture development*, New York: John Wiley & Sons.

Brooks, O.J. (1986), 'Economic Development Through Entrepreneurship: Incubators and the Incubation Process', *Economic Development Review,* **4**(2), 24-29.

Brush, C.G., Green, P.G. and Hart, M.M. (2001), 'From initial idea to unique advantage: the entrepreneurial challenge of constructing a resource base', *The Academy of Management Executives*, **15**(1), 64-78.

Bruyat, C. and Julien, P.A. (2000), 'Defining the field of research in entrepreneurship', *Journal of Business Venturing*, **16**, 165-180.

Budrock, Helen, Assistant Director, Catskill Center for Conservation and Development, Arkville, New York, interview with the author (2005).

Business Week (cover story) (2002), 'The new face of philanthropy', 2 December 2002.

Bygrave, W. and Timmons, J. (1992), *The venture capital at the crossroads*, Boston, MA: Harvard business school press.

Cafédirect (2000), 'Annual Report 1999-2000', London: Cafédirect.

Cafédirect (2002), 'Company History', September 2002 (available at http://www.cafedirect.co.uk/about/company.html.).

Cannon, C.M. (2000), 'Charity for profit: How the new social entrepreneurs are creating good by sharing wealth', *National Journal*, 16 June, 1898-1904.

Carroll, A.B. (1989), *Business and society: Ethics and stakeholder management*, Cincinnati, OH: South-Western.

Carter, N., Gartner, W. and Reynolds, P. (1996), 'Exploring start-up event sequences', *Journal of Business Venturing,* **11**, 151-166.

Cartwright, D. and Hararay, F. (1956), 'Structural Balance: a

Generalization of Hieder's Theory', *Psychological Review*, **63**(5), 277-92.

Casas, C., Lajoie, W. and Prahalad, C.K. (2003), 'Voxiva' University of Michigan Business School, November 2005 (available at http://www.bus.umich.edu/BottomOfThePyramid/ xMAP2003.htm).

Casson, M. (1982) *The entrepreneur. An economic Theory*, Totowa, NJ: Barnes and Noble.

CCCD, The Catskill Center for Conservation and Development (1997), *Summary Guide to the Terms of the Watershed Agreement*, Arkville, NY: The Catskill Center for Conservation and Development.

Censis (2002), 'Rapporto Annuale Situazione Demografica Italia', Roma.

Censis (2003), 'Rapporto Annuale Situazione Demografica Italia', Roma.

Chandler, G.N. and Hanks, S.H. (1998), 'An examination of the substitutability of founders human and financial capital in emerging business ventures', *Journal of Business Venturing*, **13**, 359-369.

Chapman, W.R. and Hamel, G. (2002). 'The World Bank's Innovation Market', *Harvard Business Review*, November 1, 2-8.

Clark, Rosenzweig, Long and Olsen (2003), 'Double Bottom Line Report'.

CNR (1998), 'Rapporto sui Servizi Home Care in Italia', Roma.

Coe, C. (2002), Telephone interview with the author, 11 November 2002, Oxford: Trading Director, Oxfam.

Cohen, W. and Levinthal, D. (1990), 'Absorptive capacity: A new perspective on learning and innovation', *Administrative Science Quarterly*, **35**, 128-152.

Cook, B., Dodds C. and Mitchell W. (2001), 'Social entrepreneurship: Whose responsibility is it anyway? The false premise of social entrepreneurship', Centre of Full Employment And Equity and Department of Social Work ,21st November.

Cook, B., Dodds, C. and Mitchell, W. (February 2003), 'Social Entrepreneurship: False promises and dangerous foreboding', *Australian Journal of Social Issues*, **38**(1), 57-72.

Cumming, D. and MacIntosh, J. (2000), *Venture Capital Exits in Canada and the United States*, University of Alberta and University of Toronto:Mimeo.

Cyert, R.M. and March, J.C. (1963), A behavioral thery of the firm, Englewood Cliffs, NJ: Prentice-Hall.

Dahle, C. (2004), 'Social Capitalists – The top 20 groups that are changing the world', Fast Company, January 2004, Issue 78.

Dart, R. (2004), 'The legitimacy of social enterprise', *Nonprofit Management & Leadership*, Summer, **14**(4), 411-424.

Davis, S. (2002), 'Social entrepreneurship. towards an entrepreneurial culture for social and economic development', February 2005 (available at http://www.ashoka.org/global /yespaper.pdf).

De Villiers, Marq (2000), *Water,* New York: Mariner, Houghton Mifflin.

Dearlove, D. (2004), 'Interview: Jeff Skoll', *Business Strategy Review*, 15(2), 51-53.

Dees, G.J. (1998a), 'The meaning of social entrepreneurship', June 2005 (available at http://www.fuqua.duke.edu/ centers/case/ documents/dees_SE.pdf).

Dees, G.J., Battle Anderson, B. and Wei-skillern, J. (2004), 'Scaling social impact: Strategies for spreading social innovations', *Stanford Social Innovation Review*, (Spring).

Dees, J.G. (1998b), 'Enterprising nonprofits', *Harvard Business Review*, **76**(1), 54-66.

Dees, J.G. and Elias, J. (1998), 'The challenges of combining social and commercial enterprise', *Business Ethics Quarterly*, **8**(1), 165-178.

Dees, J.G. and Oberfield, A. (1999), *Note on Starting a Nonprofit Venture*, Boston: Harvard Business School, 9-391-096.

Dees, J.G., Emerson, J. and Economy, P. (2001), *Enterprising Nonprofits: A Toolkit for Social Entrepreneurs,* New York: John Wiley & Sons.

Dees, J.G., Emerson, J. and Economy, P. (2002), *Strategic tools for social entrepreneurs. Enhancing the performance of your enterprising nonprofit*, New York: John Wiley & Sons.

Delmar, F. and Shane, S. (2003), 'Does business planning facilitate the development of new ventures?', *Strategic Management Journal,* **24**(11), 1165-1185.

Desa, G. and Kotha, S. (2005), 'Ownership Mission and Environment: An exploratory analysis into the evolution of a technology social venture', in Mair J., Robinson J. and Hockerts K. (eds) *Social Entrepreneurship*, NY: Palgrave.

Dew, N., Sarasvathy, S.D., Velamuri, S.R. and Venkataraman, S. (2003), 'Three Views of Entrepreneurial Opportunity', in Acs Z.J. and Audretsch D.B. (eds) *Handbook of Entrepreneurship*.

Dewan, Deborah, Gubernatorial appointee to environmental seat on the Catskill Watershed Corporation, interview with the author (2005).

Doi, T. (1971), *The Anatomy of Dependence*, Kodansha International.

Donaldson, T. and Preston, L.E. (1995), 'The stakeholder theory of the corporation: Concepts, evidence, and implications', *Academy of Management Review*, **20**(1), 65-91.

Dorado, S. and Haettich, H. (2004), 'Social entrepreneurial ventures: Worth a careful look?', Working Paper, Boston: UMASS - College of Management.

Drayton, W. (2002), 'The Citizen Sector: Becoming as Entrepreneurial and Competitive as Business', *California Management Review*, **44**(3),120-132.

Drucker, H.M. (2000), 'Wanted: UK venture philanthropists', Oxford Philanthropic.

Drucker, P. (1986), *Innovazione e Imprenditorialità*, Milan: ETAS.

DUBAI International Award Best Practices in Improving the Living Environment, (available at http://www.blpnet.org /awards/awards02.htm), Dubai Award.

Duffner, S. (2003), 'Principal-Agent Problems in Venture Capital Finance', Working Paper, University of Basel, WWZ/department of Finance.

Durate, J.E. (1993), 'Policy development: planning methods that get results', *CMA Magazine,* **67**(4), 62-84.

Eagles, Paul J., McCool Stephen F. and Haynes Christopher D. (2002), *Sustainable Tourism in Protected Areas: Guidelines for Planning and Management*, IUCN – The World Conservation Union, UK.

Eckhardt, J.T. and Shane S.A. (2003), 'Opportunities and entrepreneurship', *Journal of Management*, **29**(3), 333-349.

Elkins, L. (1996), 'Tips for preparing a business plan', *Nation Business*, June.

El-Namaki, M.S. (1988), 'Encouraging entrepreneurs in developing countries', *Long Range Planning*, **21**(4), 98-106.

Elster, J. (1989), *The Cement of Society, A Study of Social Order*, Cambridge: Cambridge University Press.

Emerson, J. (1998), 'The Venture Fund Initiative: An Assessment
of Current Opportunities for Social Purpose Business
development', San Francisco, CA: The Roberts Enterprise
Development Fund, The Roberts Foundation.

Emerson, J. and Twersky, F. (eds. 1996), *New Social
Entrepreneurs: The Success, Challenge and Lessons of Non-
Profit Enterprise Creation*, San Francisco, California: The
Roberts Foundation.

Equal Exchange (2002), 'Origins of Equal Exchange', August
2002 (available at http://www.equalexchange.co.uk/ history.
htm).

Etzioni, A. (1988), *The Moral Dimension: Toward a New
Economics*, New York: The Free Press Macmillan, Inc.

EU (1998), Commission Communication to the Council 2141
'Council Meeting Development Brussels', Communication of
the European Commission to the European Council to be
discussed in the council meeting number 2141.

Fazzolari, S., Personal interviews with staff and residents (2005).

Fenn, G.W., Liang, N. and Prowse, S. (1996), 'The Economics of
the Private Equity Market', *Federal Reserve Bulletin*, January,
Federal Reserve Bank.

Fennel, D.A. (2004), 'Deep Ecotourism: Seeking Theoretical and
Practical Reverence. New Horizons in Tourism: Strange
Experiences and Stranger Practices', T.V. Singh, CABI
Publishing.

Festinger, L. (1957), *A Theory of Cognitive Dissonance*, Stanford,
CA: Stanford University Press.

FIRCO, Fideicomiso de Riesgo Compartido, cited in draft
publication by Ashoka's Full Economic Citizenship Initiative,
December 2004.

Fleming, L. (2001) 'Recombinant Uncertainty in Technological
Search', *Management Science*, **47**, 117-132.

Fowler, A. (2000) 'NGDOs as a moment in history: Beyond aid to
social entrepreneurship or civic innovation?' *Third World
Quarterly*, 21(4), 637-654.

Fowler, K. (2002), Telephone interview with the author, 9
December 2002, Oxford: Livelihood Project Manager, Oxfam.

Frank, R.H. (1987), 'If Homo Economicus Could Choose His
Own Utility Function, Would He Want One with a
Conscience?', *The American Economic Review,* **7**(4).

Freeman, R.E. (1984), *Strategic Management: A Stakeholder Approach*, Boston: Pitman Publishing, Inc.

Friedman, V.J. (2000), 'The Incubator for Social Entrepreneurship: Creating Partnerships for Second Order Social Change', Paper presented at the Annual Conference of the International Society for Third-Sector research, Dublin, Ireland: Ruppin Institute, Israel.

Fruchterman, J. (2004), 'Technology Benefiting Humanity. Ubiquity', Association for Computing Machinery (5)', June (available at http://www.acm.org/ubiquity/views/v5i5_fruchterman. html).

Galbraith, J. (1977), *Organization Design*, Reading, MA: Addison-Wesley.

Galbraith, J. (2001), *Designing Organizations: An Executive Guide to Strategy, Structure, and Process Revised*, Jossey-Bass, 2nd edition.

Galbraith, J.R. (1995), *Designing Organizations*, San Francisco: Jossey-Bass.

Galusha, D. (1999), *Liquid Assets. A History of New York City's Water System,* Fleishman's New York: Purple Mountain Press.

Galusha, Diane, Communications Director, Catskill Watershed Corporation, interview with the author.

Gartner, W.B. (1985), 'A conceptual framework for describing the phenomenon of new venture creation', *Academy of Management Review*, **10**, 696-706.

Gartner, W.B. (1988), 'Who is an entrepreneur? is the wrong question', *American Journal of Small Business*, **13**(Spring), 11-32.

Gerwin, D. and Christoffel, W. (1974), 'Organizational Structure And Technology A Computer Model Approach', *Management Science,* **20**(12), 1531-1542.

Go, F. and Mautinho, L. (2000), *Strategic Management in Tourism*, CABI Publishing.

Goodstein, Eban S. (2002), *Economics and the Environment*, 3rd eds. New York: Wiley.

Graf, Jeffrey, Program Manager, Community Planning, New York City Department of Environmental Protection, Kingston New York, interview with the author (2005).

Grameen Foundation (2005), 'Grameen Connections', Grameen Foundation USA, Spring Issue.

Grandori, A. (1999), *Organizzazione e Comportamento Economico*, Bologna: Il Mulino.

Greenfeld, K.T. (2000), 'A new way of giving', *Time*, **156**(4), July 24.

Greening, W.D. and Turban, D.B. (2000), 'Corporate Social Performance as a Competitive Advantage in Attracting Quality Workforce', Business & Society, 39(3), 254-280.

Grenier, P. (2002), 'The function of social entrepreneurship in the UK', Paper presented at the ISTR Conference, Cape Town, July.

Guclu, A., Dees, J.G. and Battle Anderson, B. (2002), *The process of social entrepreneurship: Creating opportunities worthy of serious pursuit*, Fuqua School of Business, Center for the Advancement of Social Entrepreneurship.

Guidicini, P. and Pieretti, G. (1991), 'San Patrignano: Between Community and Society'.

Guidicini, Paolo and Giovanni Pieretti (1995), 'San Patrignano Environmental Therapy and City Effect'.

Habermas, J. (1981), *Theorie des kommunikativen handels*, Frankfurt am Main: Surkamp.

Hamel, G. and Prahalad, C.K. (1989), 'Strategic intent', *Harvard Business Review*, **67**(3), 63-76.

Harper, M. (1991), 'Enterprise development in poorer nations', *Entrepreneurship Theory and Practice*, **15**, 7-11.

Harris, R., Griffin, T. and Williams, P. (2002), *Sustainable Tourism: A Global Perspective*, Butterworth-Heinemann, An Imprint of Elsevier Science Ltd., USA.

Hayek, F.A. (1945), 'The use of knowledge in society', *American Economic Review*, **35**(4), 519-530.

Heathcote, I. W. (1998), *Integrated Watershed Management*, New York: John Wiley.

Heifetz, A.R., Kania, J.V. and Kramer, M.R. (2004), 'Leading Boldly', *Stanford Social Innovation Review*, Winter **3**(2), 89-105.

Henton, D., Melville, J. and Walesh, K. (1997), 'The age of civic entrepreneur: Restoring civil society and building economic community', *National Civic Review*, **6**(2), 149-156.

Hermann, R.E. and Gioia J. (1998), *Lean & Meaningful*, Oakhill Press.

Hertzberg, F. (1966), *The Work and the Nature of Man*, New York: Wold Pub.

Hockerts, K.N. (2003), *Sustainability Innovations, Ecological and Social Entrepreneurship and the Management of Antagonistic Assets*, Bamberg: Difo Verlag, University of St. Gallen.

Hockerts, K.N. (2004), 'Bootstrapping social change. Towards an evolutionary theory of social entrepreneurship', unpublished paper.

Hockerts, K.N. (2005), 'Desafiando el cambio social, Hacia una teoría evolutiva de las iniciativas emprendedoras socials, in J. Mair', *Iniciativa Emprendedora*, **48**, 57-68. Edición especial: 'Iniciativa emprendedora social: la empresa al servicio de los excluidos'.

Hockerts, K.N. (2006), 'Entrepreneurial Opportunity in Social Purpose Business Ventures', in J Mair, J Robertson, and K.N., Hockerts (eds.), *Handbook of Research in Social Entrepreneurship*, **1**, Edward Elgar.

Hoffman, J. (2005), 'Stratification and Management of Water Quality: New York City's Catskill/Delaware Watershed', *Environmental Values*, **14**.

Hormozi, A.M., Lucio, W., McMinn, R.D. and Sutton, G.S. (2002), 'Business plan for new or small business: paving the path to success', *Management Decision*, **40**(8), 755-763.

Hsu, D.H. and Lim, K. (2005), 'Knowledge Bridging by Biotechnology Start-ups', Wharton School Working Paper.

Hudghton, T. (2002), Telephone interview with the author, 28 August 2002, Manchester: Co-operative Retail.

Huselid, M.A., Becker, B.E. and Beatty, D. (2005) *The Workforce Scorecard: Managing Human Capital to Execute Strategy*, Harvard Business School Press.

IATP, Institute for Agriculture and Trade Policy (1997), 'Watershed Agricultural Council Catskill/Delaware Watershed Complex New York', Farmer-Led Watershed Initiatives Conference, Septmber 2005 (available at www.watero bservatory.org/library.cfm?refID=33621).

International Conference Renewable Energy Sources (RES) for Islands (2003), 'Tourism and Water Desalination', 26-28 May, Crete, Greece Organizer: EREC - European Renewable Energy Council.

International Union for the Conservation of Nature and Natural Resources (The World Conservation Union – IUCN) (1999), 'Development of Approaches and Practice for Sustainable Use of Biological Resources – Tourism', 4th Meeting of the SBSTTA.

ISTAT (2002), 'Rapporto Annuale Situazione Demografica', Roma.

ISVAP (2000), 'Rapporto Annuale Servizi Assicurativi', Milano.

Jackson, I. and Nelson, J. (2004), *Profits with Principles: Seven strategies for creating value with values*, Currency/ Doubleday.

Johnson, S. (2000), 'Literature review on social entrepreneurship', University of Alberta, Canadian Center for Social Entrepreneurship, June 2005 (available at http://www.bus. ualberta.ca/ccse/Publications).

Johnson, S. (2003), 'Young Social Enterprise in Canada', Canadian Centre for Social Entrepreneurship, University of Alberta.

Johnson, S. (November 2000), 'Literature Review on Social Entrepreneurship', Canadian Centre for Social Entrepreneurship, July 2005 (available at www.bus.ualberta.ca /ccse/Publications/Publications/Lit.%20Review%20SE%20Nov ember%202000.rtf).

Jones, T.M. (1980), 'Corporate Social Responsibility Revisited, Redefined', *California Management Review,* **22**, 59-67.

Jönsson, C., B. Bjurulf, O. Elgström, A. Sannerstedt and M. Strömvik (September 1998), 'Negotiations in Networks in the European Union', *International Negotiation*, **3**(3), 319-344.

Jungman, H. and Seppae M. (2004), 'V2C activity on a local level: qualitative cases. Tampere Valley and Silicon Valley', *Qualitative Market research*: *An International Journal,* **7**(4), 265-273, Emerald.

Kaku, R. (1997), 'The path of kyosei', *Harvard Business Review,* **75**(4).

Kanniainen, V. and Keuschnigg, C. (2003), 'The optimal portfolio of start-up firms in Venture Capital Finance', *Journal of Corporate Finance*, Elsevier Science.

Kanter, R. (1999), 'From spare change to real change: The social sector as beta site for business innovation', *Harvard Business Review*, **77**, 122-133.

Kassarjjan, J.B.M. (1992), 'Shaping Spaarbeleg: Real and Ureal', IMD Case No: GM 537.

Katila, R., and Ahuja, G. (2002), 'Something Old, Something New: A Longitudinal Study of Search Behavior and New

Product Introduction', *Academy of Management Journal*, **45**, 1183-1194.

Katz, J., and Gartner, W.B. (1988) 'Properties of emerging organizations' *Academy of Management Review*, 13(3), 429-441.

Kirzner, I. (1997), 'Entrepreneurial discovery and the competitive market process: An Austrian approach', *The Journal of Economic Literature*, **35**, 60-85.

Kodithuwakku, S.S., and Rosa, P. (2002) 'The entrepreneurial process and economic success in a constrained environment', *Journal of Business Venturing*, 17, 431-465.

Kogut, B., and Zander, U. (1992), 'Knowledge of the Firm, Combinative Capabilities, and the Replication of Technology', *Organization Science*, **3**, 383-397.

Kolm, S.C. (1994), 'The Theory of Reciprocity and the Choice of Economic Systems: An Introduction', *Investigaciones Economicas,* **18**, 67-95.

Kolm, S.C. [1983] 1995, 'Altruism and Efficiency', in Zamagni S., *The Economics of Altruism*, Hants: E. Elgar.

Kotha, S. (1998), 'Competing on the internet: How Amazon.com is rewriting the rules of competition', *Advances in Strategic Management*, **15**, 239-265.

Kotler, P. and Lee, N. (2005), *Corporate social responsibility. Doing the most good for your company and your cause*, Hoboken, New Jersey: John Wiley & Sons, Inc.

Krueger, N.F. (1993), 'The Impact of Prior Entrepreneurial Exposure on Perception on a New Venture Desirability and Feasibility', *Entrepreneurial Theory and Practice*, Fall 5-21.

Krueger, N.F. (2000), 'The Cognitive Infrastructure of Opportunity Emergence', *Entrepreneurship Theory & Practice*, **24**(3), 5-23.

Laville, F.L. and Nyssens, M. (2004), 'The social enterprise: Towards a theoretical social-economic approach', in C. Borzaga and J. Defourny (eds.), *The emergence of social enterprise*, London: Routledge, pp. 312-332.

Lawrence, P. and Lorsch, J. (1967), *Organization and environment*, Boston, MA: Harvard Business School Division of Research.

Leach, W.D. and Pelkey N.W. (2001), 'Making watershed partnerships work: a review of the empirical literature', *Journal of Water Resources Planning and Management*, **127**(6), 378-86.

Leadbeater, C. (1997), *The rise of the social entrepreneur*, London: Demos.

Lepak, D.P. and Snell, S.A. (1999), 'The human resource architecture: Toward a theory of human capital allocation and development', *Academy of Management Review*, **24**(1), 31-48.

Letts, C.W., Ryan, W. and Grossman, A. (1997), 'Virtuous capital: What foundations can learn from venture capitalists', *Harvard Business Review*, **97**, 36-41.

Lindenberg, S. (1990), 'Homo Socio-economicus: The Emergence of a General Model of Man in the Social Sciences', *Journal of Institutional and Theoretical Economics,* **146**, 727-748.

Lindsay, W.W. and Rue, L.W. (1980), 'Impact of the Business Environment on the Long Range Planning Process: a Contingency View', *Academy of Management Journal,* **23**, 385-404.

Lingane, A. and Olsen, S., (2004), 'Guidelines for Social Return on Investment', *California Management Review*, **46**(3), 116-135.

Littrell, M. and Dickson, M. (1999), *Social Responsibility in the Global Market. Fair Trade of Cultural Products*, Thousand Oaks: Sage.

Lubell, M.(1999), 'Cooperation And Institutional Innovation: The Case Of Watershed Partnerships', PhD Dissertation Stony Brook University.

Lubell, M., Schneider, M., Scholz J.T. and Mihriye M. (2002), 'Watershed partnerships and the emergence of collective action institutions', *American Journal of Political Science*, **46**(1), 148-163.

MacMillan, I. (2003). 'SE: Playing the role of change agent in society'. *Knowledge@Wharton*. May.

MacMillan, I.C. (1983), 'The politics of new venture management', *Harvard Business Review*, Nov./Dec.

MacMillan, I.C. and McGrath, R. (2000), *The Entrepreneurship Mindset*, Boston: Harvard Business School Press.

MacMillan, I.C. and Subba Narasimha, P.N. (1987), 'Characteristics Distinguishing Funded from Unfunded Business Plans Evaluated by Venture Capitalists', *Strategic Management Journal,* **8**(6), 579-585.

Mair, J. and Marti, I. (2004), 'Social Entrepreneurship: What Are We Talking About? A Framework For Future Research', WP No 546, March, IESE Business School, University of Navarra.

Mair, J. and Noboa, E. (2003), 'The Emergence of Social Enterprises and their Place in the New Organisational Landscape', Working paper No. 523, IESE Business School, University of Navarra.

March, J.G. (1991), 'Exploration and exploitation in organizational learning', *Organization Science*, 2(1), 71-87.

March, J.G. and Simon, H.A. (1958), *Organizations*, New York: Wiley.

Margolis, J.D. and Walsh, J.P. (2003), 'Misery loves companies: Rethinking social initiative by business', *Administrative Science Quarterly*, 48, 268-305.

Marino, A. (2005), *Il Finanziamento dell'Innovazione*, Padova: CEDAM.

Marketing Week (2001), 'Sainsbury's in "Fairtrade" Brand Launch', *Marketing Week*, 29 November 2001, 7.

Mathews, C.H. and Scott, S.G. (1995), 'Uncertainty and planning in small and entrepreneurial firms: an empirical assessment', *Journal of Small Business Management*, October.

Matten, D. and Crane A. (2005), 'Corporate citizenship: Towards an extended theoretical conceptualization', *Academy of Management Review*, 30(1), 166-179.

Matten, D., Crane, A. and Chapple, W. (2003), 'Behind the mask: Revealing the true face of corporate citizenship', *Journal of Business Ethics*, 45, 109-120.

Mayoux, L. (2001), *Impact Assessment of Fair Trade and Ethical Enterprise Development*, London: Department for International Development (DFID).

McBeth, W.E. and Rimac, T. (2004), 'The Age of Entrepreneurial Turbulence. Creating A Sustainable Advantage for Individuals, Organisation and Society', *ESADE MBA Business Review*.

McFadden, D. (1999), 'Rationality for Economists?', *Journal of Risk and Uncertainty*, 19, 73-105.

McGrath, R. and MacMillan, I.C. (1995), 'Discovery Driven Planning', *Harvard Business Rewiev*.

McGrath, R. and MacMillan, I.C. (2000), *The Entrepreneurial Mindset: strategies for continuously creating opportunity in an age of uncertainty*, Boston: Harvard Business School Press.

McGuire, J.W. (1963), *Business and society*, New York: McGraw Hill.

McLeod, H.R. (1997), 'Cross over, Inc.', 19, 100-105.

McWilliam, A. and Siegel D. (2001), 'Corporate social responsibility: A theory of the firm perspective', *Academy of Management Review*, **26**(1), 117-127.

Merckens, K. (2000), 'Sekem – An Egyptian initiative', Hannover: Paper presented at the EXPO 2000, 15-17 August.

Miner, A.S., Eesley D.T., DeVaughn M. and Rura T. (2001), 'The magic beanstalk vision of university venture formation', in Schoonhoven, C.B., and Romanelli E. (eds.), *The Entrepreneurship Dynamic: Origins of Entrepreneurship and its Role in Industry Creation and Evolution,* Stanford CA: University Press Stanford.

Ministero del Lavoro e delle Politiche Sociali, (2003), 'Rapporto Annuale Ministeriale'.

Mintzberg, H. (1994), *The Rise and Fall of Strategic Planning*, New York: The Free Press.

Mintzberg, H., B. Ahlstrand and J. Lampel (1998), *Strategy Safari*, The Free Press.

Mitchell, R.K., Agle, B.R. and Wood, D.J. (1997), 'Toward a theory of stakeholder identification and salience: Defining the principle of who and what really counts', *Academy of Management Review*, **22**(4), 853-886.

Moore, H., (2002), 'Social entrepreneurs and responsible economy', Fathom Knowledge Network http://www.fathom. com/feature/35522/, Accessed, June, 27, 2005.

Morino Institute, Venture Philanthropy Partners & Community Wealth Ventures (2001), 'Venture philanthropy: The changing landscape'.

Morosini, P. (1998), *Managing cultural difference*, Oxford: Pergamon Press.

Morosini, P., Ulrich, S. and Isberg (2001), 'The Delancey Street Foundation', IMD case no. GM 1020.

Mowery, D.C., Nelson R.R, Sampat B.N. and Ziedonis A.A. (2001), 'The growth of patenting and licensing by U.S. universities: an assessment of the effects of the Bay Dole act of 1980', *Research Policy*, **30**, 99-119.

Mowery, D.C., Oxley, J.E. and Silverman, B.S. (1996), 'Strategic Alliances and Interfirm Knowledge Transfer', *Strategic Management Journal*, **17** (Winter), 77-91.

Andrea Muccioli, personal interview, 2006.

Nagarajan, A. and W. Mitchell (1998), 'Evolutionary diffusion: Internal and external methods used to acquire encompassing, complementary, and incremental technological changes in the lithotripsy industry', *Strategic Management Journal*, **19**(11), 1063-1077.

Nelson, J. and Zadek, S. (2001), *Partnership Alchemy*, The Copenhagen Centre.

Nelson, J., Prescott, D. and Held, S. (2005), 'Partnering for Success: Business perspectives on multi-stakeholder partnerships', The World Economic Forum, in collaboration with the International Business Leaders Forum, and the Kennedy School of Government, Harvard.

Newman, P. (2002), Personal interview with the author, 28 May 2002, London: CaféDirect.

Newman, W.H. and Wallender III, H.W. (1978), 'Managing not-for-profit enterprises', *Academy of Management Review*, **3**(1), 24-31.

NRC, National Research Council (1999*), New Strategies for America's Water Supply,* Washington, D.C.: National Academy Press.

NRC, National Research Council (2000), *Watershed Management for Potable Water Supply,*Washington, D.C.: National Academy Press.

Ollila, J. (chairman and CEO Nokia) (2002), 'Global Focus on Youth and Education', featured company article.

Oxfam (2002), 'About Oxfam and Fair Trade', 30 August 2002 (available at http://www.oxfam.org.uk/fair_trade.html).

Page, S.J. and Dowling R.K. (2002), *Ecotourism,* Prentice Hall.

Paton, R., (2003) *Managing and measuring social enterprises*, London: Sage Publications.

Peizer, J. (2001), 'Rethinking Technology in the Nonprofit Arena: Strategic Differences & New Models of Deployment', in ICT Toolsets, OSI, November 2005 (available at http://www.sor os.org/initiatives/information/articles_publications/articles/rethi nking_20010215).

Pepin, J. (2003), 'Venture capitalists and entrepreneurs become venture philanthropists', (available at www.insp.efc.be/show. php?d=24).

Perrini, F. (1998), *Capitale di rischio e mercati per PMI*, Milano: EGEA.

Perrini, F. (2000), *e-Valuation*, McGraw Hill.

Perrini, F. and Vurro, C. (2005), 'Teoría y práctica en la innovación y el cambio social', *Initiativa Emprendadora*, 48 (July-September), 8-21.

Perrini, F. and Vurro, C. (2006), 'Social Entrepreneurship: Innovation and Social Change across Theory and Practice', in *Social Entrepreneurship*, Mair J., Robinson J. and Hockerts K. (Eds), Palgrave Macmillan Ltd., London, UK.

Peters, T.J. and Robert, H. (1982), *Waterman, In Search of Excellence: Lessons from America's best run companies*, New York: Harper and Row.

Pfeffer J. (1994), *Competitive Advantage Trough People*, Harvard Business School Press.

Porter, M.E. (1983), *La strategia competitiva*, Bologna: Tipografia Compositori.

Porter, M. and Kramer, M.R., (1999), 'Philanthropy's New Agenda: Creating Value', *Harvard Business Review*, (December), 121-130.

Post, J.E., Preston, L.E. and Sauter-Sachs, S. (2002), *Redefining the Corporation: Stakeholder Management and Organizational Wealth*, Stanford: Stanford University Press.

Prabhu, G.N. (1999), 'Social Entrepreneurial Leadership', *Career Development International*, 4(3), 140-145.

Prahalad, C.K. and Hart, S.L. (1999), 'Strategies for the bottom of the pyramid: Creating sustainable development', Unpublished Draft Paper, August 1999.

Prahalad, C.K. (2004), *The fortune at the bottom of the pyramid. Eradicating poverty through profits*, Upper Saddle River, NJ: Wharton School Publishing.

Prahalad, C.K. and Hammond, A. (2002), 'Serving the word's poor, profitably', *Harvard Business Review*, 80(9), 48-57.

Pralahad, C. and Hamel, G. (1990), 'The core competence of the corporation', *Harvard Business Review*, 63, 79-91.

Preston, L.E. and Post, J.E. (1975), *Private management and public policy: the principle of public responsibility*, Englewood liffs, NJ: Prentice Hall.

Rauter, Karen, Communications Director, Watershed Agricultural Council, interview with the author (2005).

Richter, B.D., R. Mathews, D.L. Harrision and R. Wigington (2003), 'Ecologically sustainable water management: managing river flows for ecological integrity', *Ecological Applications*, 13(1), 206-224.

Right Livelihood Award (2003), 'Press Release', 8 September 2005 (Available: http://www.rightlivelihood.org/news/event03. htm).

Riker Elizabeth, Personal Interview, October 2005.

Rimac, T. and Amstrong, A. (2005), 'Pot of Gold or Pandora Box? Early Stages of Social Enterprise within a Non-profit Organization: A Canadian Perspective', Barcelona: IESE Social Enterprise Conference.

Ritchie, B., Crouch, J.R. and Geoffrey, I. (2003), *The Competitive Destination: A Sustainable Tourism Perspective*, CABI Publishing of CAB International, UK.

Roozen, N. and Van Der Hoff, F. (2002), *L'Aventure du Commerce Équitable*, Paris: JC Lattès.

Rosenkopf, L. and Nerkar, A. (2001), 'Beyond Local Search: Boundary-Spanning, Exploration, and Impact in the Optical Disk Industry', *Strategic Management Journal*, **22**, 287-306.

Rousseau, D.M. (1989), 'Psychological and Implied Contracts in Organisations', *Employee Responsibilities and Rights Journal*, **2**, 121-139.

Rousseau, D.M. (1998). 'The "problem" of the psychological contract considered', *Journal of Organizational Behaviour*, **19**, 665-671.

Sagawa, S. and Segal, E. (2000), *Common Interest, Common Good*, Harvard Business School Press.

Sahlman, W.A. (1997), 'How to Write a Great Business Plan', *Harvard Business Review*, July/August.

San Patrignano (1998), 'The Road to San Patrignano', video-tape.

San Patrignano, the Archives.

Saxenian, A. (1994), *Regional Advantage*, Cambridge, MA: Harvard University Press.

Schumpeter, J.A. (1934), *The Theory of Economic Development*, Cambridge: Harvard University Press.

Sen, A. (1987), *On Ethics and Economics*, Oxford: Blackwell.

Seppae, M. (2000), 'Strategy logic of the venture capitalist: understanding venture capitalism by exploring linkages between ownership and strategy of venture capital companies, over time, in America and Europe', *Studies of Business and Economics*, n.3, University of Jyvaeskyla.

Seppae, M., and Rasila, T. (2001), *The V2C phenomenon: pushing ventures to capital, in Hannula, Jaervelin e Seppae, Frontiers of e-Business research*, Tampere: Tampere University of Technology.

Sethi, S.P. (1975), 'Dimensions of corporate social performance: An analytical framework', *California Management Review*, **17**(3), 58-65.

Shane, S. (2000), 'Prior knowledge and the discovery of entrepreneurial opportunity', *Organization Science*, **11**, 448-469.

Shane, S. and Khurana, R. (1999), 'Career experiences and firm foundings', Working paper.

Shane, S. and Stuart, T. (2002), 'Organizational endowments and the performance of university start-ups', *Management Science*, **48**, 154-170.

Shane, S. and Venkataraman, S. (2000), 'The promise of entrepreneurship as a field of research', *Academy of Management Review*, **25**(1), 217-226.

Shapiro, A. (1982), 'Some social dimensions of Entrepreneurships', in Kent C., Sexton D. and Vesper, D. (eds.) *The Encyclopaedia of Entrepreneurship*, Englewood Cliffs, NJ: Prentice-Hall.

Shapiro, C. and Varian, H.R. (1999), 'The art of standards wars', California Management Review, **41**(2), 8-32.

Shaw, E. and Carter, S. (2004), 'Social entrepreneurship: Theoretical antecedents and empirical analysis of entrepreneurial processes and outcomes', Paper presented at 24th Babson-Kauffman Entrepreneurship Conference, Glasgow.

Shoppingplace (2002), 'A Brief History of Coffee', 30 August 2002 (available at http://www.shoppingplace.com/coffee/history.html).

Simon, H.A. (1947), *Administrative Behavior*, New York: Macmillan.

Simon, H.A. (1985), 'Human Nature in Politics: the Dialogues of Psychology with Political Science', *American Political Science Review*, **79**, 293-304.

Smilor, R.W. (1987), 'Managing the Incubator System: Critical Success Factors to Accelerate New Company Development', *IEEE Transactions on Engineering Management*, **34**(4), 146-156.

Smith, C. [1994] 2000, 'The new corporate philanthropy', *Harvard Business Review*, May-June.

Sobel, J. (March 2002), 'Can we trust social capital?', *Journal of*

Economic Literature, **XL**, 139-154.

Stajkovic, A.D. and Luthans, F. (2001), 'Differential effects of incentive motivators on work performance', *Academy of Management Journal*, 44(3), 580-590.

Stevenson, H. and Jarillo, J. (1990), 'A Paradigm of Entrepreneurship: Entrepreneurial Management', *Strategic Management Journal*, **11**, 17-27.

Stevenson, H.H., Roberts, M. J. and Van Slyke, J.R. (1988), *The Start-Up Process*, Harvard Business School, pp. 45-59.

Swammy, R. (1990), 'The Making of a Social Entrepreneur: The case of Baba Amte', *Vikalpa*, **15**(4), 29-39.

Tallontire, A.M. (2001a), 'Challenges Facing Fair Trade: Which Way Now?', Paper presented at the DSA Conference 'Different Poverties – Different Policies', 10-12 September 2001, Manchester: IDPM, (available at http://www.bham.ac.uk/DSA/CONF01TA.doc).

Tallontire, A.M. (2001b), *Fair Trade and Development*, London: NRET.

Temtime, Z.T. (2003), 'Linking environmental scanning to total quality management through business planning', *Journal of Management Development*, **23**(3), 219-233.

Tencati, A., Perrini, F. and Pogutz, S. (2004), 'New Tools to Foster Corporate Socially Responsible Behaviour', *Journal of Business Ethics,* **53**(1), 173-190.

Teleserenità (2003), *Report*, Teleserenità.

Terenziani, A. (2001), 'Il "Progetto Anziani" della Fondazione del Monte di Bologna e di Ravenna: un modello innovativo per l'assistenza domiciliare di anziani non autosufficienti', *Sociologia e politiche sociali*, **4**(2), 89-108.

Thake, S. and Zadek S. (1997), *Practical people, noble causes: How to support community-based social entrepreneurs,* London: New Economics Foundation.

Thompson, J., Alvy, G. and Lees, A. (2000), 'Social Entrepreneurship: A New Look at the People and the Potential', *Management Decision*, **38**(5), 328-338.

Thompson, J.L. (2002), 'The world of the social entrepreneur', *The International Journal of Public Sector Management*, **15**(5), 412-432.

Tour Operators Initiative (TOI) (2004), 'Supply Chain Engagement for Tour Operators: Three Steps Toward Sustainability'.

Tourism and Coastal Zone Management in Turkey, the Çıralı Practice (available at http://216.142.137.43/utils/bp_download_document.php/Tourism%20and%20Coastal%20Zone%20Management.

Traidcraft (2002), 'Traidcraft PLC: History', August 2002, (available at http://www.traidcraft.co.uk/historyplc.html).

Triolo, Mike, Economic Development Officer, Catskill Watershed Corporation, interview with the author, (2005).

Tsoukas, H. (1989), 'The epistemological status of idiographic research in the comparative study of organizations: A realist perspective', *Academy of Management Review*, **14**(4), 551-561.

Tvesky, A. (1977), 'On Elicitation of Preferences: Descriptive and Prescriptive Considerations', in D. Bell, R. Kenney, H. Raiffa, *Conflicting Objectives in Decisions*, New York: Wiley.

Tvesky, A. and Kahneman, D. (1981), 'The Framing of Decisions and the Psychology of Choice', *Science*, **211**, 453-458.

UN HABITAT – TOGETHER Foundation best practices database, 'Tourism and Coastal Zone Management in Turkey: The Çıralı Practice'.

UNEP MAP – WTO (2001a), 'Sustainable Development of Tourism Policy Report, Prepared for the UN division of Sustainable Development'.

UNEP MAP (2004), 'Regional Strategy for Sustainable Development in the Mediterranean: Policy and Tools: A Mediterranean Partnership Initiative for the Promotion of Sustainable Development'.

UNEP MAP (2005) the Mediterranean in figures http://www.unepmap.gr/home.asp

UNEP MAP (2005), 'Mediterranean Strategy for Sustainable Development: A Framework for Environmental Sustainability and Shared Prosperity' (available at http://www.foeeurope.org/mednet/mssd/eng_277-4_mcsd10rpt.pdf).

UNEP, WTTC, IFTO, IH&RA and ICCL (2002), 'Industry as a Partner for Sustainable Development'.

United Nations (1999), 'Report of the UN Secretary General on Tourism and Sustainable Development –WWF Focus on Tourism: the Sustainability Opportunity', Discussion Paper for CSD 7 on Sustainable Tourism.

United Nations Development Program (2004), 'Human Development Report 2004. Cultural liberty in today's diverse world', Washington: UNDP.

United Nations General Assembly (1999), 'Resolution Adopted by The General Assembly for the Programme for the Further Implementation of Agenda 21'.

Van De Kragt, A.J.C., Orbell, J.M., Dawes, R.M., Braver, S.R. and Wilson, L.A. (1986), 'Doing Well and Doing Good as Ways of Resolving Social Dilemmas', in H., Wilke, Messik, D., Rutte, C., *Experimental as Social Dilemmas*, Frankfur/Main: Lang Gmbh, **1**, 177-203.

Venkataraman, S. (1997), 'The distinctive domain of entrepreneurship research: An editor's perspective', in J. Katz and R. Brockhaus (Eds.), *Advances in entrepreneurship, firm emergence and growth*, **3**, 119-138, Greenwich, CT: JAI Press.

Vogel, D. (1986), 'The study of social issues in management: A critical appraisal', *California Management Review*, **28**(2), 142-151.

Vogel, D. (2005), *The market for virtue: The potential and limits of corporate social responsibility*, Brookings Institution Press.

Waddock, S. and Post, J. (1991), 'Social entrepreneurs and catalytic change' *Public Administration Review*, 51(5), 393-401.

Wallace, S.L. (1999), 'Social Entrepreneurship: The role of Social Purpose Enterprises in facilitating Community Economic Development', *Journal of Developmental Entrepreneurship*, **4**(2), 45-66.

Watson, L. (2002), Personal interview with the author, 5 September 2002, Brussels: Voluntary consultant to the Fair Trade movement.

Weber, J.R. and Brausch, O. (1992), ,IMEDE (now IMD) case', case-study.

Weich, K. (1979), *The Social Psychology of Organizing*, Reading, MA: Addison-Wesley.

Weick, K.E. (1984), 'Small wins', *American Psychologist*, **39**(1), 40-49.

Weick, K.E., (1989), 'Theory Construction as Disciplined Imagination' *Academy of Management Review*, **14**(4), 516-531.

Weisbrod, B. (ed) (1998), *To profit or not to profit: The commercial transformation of the nonprofit sector*, Cambridge: Cambridge University Press.

Wheeler, D., McKague, K., Thomson, J., Davies, R., Medalye, J. and Prada, M. (2005), 'Creating Sustainable Local Enterprise Networks', *MIT/Sloan Management Review*, **47**(1), 37.

White, D. (2002), Telephone interview with the author, 22 August 2002, London: Twin Trading.

Wills, C. (2002), Personal interview with the author, 28 May 2002, London: IFAT.

Winter, S.G. (1995), 'Four Rs of Profitability: Rents, Resources, Routines and Replication', in C. Montgomery (ed), *Resource-Based and Evolutionary Theories of the Firm: Towards a Synthesis*, Boston: Kluwer Academic Publishers, 147-178.

Winter, S.G. and Szulanski, G. (2001), 'Replication as Strategy', Organization Science, 12(6), 730-743.

Wondolleck, J.M. and Steven, L. Y. (2000), *Making Collaboration Work*, Washington D.C.: Island Press.

Wood, D.J. (1991), 'Corporate social performance revisited', *Academy of Management Review*, **16**(4), 691-718.

Wood, D.J. and Logsdon, J.M. (2002), 'Business citizenship: From individuals to organizations', *Business Ethics Quarterly*, Ruffin Series n. 3, 59-94.

World Tourism Organization (2001a), Sustainable Development of Tourism Policy Report, Prepared for the UN division of Sustainable Development.

World Tourism Organization (2002), World Summit on Sustainable Development, Johannesburg, South Africa, 26 August - 4 September.

World Tourism Organization (2003), WSSD Final Report – Plan of Implementation-Paragraph #43 - Tourism in the WSSD Final Plan of Implementation by WTO, 2003. http://www.world-tourism.org/sustainable/wssd/final-report.pdf

World Tourism Organization, (2002) Contribution of the to the WSSD World Summit on Sustainable Development, Johannesburg .

World Travel and Tourism Council (2003), Blueprint for New Tourism. Available online at http://www.wttc.org/blueprint/WTTCBlueprintFinal.pdf

WWF (2001), Turkey Çıralı Final Report, Internal Document.

WWF (2003a), Sustainable Development Globalization and Biodiversity – WWF Position Statement, originally published 2001 – revised 2003.

WWF (2003b), WWF Mediterranean Programme: working for nature and people in the Mediterranean.

WWF (2004a), Saving Nature with People in the Mediterranean: Strategic Plan 2004 – Internal Document, WWF Mediterranean Program Office.

WWF (2004b), WWF Guidelines for sustainable tourism investments in vulnerable ecological areas of the Mediterranean coasts.

WWF (2004c), WWF Freshwater and Tourism in the Mediterranean 2004, Available online at http://www.panda.org /downloads/europe/medpotourismreportfinal_ofnc.pdf

Yin, R.K. (1994), *Case Study Research: Design and Methods*, Newbury Park, CA: Sage Publications.

Yunis, E. (2003) 'The Importance of Sustainable Practices in the Tourism Industry', presentation at the WTO.

Zahra, S.A. (1996), 'Governance, ownership, and corporate entrepreneurship: The moderating impact of industry', *Academy of Management Journal*, **39**(6), 3-26.

Zamagni, S. (1995), *The Economics of Altruism*, Hants: E. Elgar.

Zamagni, S., Antoci, A. and Sacco, P. (2000), 'The ecology of altruistic motivations in triadic social environments' in L. Gerard Varet, S. Kolm, J. Mercier Ythier, (eds), *The Economics of Reciprocity, Giving and Altruism*, London, Macmillan, 335-351.

Zucker, L.G., Darby, M.R., and Brewer, M.B. (1998), 'Intellectual human capital and the birth of US biotechnology enterprises', *American Economic Review*, **88**, 290–306.

Index

Abdul Latif Jameel (ALJ) Group
294
  corporate citizenship 294, 295
  microfinance 295, 296
Abouleish, Dr. I. 210, 211, 212, 220,
221, 222
  see also Sekem
Abouleish, H. 214
academic research centres 12
Ackerman, R. 11
Acumen Fund 86–8, 279, 292, 293,
294
Agle, B. 9
Ahuja, G. 243, 252, 256
Ajzen, I. 111, 116
ALJ Group *see* Abdul Latif Jameel
Group
Alkhafaji, A. 59
Allen, D. 49
Alter, K. 75
alternative trading organisations
(ATOs) 193, 195, 196
  difficulties for 196, 208
  strategy 201–2
    increased commercial awareness
197
  World Shops 195
  see also CaféDirect; fair trade
Altman, B. 5
Alvord, S. 16, 25, 28
Alvy, G. 7, 110
Alworth, T. 267
Amanco 288
  partnership with RASA 289
Amaral, L. 261, 262, 263
AmeriCorps 300
Andriof, J. 5
animal feed production 126, 127
  see also LocalFeed
Appropriate Technologies for

Enterprise Creation (ApproTEC)
280
  partnership with SC Johnson 290,
291
  promotion of sustainable economic
growth and employment
290–91
Aravind Eye-Care Hospitals 19, 42–3
Argyle, M. 106
Arkenstone 245
Armstrong, A. 110, 113
Ashoka 86, 88–9, 99, 277, 278,
281–2, 286
  fund impacts 103
  Hybrid Value Chain™ approach
278, 283, 286, 287, 288, 289
  investment strategy 100
  performance measurement 103–4
  selection criteria and portfolio
composition 101–3
  skills and resource transfer 101
  venture philanthropy model
100–101
ATOs *see* alternative trading
organisations
Attenborough, Sir David 151

Backman, 55, 56, 57
Balbo, L. 95
Bank of America
  City Year program 300
  see also BankBoston
Bank of England 66, 68
BankBoston 298–9
  seed funding for City Year program
299–300
  see also Bank of America
Barendsen, L. 16
Baron, R. 54
Barr, S. 198

329